Monograph Series of the Socio-Economic History Society, Japan

This monograph series is published by the Socio-Economic History Society, Japan, and Springer.

The aim of the series is to make works by Japanese scholars accessible to a wider readership and thereby enhance the global knowledge of Japanese and Asian scholarship in the fields of economic, social, and business history.

This book series will present English translations of outstanding recent academic research works, survey articles, and book reviews carefully selected from the Society's quarterly Japanese-language journal *Socio-Economic History*, which is the preeminent journal in its field in Japan, as well as from other publications of the Society. These will be edited under specific themes such as energy and the environment, the consumer society and the company system in postwar Japan, and the economic history of Japan in the early twentieth century. The content will include chapters on economic, social, and business history ranging geographically from Japan and Asia as a whole to Europe and the United States, and a small number of book reviews of recent academic works published in Japanese and other languages.

The Society was founded in 1930 and currently comprises more than 1400 registered members, mainly academics, researchers and postgraduate students affiliated with universities and research institutions in Japan.

More information about this series at http://www.springer.com/series/13569

Haruhito Takeda
Editor

Micro-Performance During Postwar Japan's High-Growth Era

Springer

Editor
Haruhito Takeda
Professor Emeritus
The University of Tokyo
Tokyo
Japan

ISSN 2364-2394 ISSN 2364-2408 (electronic)
Monograph Series of the Socio-Economic History Society, Japan
ISBN 978-981-10-9232-9 ISBN 978-981-10-0709-5 (eBook)
DOI 10.1007/978-981-10-0709-5

Printed on acid-free paper

This Springer imprint is published by Springer Nature
The registered company is Springer Science+Business Media Singapore Pte Ltd.

Preface

The aim of this book is to analyze Japan's high-growth economy, in particular to clarify the kinds of change that were generated by high economic growth in the life of the people.

Japan's postwar high-growth economy (1955–1970) was long regarded as a miracle. Today, however, it is evident that other East Asian nations, including China, Korea, and Taiwan, are enjoying high economic growth as well and are becoming leading powers in the world economy. Japan's success is thus no longer seen as an exceptional miracle but as the first in a series of cases of rapid economic growth.

It is well known that high growth based on steep industrial development generates advancements in the industrial structure and expansion of exports. That development is itself driven by improvements in international competitiveness, which are based on the active investment in plant and equipment that accompanies technological innovation. In the Japanese case, an industrial policy that promoted industrial development was regarded as particularly significant, so much so that the close relationship between government and business was dubbed "Japan, Inc." This evaluation of the high-growth economy by its contemporaries now needs to be reexamined from the vantage point of history.

The present volume focuses not on the macroeconomic mechanisms that expanded the scale of the economy but on the microeconomic changes that were effected in people's lives. The emergence of a mass consumption society as a result of economic growth suggests that people's lifestyles and consumer behavior changed in various ways. The first chapter, "The Japanese Apparel Industry and Consumer Society from 1950 to the 1970s," focuses on the apparel industry's expanding market as it corresponded to changes in consumer behavior. Increasing worker income provided the foundation for the mass consumption that in turn supported mass production, but that rise in income was not enough by itself. Key to the link between high economic growth and the improvement and enrichment of consumer life are the channels that supply consumer goods. Producers must be encouraged to turn out new products that satisfy consumer needs, and consumers must be stimulated to buy these new products, as replacement or supplementary purchases, on a short cycle. This is observable in the frequent model changes not only of clothing but also of automobiles, household electrical appliances, and other such products. The first chapter analyzes the market interactions between business firms and consumers in order to clarify their influence on industrial development.

Even as consumer life became more comfortable and abundant, consumers were becoming uneasy about the environmental deterioration associated with high growth. Among environmental problems, the air pollution caused by automobile exhaust gases in urban areas loomed particularly large. The second chapter, "The Legislative Process of Automobile Exhaust Emissions Control in Japan: The 1966 Regulation and the Role of the Ministry of Transport," focuses on how the Japanese government addressed emissions regulations while drawing on the lessons of America's experience with the same issue. With public opinion demanding strong controls, the government took the approach of gradually strengthening emissions regulation in conjunction with technical development at the company level. The development of technologies corresponding to appropriate regulation strengthened the international competitiveness of Japan's automobile industry and expanded its share in the U.S. market.

While the automobile industry and others were apparently enjoying rapid development, the change in industrial structure brought about by economic growth inevitably resulted in the decline of other industries. Chief among these was the coal-mining industry, which, with the onset of a full-scale energy revolution, lost its role as energy supplier to the importers of cheap crude oil. Because the coal industry had played an important role in local economies around Japan, its decline resulted in the stagnation of regional economies and a serious unemployment problem. Those faced with unemployment did not share in the improvements to consumer life engendered by economic growth. The third chapter, "Adjustment Policies in the Japanese Coal-Mining Industry During the Period of High Economic Growth," discusses the government's industrial policies as they addressed the coal industry's adjustment in the high-growth era, concluding that they reduced such problems as stagnation, unemployment, and local industrial decline. With an eye to social stability, the government decided that it would not be sufficient to entrust the adjustment task to market processes alone, and it made significant efforts to address the friction associated with changes in the industrial structure. Similar approaches became characteristic of the policies addressing structurally depressed industries after the oil crisis of the 1970s. This chapter examines the role of industrial policy from a wider perspective than has been usual.

The adjustments in employment practices contributed positively to the gradual shift of labor from declining industries to growth industries. What these new job opportunities offered by way of working conditions, including wages, however, may be another story. The effort to devise a reasonable wage system—one that would bring out the best in worker performance and evaluate it fairly—was a trial-and-error process. The fourth chapter, "The Relationship Between Labor–Management Rationalization and Industry-Level Business Relations: A Case Study of the Japanese Steel Industry," investigates changes in labor management in the steel industry, which was one of the high-growth era's leading industries. Although a case study, it demonstrates that, in an environment of strained relations between management and labor, rationalization measures were accepted alongside an improvement in working conditions and cooperative relations. The cooperative industrial relations that became such a signal characteristic of Japanese management resulted from microlevel discussions between employers and employees.

In addition to these four chapters, this book includes reviews of four books that introduce the research set forth in those chapters: *The History of Technological Innovation in Liquid Crystal Displays* by Tsuyoshi Numagami; *"Transactions over Status" and Japan's Employment Practices* by Woo Jong-Won; *The Economic History of Industrial Development and Decline* by Junko Watanabe; and *The Structure of Postwar Japan's Economic Growth* by Juroh Hashimoto. These studies present important research concerning product development, industrial relations in the national railways, industrial policy on declining industries such as cotton, and the relations between government and business.

As stated above, this volume, by investigating historic changes at the microlevel, illuminates the kinds of transformations that were wrought by the high-growth economy.

I must thank Dr. Koichi Inaba, who translated Chaps. 2, 3, and 4, and Ms. Louisa Rubinfien, who translated all the book reviews and checked all the chapters to improve the drafts.

Tokyo, Japan

Haruhito Takeda

Contents

About the Contributors

Jin Sung Chung is a professor of Japanese studies at Korea National Open University. He obtained an M.A. in economics from Seoul National University and a Ph.D. in history from the University of Tsukuba. His main research field is the economic history of Japan. His publications include *Juyosangyō Tōseihō Ka ni okeru Sekitan Dokusen Sosiki no Shijō Tōsei Seisaku* (Japanese Coal Cartels and The Major Industries Control Law, 1933–1936) in *Shakai Keizai Shigaku* (Socio-Economic History), 59(4).

Juroh Hashimoto was a professor at Hosei University. He obtained a Ph.D. in economics from The University of Tokyo in 1984. His main research field is the economic history of modern Japan. His publications include *Daikyōkōki no Nihon Shihonshugi* (Japanese Capitalism during the Great Depression) (University of Tokyo Press, 1984) and *Nihon Keizai no Seichō Kōzō* (The driving forces of high economic growth in postwar Japan) (Yuhikaku Press, 2001).

Kyohei Hirano is an associate professor of business history at Kobe University. He obtained a Ph.D. in business administration from Kobe University in 2008. His main research field is the economic and business history of Japan. His publications include *Senjiki Nihon no Daiyō Sen'i Kaihatsu to Sengo heno Keishō* (The Development of Substitute Fibers in Wartime Japan and Their Postwar Evolution: The Failure of Kanegafuchi Spinning Company's Kanebian) in *Rekishi to Keizai* (The Journal of Political Economy and Economic History), 57(1).

Hiroshi Ichihara is a professor of Japanese economic history at Dokkyo University. He obtained a Ph.D. in economics from Hitotsubashi University in 1998. His main research field is Japanese labor history. His publications include *Tankō no Rōdō Shakaishi* (A Social History of Japanese Coal Miners) (Taga-Shuppan, 1997).

Susumu Ishii is a professor of economics at Gakushuin University. He obtained a Ph.D. in economics from The University of Tokyo in 2000. His main research field is the economic and business history of Japan. His publications include *Sengo Nihon no Shikin Haibun* (Fund Allocation in Early Postwar Japan) (University of Tokyo Press, 2001).

Akira Itagaki is an associate professor of economics at Hokkai-Gakuen University. He obtained a Ph.D. in economics from The University of Tokyo in 2011. His main research field is the economic and business history of Japan. His publications include *Fukkōki Gaikokusha Yunyū wo Meguru Ikentairitsu to Sono Kiketsu* (Opposition to Car Imports in the Postwar Reconstruction Japan) in *Keiei Shigaku* (Japan Business History Review), 38(3), and *Nihon ni Okeru Jidōsha Haishutsu Gasu Kisei no Seiritsu Katei* (The process of enactment of exhaust emission control in Japan), *Shakai Keizai Shigaku* (Socio-Economic History), 72(4).

Hiroshi Sugiyama is an assistant professor of Japanese economy at the Osaka University of Economics and Law. He obtained a Ph.D. in economics from Hitotsubashi University in 2007. His main research field is the economic history of Japan. His publications include *Kōdo Keizai Seichōki no Shokuba Kanri to Jinji Shōgū Seido: Rīdingu Indasutorī to shite no Tekkō Sangyō no Bunseki kara* (Workplace Management in Japan's High Growth Era: From the Perspective of Connections to Personnel Management Systems) in *Keiei Shigaku* (Japan Business History Review), 47(4).

Haruhito Takeda is a professor emeritus at The University of Tokyo, where he obtained a Ph.D. in economics in 1988. His main research field is the economic and business history of Japan. His publications include *Nihon Sandougyō shi* (A History of Copper Mines in Japan) (University of Tokyo Press, 1987).

Seiichiro Yonekura is a professor at Hitotsubashi University's Institute of Innovation Research. He obtained a Ph.D. in history from Harvard University in 1990. His main research field is the business history of Japan. His publications include *The Japanese Iron and Steel Industry 1880–1990: Continuity and Discontinuity* (Palgrave Macmillan, 1994).

Part I
Micro-Performance During Postwar Japan's High-Growth Era

Chapter 1
The Japanese Apparel Industry and Consumer Society from 1950 to the 1970s

Susumu Ishii

Abstract The purpose of this paper is to analyze the development of the apparel industry in post-war Japan. Previous studies have emphasized how unique customary practices in the transactions between wholesalers and retailers contributed to the development of the industry. This paper proposes a broader historical view, arguing that the apparel industry experienced three different phases in the post-war period.

In the first phase (the 1950s), there was little progress in apparel production because the procurement of textiles was such an important factor in determining the competitiveness of apparel companies. In the second phase (the 1960s), apparel products saw rapid improvement, and ready-made apparel became available in various sizes and designs. In this phase, department stores and specialist shops provided different types of products and were drawn into fierce competition with each other. In the third phase (from the 1970s onwards), apparel companies began to develop sophisticated strategies in the management of retail outlets and the pricing of products. This new phase occurred alongside a general rise in income levels and the appearance of a range of designs. Consumers developed diverse tastes that fluctuated in unpredictable ways. This paper identifies the third phase as marking the emergence of consumer society and treats it as a typical socio-economic phenomenon of our time.

Keywords Apparel industry • Consumer society • Developmental phase

1 Introduction

This paper is an analysis of the development process of the apparel industry in post-World War II Japan, with a focus on women's apparel. I will discuss the diffusion of ready-to-wear clothes in the 1950s and 60s and the ways consumer behavior changed in the 1970s. This study will serve as a lens for considering the Japanese economy's development since the end of the Second World War.

S. Ishii (✉)
Faculty of Economics, Gakushuin University, Tokyo, Japan
e-mail: susumu.ishii@gakushuin.ac.jp

H. Takeda (ed.), *Micro-Performance During Postwar Japan's High-Growth Era*, Monograph Series of the Socio-Economic History Society, Japan,
DOI 10.1007/978-981-10-0709-5_1

The significance of the study of the apparel industry from the vantage point of economic history is as follows. First, it clearly illustrates the rapid transition from one economic phase to another that characterized post-war Japan's economic development. The market prices of basic materials, including fiber and textiles, and iron and steel, fluctuated wildly in the 1950s. Apparel makers were forced to adapt to the gyrations. (Phase 1: pursuit of "market value")[1] Baffled by the fluctuations in textile prices, apparel makers could not afford to improve their production processes. In the 1960s, by contrast, apparel makers were able to purchase raw fabric more easily because of cooperation among textile firms, increasing production, and industrial policy concerning the fiber and textile industry. Apparel makers upgraded production processes through streamlining, quality improvements, and enhancements in their product portfolio of clothing sizes. (Phase 2: pursuit of "production value") However, there was less room for improvements in production in the textile industry than in other industries like metals and machinery. After the 1970s, the variety of apparel products increased dramatically because of quality improvements and diversification in size and design. At the same time, the increase of leisure time, the rise of working women living in the cities, and the growth of income diversified fashion as well. As a result, the consumer's preference became more varied, less stable, and more ambiguous. Apparel makers began to adopt new sales strategies in order to create and capture unstable consumer surplus. (Phase 3: pursuit of "consumer value") Consumers are likely to adopt noncomplementary heuristic strategies when merchandise variety and quality expand and the ownership of products spreads. Consumer preferences come to depend on the order in which they discover outlets (the result of their information searches) and they become unstable and ambiguous (Tetsuo Sugimoto 1997; Payne et al. 1993).

Second, it is assumed that the apparel industry took the lead in the shift to a consumer society that was characterized by its pursuit of "consumer value" viz. consumers who were becoming more diverse, fluid, and ambiguous. In this paper, 'consumer society' is not synonymous with 'mass consumption society'. The concept of 'mass consumption society' suggests that undifferentiated goods are mass-produced and widely diffused and assumes that consumer preference is homogeneous, with firms competing for "production value." The 'consumer society,' by contrast, is characterized by consumer behavior that is unstable and susceptible to business strategies. Previous studies have taken up the subject of 'consumer society' from a semiological perspective (Jean Baudrillard 1970; Ryuzo Uchida 1987), while economic history discussions of 'consumer society' focus on the interaction between demand and supply and on competition among firms (Herbert Blumer 1969; Susan Kaiser 1985; Susumu Kamiyama 1999). In this paper, I define 'consumer society' as the widening pursuit of consumer value by firms in response to a consumer preference that is diversified, unstable and ambiguous.

---

[1] I will discuss post-war Japan's economic phases in the last section of this paper.

Research on the history of the apparel industry has not been very extensive. The first to address Japan's postwar apparel industry were Hiroshi Ejiri (1979, 2003) and Mika Takaoka (1997, 2000) in their studies of department stores.[2] They both argued that the system established in the post-WWII reconstruction period led to the decline of the department stores and the growth of apparel makers.[3] They argued that the department-store/apparel-maker relationship was increasingly characterized by consignment buying (*itaku shiire*), purchase according to performance (*uriage shiire*), and the dispatching of salesclerks by apparel makers (*haken hanbai-in*). In consignment buying, goods are consigned to retailers, accounts are settled after sale, and unsold goods are returned to the apparel makers. The retailers themselves are responsible for goods on the sales floor. In "purchase according to performance", the apparel makers are responsible for selling and managing the goods on the sales floor. The retailer's "purchase" of an item coincides with its sale to a consumer.

Kashiyama (later Onward Kashiyama Co. LTD.) and other leading apparel makers made good use of these business practices. They devised systems to handle returns of merchandise, controlled retail prices and increased their margins, gathered information about consumer preferences through the salesclerks they dispatched, and initiated vertical integration. These strategies promoted rapid growth. The Ejiri and Takaoka studies mentioned above were correct in asserting that business practices like consignment buying and sending salesclerks to the retailers served to reduce the risk of unsold stock. These arrangements should not, however, be considered the main causes of the apparel makers' growth. The studies overlooked the apparel industry's diversified development process and the historical changes in the economic and social environment that affected availability of materials, production technology and consumer behavior.

The essential points of this paper are as follows.

(A) The growth of apparel suppliers is not a direct result of the distinctive business practices described above. Their advantage in buying raw fabrics and their cooperative relationships with department stores also contributed. From around 1960, when apparel makers gained readier access to raw fabrics, innovative apparel makers began to emerge from outside the networks of suppliers to department stores. The expansion of those new makers diversified the development of the apparel industry.

(B) As a result of this diversified development, the apparel industry began to pursue 'consumer value,' marking the beginning of the shift to the 'consumer society' phase.

[2] Shozo Nakagomi (1975) and Tomizawa Konomi (1995) should be noted as major references on the history of the apparel industry in Japan.

[3] 'Apparel makers' are defined as firms that plan products, produce apparel in their own or subcontracted factories and sell their products to retailers and consumers.

In the first section of this paper, I will investigate the process by which transactions were resumed between department stores and wholesale dealers in the postwar reconstruction period. It was during this phase that business practices like consignment buying and dispatched salesclerks spread across the apparel industry.

The second section will show that the competitive advantage of ready-to-wear apparel makers depended on the smooth acquisition of raw fabric and the close relationship with department stores in the 1950s.

The third section covers the 1960–1970s. The growth in production of raw fabric equalized the competitive conditions among apparel makers and retailers. At that point, the apparel industry as a whole began developing in one of two directions, department store and specialty store. In the 1970s, consumer preference became more diverse, less stable, and more ambiguous, and the apparel industry began pursuing consumer value.

The last section consists of concluding remarks and prospects for further study.

2 The Controlled Economy and the Reorganization of Wholesalers: From Wartime to the Early 1950s

The conventional distribution system was disbanded under wartime controls, and the position of long established wholesalers weakened further as newly emerging wholesalers rose in the controlled economy of the postwar. When department stores selected wholesalers to work with and began reconstruction of the distribution system, they adopted business practices such as consignment buying and the dispatched salesclerks by apparel makers. Takaoka (1997) suggests that department stores used these strategies to expand their assortment of Western-style and ready-to-wear clothes amidst the ongoing resource shortages of the time (Takeo Kikkawa and Mika Takaoka 1997). It was really only later, though, that Japanese department stores came to offer Western-style and ready-to-wear clothing on a large scale. The practice of returning unsold goods was not limited to department stores viz. their ready-to-wear suppliers, but also prevailed in transactions of other goods, such as silk and rayon textile (Isamu Kanai 1954).[4] Therefore, we have to understand consignment buying and the other practices in the context of the general relationship between department stores and wholesalers.

[4] Takaoka's interpretations (1997) are open so question, but her paper clearly shows the replacement of suppliers and the rising number of wholesalers dealing in Western-style clothes.

2.1 Wartime and Post-war Controlled Economy

With the outbreak of the Sino-Japanese War in 1937, the government strengthened its control over the economy. The controls on fiber and textile products were of particular importance. Sales of pure cotton cloth were prohibited as of 1938, and restrictions were placed on the manufacturing, processing, and sale of cotton products. The Regulation of the Production and Sale of Luxury Items (*Shashi-hin to Seizo Hanbai Seigen Kisoku*, called '*7-7 Kinrei*') was promulgated in July 1940. The '*7-7 Kinrei*' delivered a decisive blow to Japanese clothing (*gofuku*) and high-quality textile wholesalers, who had been major suppliers to department stores. It was followed in 1942 by the Regulation of Rationing and Consumption of Textile Goods (*Sen'i Seihin Haikyu Shohi Tosei Kisoku*) and the Coupon for Clothes System (*Iryo Kippu Sei*) were introduced. The Ready-to-wear Manufacturing and Rationing Company (*Kiseifuku Chuo Seizo Haikyu Tosei Gaisha*) was established in the same year. All wholesalers dealing in textile goods and clothes were integrated into the Nippon Orimono Tosei Co., Ltd. and Nippon Iryo Seihin Tosei Co., Ltd. in compliance with the Corporation Control Ordinance (Tosei Kaisha Rei) in 1943.

Some major wholesalers were permitted to continue trading as agent companies under state control.[5] The major wholesalers (those with sales of one million yen or more and holdings of 50 or more sewing machines) dealing in ready-to-wear for women and children were reorganized into 16 agent companies (Tokyo Fujin Kodomo-fuku Seizo Oroshi Kyodo Kumiai 1960, pp 368–369). As an agent company, a wholesaler could only distribute designated goods at official prices within the rationing system.

The devastation caused by the war, followed by defeat and occupation, damaged established wholesalers. For example, Ichida Co., Ltd. suffered airstrikes and the wartime loss of their overseas assets, but also the damage of taxation for war compensation after the war, and ultimately was designated a special accounting company (Tokubetu Keiri Gaisha) in order to be able to clear its debts. Another wholesaler, Takihyo, had its headquarters building seized by the Occupation Army, which delayed its resumption of business.[6]

Post-war economic controls constrained their management. Silk, hemp and rayon products were controlled until 1949, woolen and cotton products and staple fiber until 1950, and clothing until 1951. These controls did not function perfectly, however. Surplus ration goods, as well as commodities from the dissolved Imperial

[5] Ichida and Kashiyama (later Onward) were embedded in the rationing system as agent companies. Ichida was a Japanese clothing (*gofuku*) and textile wholesaler established in the nineteenth century. The company also dealt in Western style women's clothing and had been one of the major suppliers to department stores before and after the Second World War (Ichida Co., Ltd., 1974, pp 260–263. Junzo Kashiyama 1998, pp 56–59).

[6] Takihyo was a major textile wholesaler in Nagoya dating back to the Edo period, and began to handle ready-to-wear clothes before the war (Takihyo Co., Ltd. 2002, pp 53–59).

Japanese Army and the Occupation Army, were put on the black market. Some tradespeople engaged in business that skirted the edge of legality and discovered business opportunity in market niches hidden by the controlled economy. Leading old-time wholesalers, however, avoided such businesses in order to maintain their reputations.[7]

The newcomers flourished in the apparel industry and built their foundation in the era of post-war economic controls. For example, Nobuyuki Yoshiwara, who established San-yo Shokai in 1942, acquired air-defense netting through information from a friend in the navy after the war, and made them into children's cloaks that he could sell. In 1947, he purchased *habutae* (fine silk) that had been used for parachutes, dyed it and made it into women's raincoats (Yoshikazu Hiraishi 1974; Junko Ouchi and Yuriko Tajima 1996, pp 97–100). Koichi Tsukamoto was discharged from military service and established Wako Shoji (later Wacoal), selling women's accessories that were not controlled by the government (Wacoal Co., Ltd. 1999, pp 86–98). With his sale of the 'Bra Pad,' he became a maker and wholesaler of women's underwear. Tokyo Hosei (established in 1949, later Tokyo Style Co., Ltd.) made women's clothes from fine fabric through Occupation Army channels and succeeded in selling them to Mitsukoshi department store, thereby establishing a relationship with it (Tokyo Style Co., Ltd. 2000, pp 10–11).

Ready-to-wear apparel makers in Gifu city often violated government controls. Many repatriates from former Japanese colonies settled in 'Harbin' Street in Gifu upon their return, and went into business by selling extra ration goods on the black market. In the summer of 1947, they won permission to trade in secondhand clothing: they did not limit themselves to purchasing used clothes, however, covertly purchased fabric that had been under government control and sold it as is or made it into clothes to sell illegally with used-clothes certificates. Early on, the Harbin Street merchants peddled their wares around the country. Wholesalers from other areas soon began coming to Gifu to buy in ready-to wear apparel (Tokai Sen'i Shimbun-sha 1975; Yoshiaki Ogikubo and Hideyuki Negishi 2003), and ultimately, Gifu became one of Japan's major production centers of ready-to- wear apparel.

The changes in control methods influenced the apparel and textile industries. Nippon Iryo Seihin Tosei Co., Ltd. was ordered to close; the ration rule (*Iryohin Haikyu Kisoku*), coupon rule (*Iryohin Kippu Kisoku*), and tuition rule (*Shitei Sen'i Shizai Haikyu Kisoku*) were enacted, and a system for registering clothing distributors was introduced in September 1947. All clothing wholesalers who met minimum qualification were supposed to register, which opened the way for new entrants and wholesalers that had closed or changed their trade in wartime. Under the post-war control system, the competition among clothing wholesalers became more intense than it had been under the wartime control system (Tokyo Fujin Kodomo-fuku Seizo Oroshi Kyodo Kumiai 1960, pp 471–481).

The major clothes wholesalers of the pre-war were allowed to resume handling apparel and textile products after the abolition of economic controls between 1949

[7] Ichida sold miscellaneous goods. It earned less than expected (Ichida 1974, p. 267).

and 1951. This deregulation stimulated competition with the new entrants who had expanded in the post-war controlled economy. Around the same time, department stores were permitted to resume business at their prewar scale. The department stores confronted a new business environment in which leading older wholesalers had lost their power and post-war new entrants were aggressively pushing their products.

New entrant Wako Shoji negotiated with Kyoto Takashimaya Department Store to sell brassieres and corsets in 1950. They repeatedly visited the person in charge of buying and promoted their products when they learned that Seiseisha had priority as a supplier to Takashimaya. Seiseisha was a long established wholesaler of accessories for women. Wako Shoji won approval as designated supplier to Takashimaya, a victory over Seiseisha (Wacoal Co., Ltd. 1999, pp 86–98). The corporate history of Takashimaya describes the process as follows (Takashimaya Co., Ltd 1982, p 141, p 242). "The new wholesalers established in the post-war turbulence and the traditional wholesalers who had had business connections with department stores since before the war were all jumbled together. They dispatched large numbers of salespeople and took part in various events like exhibitions, without regard for profit, in order to deliver sales results." "New entrants proposed favorable terms such as accepting returned goods without any charge or sales support." "It was very convenient for the department stores to adopt merchandise purchasing methods like consignment buying when the suppliers were not trustworthy and the products were not reliable."

Business practices like consignment buying and dispatched salesclerks were used as a performance-based system for screening suppliers. The dispatched salesclerk system may also have been related to the increase in labor costs. Confronted by the ascendance of labor unions and cost-of-living-linked wage structures, department stores hesitated to employ more workers. Mitsukoshi and Takashimaya Department Store faced strikes by workers, while Isetan Department Store built a cooperative labor-management relationship under the slogan 'High Wages and High Efficiency'.

The department stores had to reconstruct their relationships with wholesalers because the pre-war distribution system had been destroyed by wartime controls and was in a further state of disarray due to the postwar controls. Leading pre-war wholesalers had not yet recovered enough to supply goods that were sufficient either in quantity or quality. It was not yet apparent whether the new entrants who expanded with their idiosyncratic business methods under postwar controls would prove reliable. Short-term needs such as reducing the risk of unsold stock were therefore not the only concerns of department stores, as some previous studies have argued. They also had longer-term views and reconstructed relationships with wholesalers, anticipating that their future development would be based on the information they gained through the screening process.

The competition among department stores forced them to screen their suppliers. Seibu Department Store was faced with falling revenues in 1954–1955 even though it had enlarged its shopping floors after 1951. It was Seiji Tsutsumi, inaugurated as director and shop manager in November 1955, who took on the screening of suppliers. According to Seibu's corporate history, he himself checked into all of them as well as the suppliers of other leading department stores. Seibu replaced a number of its suppliers and strengthened business relationships with Ichida, Renown, Kashiyama, Itokin and other leading apparel makers.[8]

2.2 *Discussions on Consignment Buying (*Itaku Shiire*)*

As stated above, business practices such as consignment buying and dispatched salesclerks were means for reviving a distribution system. They were not intrinsic to the apparel industry. Previous studies emphasized that while department stores sought to reduce the risk of unsold stock, apparel makers undertook that risk in their stead. Department stores were accordingly regarded as having avoided risk and lost their ability to carry the goods that sold the best, and therefore to have fallen into decline. Apparel makers, conversely, were seen as having undertaken the risk, researched consumer demand and expanded their businesses. This interpretation is too simple, however, because the effects of the apparel industry's business practices were more varied than it implies.

First, department stores did see a gradual decline as they lost their advantage in purchasing and certain major apparel makers took on retailing functions. The result was that both came to have an incentive to maintain their joint business practices. However, there was wide disparity among apparel makers in the ability to undertake the risk of unsold stock. The incentive for them to maintain their practice of receiving returns was therefore unpredictable, and tensions between department stores and apparel makers in fact persisted until the 1970s, with frequent changes in the business practices governing their transactions.

Second, the particular means of undertaking the risk depended on suppliers' management policies. Some makers purchased only those products that sold well.[9] This management policy may suit those situations in which the maker can easily predict consumer demand, but it is not desirable in unpredictable markets, as demand is likely to suffer at both suppliers and department stores. Other business practices may well be more effective in periods of fluctuating demand.

We therefore need further investigation of the history of the apparel industry's development before we can accept the conclusion of previous works that apparel makers' growth was attributable to consignment sales.

[8] Tsunehiko Yui (1991), pp 99–102. The author of this section is Asobu Yanagisawa.

[9] On the effects of trade practices, see Yoshiro Miwa (1990).

3 Raw Fabric and Its Price Fluctuations in the 1950s

The largest issue confronting apparel makers in the 1950s was the difficulty of acquiring raw fabric. The ability to accommodate the price fluctuations of raw fabric had a great effect on the competitive advantage of apparel makers.

3.1 Financing and Acquisition of Raw Fabric

In general, apparel makers used to be small in scale and struggled to procure capital. An investigation by the Tokyo Metropolitan government in 1956 found that medium-sized apparel wholesalers and makers were financed mainly by kindred or close companions (Tokyo-to Keizaikyoku 1957). Their business consisted of product planning (creating designs and dress patterns), the purchase of raw fabric and subsidiary material, the consignment of processing to clothing makers, and the sale of products to retailers and wholesalers. Few makers had their own factories. Almost all women's apparel makers consigned processing work to subcontractors or makers with exclusive contracts. Processing charges were usually paid in cash (Tsusho Sangyo-sho Kigyokyoku 1964, p 378). Even makers with their own factories frequently depended on subcontractors because of sharp seasonal fluctuations in production. It was relatively easy to enter the apparel business by using an off-season subcontractor's factory or home workers, if only one could obtain the raw fabric.

According to the above Tokyo Metropolitan Government's report, the prices of raw fabric varied between 40 and 50 % of the sales price. Another report by the Tokyo Metropolitan government in 1963 recorded that the purchases of raw fabric constituted 57.2 % of total sales.[10] The wholesalers generally purchased raw fabric from two to five textile suppliers (the No. 14 company was exceptionally large, with 11 suppliers). The means of settlement depended on the wholesalers: an average 44.2 % of the sample firms settled with cash and 55.8 % with commercial bills (Table 1.1). The report, however, noted that cash had been the major means of settlement until 1954.

The raw fabric transactions between Gifu, Bisai and Ichinomiya were settled mainly in cash as long as prices were still fluctuating violently, until 1953 (Tokai Sen'i Shimbun-sha 1975, p 15), as described below (Tokyo-to Keizaikyoku 1957, pp 152–155): "The wholesale prices of raw material rose in busy seasons and fell gradually toward the end of the season. Wholesalers with sufficient financial resources to pay for the purchase in cash are in an advantageous position." "The price of purchases in commercial bills is automatically 10 % higher than that for

[10] Tokyo-to Keizaikyoku (1965). The report data was from a 1964 survey of 13 women's and children's clothing wholesalers and 15 men's-wear wholesalers in the Kanda and Akihabara districts.

Table 1.1 Data on apparel makers (year-end of 1956)

Maker	Business category	Capital fund (million yen)	Number of Employees	Sales (thousands of yen)	Operating profit (thousands of yen)	Raw fabric transactions (ratio)	Transactions with department stores	Major products
No.1	M.W.	200	34	41,139	742	cash0· notes100	T.W.	Shirts
No.2	M.W./S.C.	1200	97	230,823	8187	cash0· notes100	D.T.	Shirts
No.3	M.W.	50	12	13,104	693	cash100· notes0		Shirts
No.4	M.W.	50	24	48,518	2334	cash50· notes50		Shirts
No.5	M.W.	100	14	n.a.	n.a.	n.a.		Shirts
No.6	C.O.	80	21	19,454	420	cash30· notes70		Ready-to-wear men's suits
No.7	S.C.	100	93	n.a.	n.a.	n.a.		Ready-to-wear men's suits
No.8	S.C.	n.a.	11	n.a.	n.a.	n.a.	T.W.	Ready-to-wear clothes for women and children
No.9	S.C.	45	18	4967	138	n.a.	T.W.	Ready-to-wear men's suits
No.10	D.O.	n.a.	63	n.a.	n.a.	n.a.		women's clothes
No.11	M.W.	150	52	n.a.	n.a.	cash0· notes100		Ready-to-wear clothes for women and children
No.12	M.W.	200	90	n.a.	n.a.	n.a.	D.T.	Ready-to-wear men's suits
No.13	M.W.	15	6	22,187	–695	n.a.		Ready-to-wear clothes

No.14	M.W.	400	67	292,192	7516	cash0・notes100	D.T.	Ready-to-wear clothes for women and children
No.15	M.W.	200	16	n.a.	n.a.	cash100・notes0		Ready-to-wear men's suits
No.16	M.W.	30	20	3410	n.a.	cash20・notes80		Work clothes
No.17	M.W./S.C.	60	17	1872	325	cash70・notes30	T.W.	Raincoats
No.18	M.W.	3000	26	147,000	19,800	cash60・notes40	T.W.	Neckties
No.19	M.W.	90	26	70,158	1627	cash45・notes55	D.T.	Neckties
No.20	M.W.	200	23	49,659	7633	n.a.	n.a.	Neckties

Source: Tokyo-to Keizaikyoku (1957)
Note1: Business category
M.W manufacturer and wholesaler
S.C subcontracting manufacturer
D.O manufacturer directly operated by wholesaler
C.O manufacturer designated by a CO-OP
Note2: Transactions with department stores
T.W through wholesalers
D.T direct transaction

cash purchase. The later the due date of the bill, the higher the purchase price. That makes it difficult for the buyer to get good quality raw fabric."

Another document pointed out that clothing fabric wholesalers did not prefer dealing with ready-to-wear merchants over selling to department stores because transactions with ready-to-wear merchants were subdivided into many small portions, were costly and were uncertain as to credit in the 1950s (Yoshikazu Hiraishi 1974, p 139). Smaller wholesalers had to watch price changes closely and purchase with cash in order to get good quality raw fabric at reasonable prices (Tokyo Style Co., Ltd. 2000, pp 70–71).

The problem of violent fluctuations in raw fabric prices had diminished by around 1960. However, it continued to be very important for apparel makers to acquire good quality raw fabric in the early 1960s. According to a 1964 Tokyo Metropolitan Government report, nine out of thirteen women's apparel makers set a high value on the purchase of raw fabric when they chose the location for their shops, situating them near raw fabric wholesalers in order to exchange information closely (Tokyo-to Keizaikyoku 1965, p 30, p 34, p 49). One of the leading apparel makers, Tokyo Style Co., Ltd. deepened its relationships with Takiyo, Suzukura Orimono and other major raw fabric wholesalers in order to secure sources of raw fabric.

The means chosen for settling transactions depended on the customers in question. According to the report by Tokyo Metropolitan Government in 1956, 72 % of sales were paid for in cash and 28 % with commercial bills. Some apparel makers spread their risk by diminishing the transaction amounts with individual retailers whose credit standing was uncertain. Transactions with department stores, on the other hand, were notably large (Tokyo-to Keizaikyoku 1957, pp 160–162, p 380). Individual customers' transactions with general retailers came to 126,000 yen with general retailers, 13,320,000 yen with wholesalers, 20,010,000 yen with department stores and 690,000 yen with other traders. Department stores were reliable about credit. Transactions with department stores were settled mainly in cash, and the bill matured sooner in the case of draft transactions.

3.2 Fluctuation of Raw Fabric Prices

The term *tsubushi-ya* in the Japanese textile industry refers to apparel traders in general ready-to-wear. It was often used to indicate traders who purchased raw fabric at low market prices, and then made it into clothing that they sold in expectation of rising product prices (Shozo Nakagomi 1975, p 168). It reflects a time when fabric was the textile industry's main product and garment manufacture processing was of little importance. The price of raw fabric fluctuated sharply until the late 1950s (Fig. 1.1). Most ready-to-wear traders were regarded as "tsubushi-ya". The war damage and controls on the textile industry, the intensification of competition and Occupation policies, Antimonopoly Act regulation of price cartels

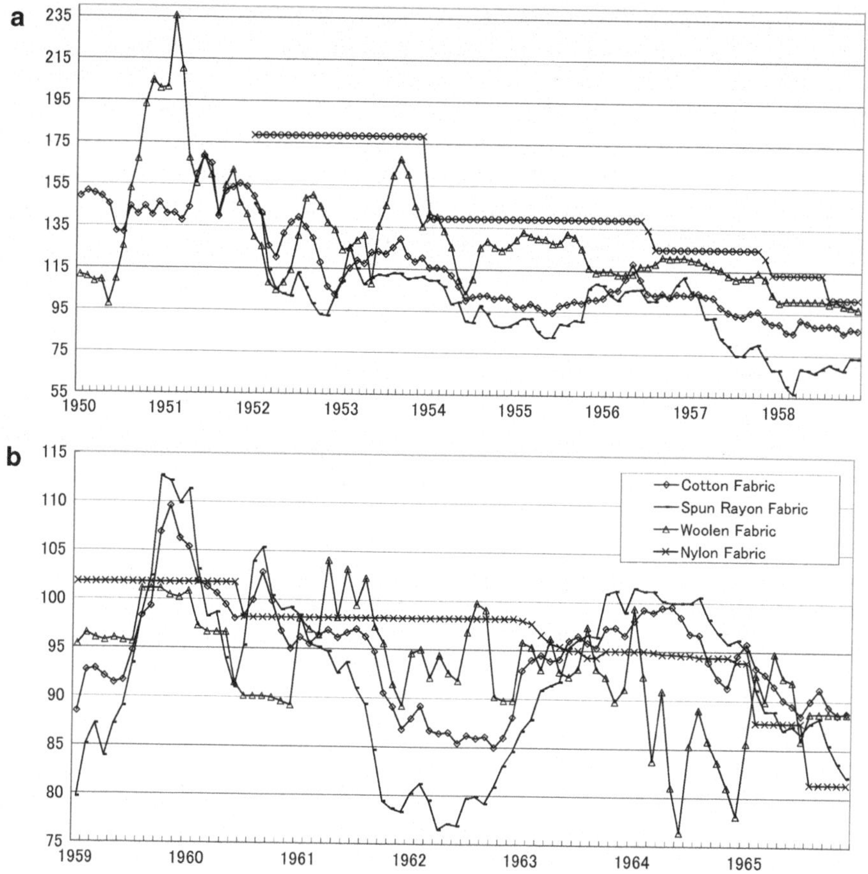

Fig. 1.1 (**a**) The price of fabric (1950–1958); (**b**) The Price of Fabric (1959–1965) (*Source:* Bank of Japan wholesale Price Index (1960 Base:100))

and the demand shock caused by the Korean War – all these formed the background of the violent price fluctuations.

Until 1953, ready-to-wear apparel makers in Gifu city purchased raw fabric at low prices in cash and made high profits, except during the steep fall of the textile market after the "Flannel Sempu" in April 1951 (Tokai Sen'i Shimbun-sha 1975, p 15).[11] Ready-to-wear makers always kept an eye on the movement of raw fabric market. The TFKSOK history refers to market fluctuation every year during the

[11] The apparel traders in Gifu often made deals within the fellow wholesalers. They were also affected by fluctuations in apparel prices. To cope with violent fluctuation, traders of the Gifu Kiseifuku Oroshi-sho Dogyo-kai (Gifu Ready-to-wear Apparel Wholesalers Association) agreed on a settlement method for raw fabric purchases and requested fabric suppliers in the Bisai district to cooperate for the stability of raw fabric price. (Tokai Sen'i Shimbun-sha 1975, pp 115–116).

1950s (Tokyo Fujin Kodomo-fuku Seizo Oroshi Kyodo Kumiai 1960, p 521). Even major suppliers to department stores, such as Kashiyama, managed their business like "tsubushi-ya". Face with the price plunge after the April 1951 "Flannel Sempu", Kashiyama swiftly cleared its stock, purchased raw fabric at the lowest price, sold it by the piece at department stores and made a large profit (Junzo Kashiyama 1998, pp 67–69). Kashiyama explained: "You should purchase against the declining trend. You can do this only if you maintain sound financial conditions so as to be able to take risks when it comes to the point."

3.3 *Management of the Apparel Makers*

The above documents and data indicate that most apparel makers in the 1950s were very small and unstable. Their credit was poor, which meant they needed liquidity in order to purchase fine raw fabric at whatever the fluctuating price. They had to have cash ready for processing charges. The cost required to collect sales proceeds was high because their customers numbered over 100. It took 3–4 months from the purchase of raw fabric to the shipment of sewn products to retailers (Tsusho Sangyo-Sho Kigyokyoku 1964, p 380; Tokyo-to Keizaikyoku 1957, p 152). The cash flow issue may have put constraints on the purchase of raw fabric until the mid-1950s.

Suppliers to department stores, by contrast, were quite different from general apparel makers (Table 1.1). No. 14 was one of the major apparel makers that did business with Takashimaya (Tokyo, Osaka and Kyoto), Seibu Department Store and Sogo. The settlement method with department stores was 30 % cash and 70 % by 60-day-draft. Raw fabric was generally paid for with 90-day-drafts. This maker also had about 40 exclusive subcontracting factories. Its business transactions with department stores had various effects. No. 14's sales were much larger than others' except No. 2 and could collect bills at a lower cost. The maker might have acquired fine raw fabric on favorable terms because of its good credit and large purchase volume. The apparel suppliers to department stores definitely had the competitive advantage when it came to raw fabric purchases. Their advantage in the apparel industry was considered remarkably strong in the 1950s.

Apparel makers had the option of selling their products to wholesalers, which enlarged their transaction volumes and made collection of bills easier. However, the transactions with wholesalers were somewhat unstable because the price of products was affected by the fluctuation of the price of raw fabric. Thus the management of wholesalers was not itself necessarily stable.

3.4 The Reality of Apparel Products

Western-style clothing spread to the public in post-war Japan, but in the early 1950s, Japanese clothes (*gofuku*) were still the main merchandise line in department stores. Isetan, the leading fashion department store, was no exception (Isetan Co. Ltd. 1990, p 158, pp 175–182). The sales floor at Isetan's main store in 1953 was allocated as follows: Japanese clothes were on the 4th floor; raw fabric, suits for gentleman, student and women (both ready-to-wear and made-to-order) were on the 3rd floor; children's clothing, shoes, sweaters, underclothes, blouses and other casual wear for women and children were on the second floor. Ready-to-wear apparel was regarded as lower rank than Japanese clothes and raw fabric. Ready-to-wear apparel was limited in variety and sizes, and "its selling space was as small as its quantity". Semi-order-made suits began to increase around 1953, and reached their peak in 1957–1959.

Tokyo Takashimaya, like Isetan, divided its apparel floors equally among three: raw fabric, semi-order-made suits and ready-to-wear apparel (Junko Ouchi and Yuriko Tajima 1996, pp 311–312). Renown, one of the major apparel makers, created a raw fabric section in 1949 and grew with the expansion of fabric sales (Akihiro Kinoshita 2001, p 200).

Ready-to-wear apparel products remained on the humble end in the last half of the 1950s. "Fujin Koron", a respected women's journal, surveyed readers about women's wear in 1958. According to the survey, as many as 70–90 % of ready-to-wear apparel users bought blouse, sweaters and inner wear, and fewer than 10 % sought one or two-piece dresses, suits and skirts. Consumers of ready-to-wear apparel complained that sizes were limited, design was unsophisticated and too ornate, and that clothes were often made with the same design or sewn coarsely.[12]

Masayo Murata points out that women's magazines like "Fujin Koron", "Shufu no Tomo", and "So-en" carried many more complaints about ready-to-wear apparel in the 1950s than after 1960 (Masayo Murata 1988). There was certainly demand for ready-to-wear suits, dresses and other clothes because these had already spread and were easy to resize and to mass-produce.[13] In the 1950s, apparel makers tried to improve quality and design and refine the size range. Their effort was insufficient, however. General consumers were not willing to buy ready-to-wear clothes.

Women's Ready-to-wear clothes spread rather slowly. According to an International Wool Secretariat survey in 1964, 26 % of women's suits were ready-to-wear, 11 % were semi-order-made, 41 % were order-made and 18 % were self-made. Ready-to-wear suits became the majority in the 1970s according to the same

[12] The survey was conducted with about 70 each of female college students, dressmaking school students, working women and housewives (Fusako Kumon 1958).

[13] Isetan department store recognized that semi-order-made seemed suits halfway and unsatisfactory to consumers and aimed to carry fully ready-to-wear clothing in the future (Isetan Co. Ltd. 1990, pp 176–177).

survey.[14] Ready-to-wear clothes for married women had not yet been developed at that time. In the fashion world, "sack dress",[15] which was in vogue in 1958, was said to have been first accepted by the youth in the ready-to-wear apparel history.

It seems to have taken a long time for ready-to-wear apparel to spread in Japan. First, it took a long time to collect data on Japanese physique types, which was needed in order to expand the range of sizes. Second, semi-order-made clothes were popular in the 1950s, and there was little incentive for makers to improve ready-to-wear.

Moreover, there was a big market for raw fabric. The post-war boom in dress-making schools promoted self-made clothes, which were a major competitor to ready-to-wear (Tokyo Fujin Kodomo-fuku Seizo Oroshi Kyodo Kumiai 1960, pp 542–544). Third, as considered in this section, the competitive advantage of apparel makers lay in their ability to acquire fine raw fabric amidst the violent fluctuations in raw fabric prices. Production improvement in ready-to-wear was therefore not beneficial to them.

There were some exceptions. Wacoal, a leading underwear maker, began to use grading technology to expand the range of its sizes. The company worked to understand the characteristics of Japanese consumers, developed new merchandise and improved its sewing techniques (Wacoal Co., Ltd. 1999, pp 59–86, pp 142–145).[16]

4 Production Improvements and Consumer Change from the 1960s to the 1970s

4.1 Improvement of the Condition in Raw Fabric Market

The production of textiles increased from the second half of the 1950s on. However, textile prices were still volatile. Industrial policies were imposed, including the curtailing of fiber production through administrative guidance and the temporary closure of textile facilities. Price fluctuations in raw fabric gradually diminished. As fiber prices decreased, wool and cotton spinning makers began to integrate the production of raw fabric into their operations. Synthetic fiber makers also integrated downstream products to expand their market in fibers. Some fiber makers tried to enter the apparel business but they often failed because the logic of fiber market expansion was not in accord with apparel production. The few successes were found in such products as shirts and blouses (Shozo Nakagomi 1975, pp 308–425).

[14] In women's wear, ready-to-wear clothes became the majority around 1962 (Kunio Hayashi 1987, p 82; Yoko Yanagi 1985, p 175).

[15] "Sack dress" was loosely tailored and designed to obscure the body line. Across Henshubu (1995), pp 68–74.

[16] See the Kashiyama case (Junzo Kashiyama 1998, pp 70–80; Akihiro Kinoshita 1997).

By about 1960, price stability and the integration of raw fiber production into their operations had improved the ability of ready-to-wear apparel makers to acquire raw fabric. Some fiber makers financed apparel makers. The 1964 investigation by MITI showed that more ready-to-wear apparel makers purchased raw fabric from spinning makers than before. Spinning makers' bills matured over a period as long as 120–150 days, which meant that apparel makers could in effect obtain rather long-term loans (Tsusho Sangyo-sho Kigyokyoku 1964, p 375). Furthermore, polyester fabric began to appear on the market and diffused rapidly through advertising by synthetic-fiber makers.

Meanwhile, growing apparel markets and their concomitant rise in income attracted new entrants to the market. The output of women's ready-to-wear clothes grew rapidly, from an indexed 100 in 1952 to 238 in 1958, 243 in 1959, 329 in 1960, and 477 in 1961.[17] Improvement in the procurement of raw fabric as well as increased demand gave medium and small makers without credit the chance to play an active part in the apparel market.

The advantages enjoyed by department stores and their supplies slackened as a result. Competition between apparel makers and retailers became considerably more equal. In the 1960s, the main source of competitive advantage in the apparel industry came from upgrades in product quality, expansion of size ranges and other production improvements. Juki Synchronization System, developed by Tokyojuki Kogyo Co., Ltd., was spreading in sewing factories, improving their productivity and upgrading the quality of apparel products (Tokyojuki Kogyo Co., Ltd. 1979, pp 41–51). This new equipment boosted production improvements in the apparel industry.

In this section I will discuss the following four points: (1) Department stores led the expansion of size rages and quality upgrades. (3) Specialty stores and their suppliers sought to divide customers into segments and grow with a design-oriented strategy.[18] (4) Specialty stores prospered in the 1970s. (5) The apparel industry and consumer behavior both experienced big changes.

4.2 *Quality Improvement Led by Department Stores*

Apparel suppliers to department stores were not motivated to widen the assortment of sizes and designs on any lines other than the best selling because they sought to avoid the risk of returning goods (Tokyo Fujin-Kodomo-fuku Kogyo Kumiai 1982, p 303). Accordingly, department stores themselves led the drive to improve the

[17] The data comes from the survey by Nihon Kiseifuku Seizo Kogyo Kumiai Rengo-kai (Japan Ready-to-wear Clothes Manufacturers Association).

[18] A 'Specialty Store' is not clearly defined. In general, it is distinguished from a local clothing store and denotes a fashion-oriented retailer located mainly in cities and specializing in men's or women's apparel.

Table 1.2 Raw fabric component ratios

	Value of raw fabric laid in (ten thousand yen)	Pure wool	Wool blending	Cotton and staple fiber	Nylon	Polyester	Acrylic resin	Silk and rayon
1955	76,535	42.2 %	16.7 %	22.8 %	3.3 %			10.0 %
1963	450,535	35.5 %	14.2 %	9.4 %	5.6 %	21.2 %	6.7 %	3.5 %

Source: Tokyo-to Keizaikyoku (1965)

quality of ready-to-wear clothes, upgrade the assortment and expand the range of sizes. Apparel makers cooperated with department stores. In the process, makers cultivated their sewing, pattern making, and size grading skills.

Isetan Department Store, one of the pioneers in ready-to-wear apparel, had been making plans for semi-order products since the 1950s and had therefore accumulated massive data about the body shapes of customers. In 1957, Isetan established its Dresses and Accessories Laboratory (Fukushoku Kenkyu-shitsu) and launched research on ready-to-wear, focusing on size and color (Isetan Co. Ltd. 1990, pp 176–179, pp 216–221) and developing sizes and designs suitable to Japanese bodies. Production of Isetan's designs was consigned to Renown and Yoshida Hosei. Seibu and Takashimaya followed this development.

In 1963, Isetan, Seibu and Takashimaya jointly published standard specifications for women's wear sizes.[19] Women's wear was limited two common sizes until the mid-1960s, however (Tokyo Style Co., Ltd. 2000, p 24). The publication of the standard did not lead immediately to an expansion of size rages. Size variety was essential to spreading ready-to-wear in Japan. Traditional Japanese clothing (*gofuku*) was not made to fit the individual body, but Western clothes were. Accordingly apparel makers had to master pattern making, size grading, draping, sewing and other skills to fit the bodylines of Japanese women. The introduction of pattern making smoothed the sewing process and stabilized the quality of the product (Table 1.2).

Some department stores launched business partnerships with overseas brand in the 1960s. Raw fiber makers also contributed to the improvement in ready-to-wear clothing through business partnerships with overseas brands. This was often interpreted as a strategy oriented to the high end (Kazutoshi, Maeda 1991, pp 40–41). Department stores, too, tried to upgrade ready-to-wear quality through such partnerships. Isetan expanded its Dresses and Accessory Laboratory into the Merchandise Laboratory of Sales Division (Hanbai-bu Shohin Kenkyu-shitsu) in 1963, then into Isetan Laboratory Co., Ltd. in 1967 (Isetan Co. Ltd 1990, pp 219–221). During this period, Isetan established an exclusive contract with Norma Tullo, an Australian designer. The products under license were rigidly inspected and the management system covering production to sales was established. Tokyo Style cooperated with Isetan to undertake the production of

[19] Some other standards coexisted like JIS standard and others.

Table 1.3 Tokyo Style Co. management performance

Accounting month		Sales (thousand yen)	Ordinary profit to sales ratio
1950	Dec.	120,584	3.0 %
1955	Dec.	507,479	3.0 %
1960	Sep.	1,168,406	6.1 %
1961	Sep.	1,436,138	4.5 %
1962	Sep.	1,561,374	5.6 %
1963	Sep.	1,940,925	7.3 %
1964	Sep.	2,187,638	5.7 %
1965	Sep.	2,403,871	6.4 %
1966	Sep.	2,437,896	5.4 %
1967	Sep.	2,763,391	5.9 %
1968	Sep.	3,580,576	7.9 %
1969	Sep.	5,065,061	5.1 %

Source: Tokyo Style Co., Ltd. (2000)

Norma Tullo products. The company mastered the knowledge and skill required to produce ready-to-wear clothes and increased its profit margin (Table 1.3). Tokyo Style also made its own effort, through draping techniques, to take the lead in producing ready-to-wear in 1964 (Tokyo Style Co., Ltd. 2000, pp 24–26).

Isetan Laboratory continued its cooperation with Tokyo Style and established new brands: 'Five In One' in 1967 and 'Strawberry Shop', specializing in small sizes, in 1969. Isetan Laboratory played an important role in improving ready-to-wear clothes. The company also contracted with a US apparel maker and had Yoshida Hosei, one of its sewing subcontractors, acquire pattern-making and size-grading skills, which were then transferred to Tokyo Style, Hanasaki, Kashiyama and other apparel makers. Takashimaya tied up with Pierre Cardin in 1959 and started pret-a-porter from 1962. Toray CO., Ltd. contracted with Yves Saint-Laurent in 1963 and Kashiyama acquired a sublicense from Toray. Bunka Fukuso Gakuin, one of the leading dressmaking schools, started draping classes from the second half of the 1950s. All these contributed to developing human resources in the industry (Junko Ouchi and Yuriko Tajima 1996, pp 436–437).

4.3 *Specialty Stores and Designers*

The transactions between apparel makers and department stores expanded with the growth of apparel market (Table 1.4). Consequently returned goods also increased along with tensions around consignment buying. In 1959, women's apparel makers reported that they were forced to accept returns of a large amount of winter clothing from department stores during the department stores' special bargain sales. In response, the National Ready-to-Wear Clothes Association (Zenkoku Kiseifuku Rengo-kai) made an effort to improve the terms of trade and distributed posters to

Table 1.4 Customers of women's apparel makers

	General retailers	Department stores	Supermarket	Installment-sales stores	Wholesalers
1955	68.4 %	14.4 %	n.a.	9.4 %	0.5 %
1963	48.3 %	24.9 %	0.1 %	10.4 %	10.6 %

Source: Tokyo-to Keizaikyoku (1965)

its members to promote suppliers' awareness (Tokyo Fujin Kodomo-fuku Seizo Oroshi Kyodo Kumiai 1960, pp 611–623). The poster taught that: (1) Consignment buying required a formal contract. (2) Suppliers had to restrain from speculative shipping. (3) Cancellation or returns of goods must not be accepted without special cause. According to the MITI's 1964 investigation, returned goods accounted for 20–30 % of shipments, though the reasons for the returns were unknown (Tsusho Sangyo-sho Kigyokyoku 1964, p 383, p 471).

The tension between suppliers and department stores reached its peak in the early 1960s. Of the so-called Big Four among Tokyo women's apparel makers at the time, Hanasaki, Tokyo Style and Hanamura continued to expand their business focusing on trade with department stores (Table 1.5). Meanwhile, President Wataru Ono of the fourth, Sanshi (established in 1924), became chairman of the Tokyo Women's and Children's Wear Manufacturers' Association. In this role, he was forced to bear the brunt of the negotiations with department stores for improved terms of trade. The negotiation did not progress well. During the time, Sanshi withdrew its trade from department stores, which had accounted for 80–90 % of its sales, and shifted its sales to specialty stores. In the second half of the 1970s, department stores accounted for only 10 % of Sanshi's total sales of Sanshi, as against the specialty stores' 90 % (Yano Research Institute 1979).

During this tense period, Tokyo Women's and Children's Wear Manufacturers' Association promoted organized action to improve apparel products on their own terms. Under chairman Ono, Teruo Takada from Tokyo Blouse Co. (one of leading apparel makers, established in 1941) took the initiative in various activities such as inviting instructors from the US and holding workshops. As a result, draping skills spread and the size range for clothing size widened (Junko Ouchi and Yuriko Tajima 1996, pp 325–326).[20]

In the early 1960s, some apparel makers began to prefer specialty stores as their customers. Five apparel makers, including Sanshi, Tokyo Blouse, Sanki, Kanto Dress and Stella, and nine retailers specializing in apparel, formed the 'R9 Group' (Yoshikazu Hiraishi 1974, pp 166–170).

In 1963, Hajime Yanagisawa left his old ready-to-wear maker and established apparel maker Ichiju with 5 people, aiming to create new and unprecedented products. Fashion-oriented Ichiju prospered with leading specialty stores like San'ai and Suzuya. In the late 1960s Ichiju commercialized dresses designed by

[20] At the same period, press machined were introduced in sewing factories (Tokyo Fujin-Kodomo-fuku Kogyo Kumiai 1982, p 267, p 302).

Table 1.5 Sales of leading makers of women's apparel (FY1973)

Ranking	Company	Headquarters location	Sales (million yen)	Ordinary profit to sales ratio	Major customers
1	Itokin	Osaka	30,248	10.2 %	Various
2	Tokyo Style	Tokyo	21,385	7.1 %	Department stores
3	Micalady	Tokyo	19,098	2.3 %	Department stores
4	World	Kobe	15,389	15.3 %	Specialty stores
5	Kashiyama*	Tokyo	13,200	9.5 %	Department stores
6	Hanasaki	Tokyo	12,790	1.2 %	Department stores
7	Naigai Amimono*	Tokyo	10,216	2.7 %	Department stores
8	Fujii	Osaka	9245	–	–
9	San'yo Shokai*	Tokyo	9212	4.4 %	Department stores
10	Renown*	Tokyo	9026	6.2 %	Department stores
11	Yokoyama	Nagoya	7168	7.1 %	Specialty stores
12	Sakuraya Shoji	Nagoya	7124	3.1 %	Supermarkets
13	All Style	Kobe	7047	4.7 %	Specialty stores
14	Caravan	Tokyo	6796	3.8 %	Specialty stores
15	Yamamoto Group	Tokyo	6579	3.0 %	Supermarkets
17	Sanshi	Tokyo	6205	5.0 %	Specialty stores
19	Mikura	Tokyo	5797	4.2 %	Specialty stores
20	Renown Look	Tokyo	5749	2.7 %	Department stores
21	Tsubame Coat	Tokyo	5008	1.9 %	Various
22	Tokyo Blouse	Tokyo	4866	5.2 %	Department stores
28	Hanamura	Tokyo	3981	0.0 %	Department stores
35	Ichiju	Tokyo	3390	6.3 %	Specialty stores
39	Barbizon	Tokyo	2940	15.7 %	Specialty stores

Source: Yano Keizai Kenkyu-jo (1977)
Note: The sales of each company with asterisk includes only the sales of its women's apparel division

Issei Miyake and Takada Kenzo, who in the later 1970s would enjoy international reputations (Junko Ouchi and Yuriko Tajima 1996, pp 368–370, pp 465–466).

Another leading fashion apparel maker, Mikura, reduced its trade with department stores in favor of specialty stores in the mid-1960s. Mitsuhiro Matsuda, the founder of Nicole in 1967, and Kenzo Takada, the founder of Jungle Jap in Paris in 1970, worked for Mikura and then San'ai as designers in the early 1960s after graduating Bunka Fukuso Gakuin, one of the leading dressmaking schools. San'ai and Suzuya were the most popular retailers specializing in apparel products in the 1960s. Unlike traditional, regionally-oriented clothing stores or department stores with their diverse customers, Suzuya divided customers into fine categories and targeted women in their 20s who were sensitive to fashion. Suzuya aggressively opened new shops including Sukiyabashi-ten in 1957, Ginza-ten in 1960, Tachikawa-ten and Ikebukuro-ten in 1962. Suzuya centralized its procurement and promoted an assortment corresponding to character of each outlet. Suzuya also cooperated with small and medium apparel makers to develop original product and discovered talented designers. Suzuya obtained cooperation of Yoji Yamamoto and Rei Kawakubo, who later became distinguished designers and developed original products (Suzuya Co., Ltd. 1975, pp 40–49; Junko Ouchi and Yuriko Tajima 1996, pp 328–330, pp 478–479, pp 518–519).

These shifts among specialty stores and suppliers came about because once the constraints on the raw fabric supply were lifted, department stores and their suppliers lost their advantage while small and medium makers and retailers enjoyed new opportunities. At this point specialty stores and their suppliers adopted strategies that differed from those of department stores. They did not provide either high-class, high-quality products or the standard products for the taste of general customers, but created uniquely designed clothes and reinforced their competitiveness (Yoshikazu Hiraishi 1974, pp 169–170).

It should be noted that the trade between specialty stores and their suppliers was conducted generally in the form of spot sales (*kaitori*) basis, rather than on a consignment basis. Table 1.6 shows the transaction method of later years, which may have been the same in the early 1960s according to the recollections of people in the apparel business. Iwashima, Sanshi, Tokyo Blouse and other apparel makers promoted the trade on a spot-sales basis. According to the memoir of Hajime Yanagisawa, who founded Ichiju, trade with San'ai had been on a consignment basis, but on a spot-sales basis with other specialty stores (Yoshikazu Hiraishi 1974, pp 167–168; Junko Ouchi and Yuriko Tajima 1996, p 369, pp 494–496).

Specialty stores aimed for a distinctive assortment, for a limited group of customers. This concentration strategy fostered expert buyers and enabled the spot-sales trade Small and medium makers, who sometimes took risks to provide opportunities to creative designers, preferred spot sales to consignment sales, the assortment of which tended to be from well-selling lines (Yoshikazu Hiraishi 1974, pp 167–178).[21] The terms of trade with department stores remained unimproved,

[21] There were a few return goods in the spot-sales trade as well.

Table 1.6 Types of contracts between apparel makers and retailers, and ratios of returned goods (August–October 1977)

1. Sales ratios by contract types (%)

	Urban department stores	Local department stores	Installment department stores	Supermarkets	Specialty stores	General retailers	Wholesalers
Spot Buying (*kaitori*)	40.1	64.2	51.4	94.6	90.2	84.6	92.9
Consignment buying (*Itaku Shiire*)	56.5	35.5	48.6	3.6	9.1	15.3	7.2
Purchase according to performance (*Shoka Shiire*)	3.4	0.3		1.8	0.7	0.2	

2. Ratio of returned goods to sales

Spot buying		Consignment buying or purchase according to performance	
0–4.9 %	11	0–4.9 %	0
5–9.9 %	29	5–9.9 %	0
10–14.9 %	11	10–14.9 %	6
15–19.9 %	9	15–19.9 %	6
20–24.9 %	2	20–24.9 %	9
25 %–	2	25–29.9 %	8
		30–34.9 %	12
		35 %–	7

3. Reasons for returns in spot buying

Inferior quality	52
Late delivery	60
Unsold goods	38
Inventory adjustment of retailers	36
Different from sample	11
Others	3

Source: Tsusho Sangyo-sho (Ministry of International Trade and Industry) (1978)

which also made some apparel makers specialty-store-oriented. In the meantime, specialty stores needed distinctive products in order to be able constantly to update their assortments in accordance with changes in fashion. Specialty stores aggressively promoted this strategy, and they were able to open new stores more easily than department stores, which were subject to Department Store Law regulation (Hyakka-ten hou).

4.4 *The Growth of Specialty Stores*

In 1960s, the apparel industry showed rapid growth. The women's apparel market in particular saw remarkable expansion (Table 1.7). During the same period, ready-to-wear clothes became more widely accepted (Table 1.8). Department stores, specialty stores and apparel makers grew respectively, constituting two different markets. The suppliers of department stores and specialty stores were very different (Tables 1.9 and 1.10). In short, department stores were high-class and high-quality-oriented while specialty stores were uniqueness- and design-oriented. Department stores and specialty stores competed in alternative goods.

In 1970s, the apparel market expansion continued, but changed such that department stores' sales began to stagnate while specialty stores continued their notable growth. Not only Suzuya, San'ai and other established specialty stores, but also affiliate and shops directly operated by new apparel makers achieved rapid growth. Specialty stores mainly targeted young generation or post-war baby boomers who were likely to seek an unfettered and unique sense of fashion (Table 1.11).

At the same time, the so-called 'Mansion Makers' mushroomed and targeted women from their high teens to thirties. They produced unique products mainly for specialty stores and created a great sensation. Most leaders of the 'Mansion Makers' were baby boomers, which suggested that those who were of the same generation as

Table 1.7 Performance of apparel wholesalers

	Average sales per wholesaler			Total sales by wholesalers		
	Fiber products	Clothes	Women's and children's clothes	Fiber products	Clothes	Women's and children's clothes
1962	100.0	14.5	11.9	100.0	3.2	2.1
1972	186.2	35.6	64.9	190.6	9.2	22.1

Source: Ministry of international trade and industry, census of commerce
Note: Values indexed to the value of Fiber Products in 1962

Table 1.8 Composition of women's ready-to-wear apparel

	Suits	Dress	Skirts	Sweaters
1965	25.8 %	34.9 %	34.5 %	77.6 %
1970	43.2 %	51.2 %	69.3 %	86.5 %
1975	71.4 %	79.1 %	89.2 %	97.1 %

Source: International Wool Secretariat

Table 1.9 Specialty stores and apparel makers (1973)

Retailers	Sales (hundred million yen)	Number of stores	Major suppliers
San'ai	244	27	Itokin, Sanshi, Ichiju, Tokyo Blouse, Hanasaki, All Style, Liberal Nakamura, Seven Mode, World, Mock, Java, Orion, San-yo Shokai
Suzuya	205	33	Ichiju, Roma Iwashima, Tokyo Blouse, Jardin, Caravan, World, Merino
Mammina	90	17	Hanasaki, Kashiyama, Sanshi, Tokyo Style, New Star, Caravan, Artemodo
Hiyoshiya	50	27	VIVID
Tamaya	50	18	World, All Style, Akagawaei, Okura, Mock, Viron, Barbizon, Itokin, Sanshi, Okura, Heidi

Source: Nihon Sen'i Keizai Kenkyu-jo (1974)
Note: Mamina is an affiliated company of Isetan

Table 1.10 Department stores and apparel makers (1982/83)

Department store	Sales by apparel supplier (million yen)
Isetan Main Store	Kashiyama 1751, San'yo Shokai 1376, Renown 1080, Daido 660
Takashimaya Nihonbashi Store	San'yo Shokai 828, Renown 430, Kashiyama 418, Kosugi Sangyo 156, Issey Miyake 94, Naigai Amimono 70, Intermode 60, Igin 56
Seibu Ikebukuro Store	San'yo Shokai 1325, Renown 940, Kashiyama 432, Daido 490, Eruka Hanbai (KENZO) 100
Tokyu Shibuya Main Store	Kashiyama 680, Renown 165, Intermode 148, San'yo Shokai 118, Kansai Yamamoto 55, Igin 33, Kosugi Sangyo 24
Hankyu Sukiyabashi Store	Renown 278, San'yo Shokai 160, COMME des GARÇONS 80, Daido70, Naigai Amimono 50
Matsuya Ginza Main Store	Kashiyama 388, Renown 205, San'yo Shokai 162, Issey Miyake 160, Kansai Yamamoto 130, Eruka Hanbai (KENZO) 120, COMME des GARÇONS 90、Kosugi Sangyo 48
Mitsukoshi Nihonbashi Main Store	San'yo Shokai 437, Kashiyama 412, Intermode 145, Igin 87, Kosugi Sangyo 84, Eruka Hanbai(KENZO) 40

Source: Yano Keizai Kenkyu-jo (1983)

Table 1.11 The purchase of women's apparel by age and shop (1977)

	Suits			Dress		
Age	Department stores	Supermarkets	Specialty stores	Department stores	Supermarkets	Specialty stores
16–19	22.8 %	21.2 %	38.6 %	23.2 %	25.9 %	36.7 %
20–24	29.3 %	10.7 %	39.7 %	29.3 %	15.9 %	33.0 %
25–29	34.6 %	12.0 %	40.3 %	26.5 %	24.6 %	24.5 %
30–34	20.1 %	13.1 %	39.9 %	25.0 %	27.2 %	20.0 %
35–39	34.5 %	16.7 %	21.8 %	29.8 %	26.4 %	20.4 %
40–44	34.6 %	15.8 %	17.2 %	29.0 %	20.9 %	17.4 %
45–49	41.8 %	13.5 %	25.8 %	27.7 %	23.2 %	19.6 %

Source: International Wool Secretariat
Note: Ready-to-wear and semi-order-made apparels

Table 1.12 The actual condition of women's apparel 'Mansion Maker'

Representative person				Performance of company			
Age		Years of experience		Sales (million yen)		Ratio of profit to sales	
–29	3.0 %	0–5	2.4 %	0–100	12.3 %	0–1 %	29.5 %
30–32	14.8 %	6–10	22.4 %	100–200	31.1 %	1–2 %	21.1 %
33–35	30.9 %	11–15	40.0 %	200–400	31.6 %	2–4 %	21.1 %
36–38	17.0 %	16–20	18.1 %	400–600	15.6 %	4–6 %	10.5 %
39–41	12.2 %	21–25	9.5 %	600–800	3.8 %	6–8 %	5.3 %
42–44	9.1 %	26–	7.6 %	800–1000	1.9 %	8–10 %	5.3 %
45–47	4.3 %	Sex		1000–	3.8 %	10 %–	7.4 %
48–	8.7 %	Male	91.4 %				
		Female	8.6 %				

Source: Yano Keizai Kenkyu-jo (1982)

their customers enjoyed advantages in the market (Table 1.12). The business strategy of specialty stores was said to be suited to an age of diversity and uniqueness (Tomizawa Konomi 1995, p 582). New developments occurred in the 1970s, including product differentiation corresponding to the diversification of consumers.

4.5 Diversification, Instability and Ambiguity of Consumers

From the early 1970s, apparel prices had shown amplified seasonal fluctuations (Fig. 1.2). This suggested that high markup prices were set at the beginning of the season (June for summer goods and September/October for winter goods) with a substantial markdown following the end of the season.

We cannot obtain time series of markup and markdown rates. Figure 1.2 shows estimates from the following regression model: The dependent variable is the price of clothing in a given month and the independent variables are the general consumer price index and price of clothing in the previous month. The predicted price is calculated in the regression equation. The ratio of predicted price to actual price is shown to fluctuate in parallel with the markup rate.

The change of contents in the price index of clothing has to be taken into consideration, which is difficult because we do not have long-term data series on the same item. We can only obtain fragmentary data. The markdown index for a two-piece women's dress (highest price/lowest price, in the same season for winter goods) changed from 99.9 % (1965–1966), to 96.5 %(1966–1967), to 95.8 % (1967–1968); the women's dress index, from 77.3 %(1971–1972), to 91.4 % (1972–1973), to 80.1 %(1973–1974), to 85.8 %(1974–1975); a women's suit: 88.8 %(1975–1976), 81.4 %(1976–1977), 81.3 %(1977–1978), 67.9 % (1978–1979), 66.8 %(1979–1980), 71.6 %(1980–1981).

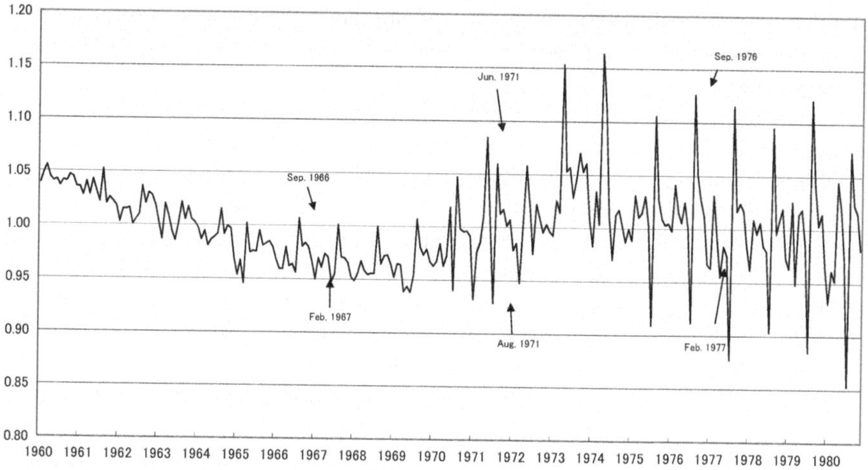

Fig. 1.2 Actual price/predicted price of clothes
$\text{CPI}\cdot\text{cloth} = -0.836 + 0.601 * \text{CPI}\cdot\text{cloth}(-1) + 0.405 * \text{CPI}\cdot\text{general}$. Adjusted $- R^2 = 0.988$
(t−value) (12.110) (8.089)
Period: Jan. 1960–Dec. 1980 (*Source*: Consumer Price Index in Tokyo's special wards)

According to this data and Fig. 1.2, it appears that since the 1970s, the markup rate was set higher at the beginning of the season and that the markdown accelerated in the same season. A similar trend was observed in the US from the last half of 1960s (Peter Pashigian 1988).[22]

Theoretically the rational pricing strategy for a firm is to set high markup prices at the beginning and probe demand trends, then mark it down based on sales, in cases where the variability in consumers' reservation price (the price which consumers are willing to buy) is large or uncertain. Firms can absorb consumer surpluses effectively through such strategies (Edward P. Lazear 1986; Peter Pashigian and Brian Bowen 1991; Peter Pashigian 1988; Bernard Van Praag and Ben Bode 1992; Alvaro Rodriguez and Luis Locay 2002).

Figure 1.2 suggests that apparel firms set high markup prices, differentiated by product, at the beginning of the season, failed to maintain the prices and marked them down in the same season, as they confronted intense competition by other apparel makers, increased variability in consumers' reservation prices (diversification), intertemporal changes in consumers' reservation prices (instability), and increased uncertainty about consumer's reservation prices (ambiguity).[23]

These changes were the result of the following: As discussed previously, consumers had become able to choose from among various goods thanks to developments in the quality of ready-to-wear clothes, wider size ranges, and growing

[22] Shinobu Majima suggested a similar trend in the UK in her presentation at the 72th Conference of Socio-Economic History Society, Japan in June 2003.

[23] Tatsuya Nakamura (1992) referred to consumer 'ambiguity'.

diversity in design. In ladies' magazines, complaints about ready-to-wear clothes gradually disappeared while advice on ready-to-wear choices increased (Masayo Murata 1988).

The increase of leisure time and growing numbers of working women in the city diversified the kinds of occasions requiring particular clothing, which multiplied the kinds of goods required. The choice of goods became dependent on the search process and difficult to predict. In 1970s, new types of clothes and styles emerged one after another, including miniskirts, pants, jeans, sporty wear, and others. The ideas of wearing clothes appropriate to time, place, and occasion, which prevailed in the 1960s, went out of fashion. Uniformly accepted styles such as the miniskirt or those that had been promoted in advertising campaigns by synthetic fiber makers in the 1960s disappeared. It became hard to predict consumer preference. Newly designed products became ever shorter-lived (Kunio Hayashi 1987, pp 149–167; Tsusho Sangyo-sho Seikatsu Sangyokyoku 1984, pp 65–99).

New fashion journals were born one after the other, introducing the latest styles (Teruko Inoue and Jose Zasshi Kenkyu-kai 1989, Chap. 1). Consumer preference came to be influenced by fortuitous encounters with information presented in the mass media and by word-of-mouth. The above suggests that consumers became more diversified, unstable and ambiguous from around 1970 because of economic changes and developments in the production of apparel goods. As a result, apparel makers started full-fledged endeavors to pursue "consumer value".

I previously analyzed the details of the history of apparel industry in the 1970s (Susumu Ishii 2004) as follows. Apparel makers established their own brands, developed multiple brands and took on retailing functions, while some big apparel makers adopted a new strategy of maintaining multiple original brands (Table 1.13). According to a 1976 report on 13 leading women's-wear makers, all had their own original brands.[24] The number of brands was 7.54 and the sales share of their original brands was 74 % on average. Many makers (9 in the above report) introduced divisional systems based on product types and brands from the 1970s. The subdividing of customers and brand marketing were management strategies aimed at diminishing the dispersion of customers and the uncertainty about their reservation prices, and at effectively absorbing the consumers' surplus.

Another remarkable development in the 1970s was the apparel makers' taking on the retailing function. World Co., Ltd., for example, a major supplier to specialty stores, developed a new brand focused on coordinates. In the development process, World even considered dyeing raw yarn and organized medium-sized specialty stores into 'Only Shops' that mainly sold World products. World Co., Ltd. grew rapidly and eventually opened direct management stores (Yasuji Yamakawa

[24] This investigation was conducted by the Japan Apparel Federation (Nihon Iryo-hosei-hin kyokai) in Feb. and Mar. 1976. Ichiju, Itokin, Kashiyama, Command, Sanyo-Shokai, Genet, Tsubame-Coat, Tokyo Style, Nihon Iryo, Hanasaki, Micalady, Rome Iwashima, and Renown Look were the companies examined.

Table 1.13 The brands of Tokyo Style Co., Ltd

(1) Number of new brands emerging in each period

Period	
1950s	1
1960–64	3
1965–69	3
1970–74	19
1975–79	22

(2) Number of brands by customer segment in 1980

	Mail sales channel						
	Department stores				Supermarkets		Specialty stores
	Limited brand		General brand		Limited brand	General brand	General brand
Target by age	High end	Mid range or low end	High end	Mid range or low end	Mid range or low end	Mid range or low end	Mid range or low end
Young							
Young and young married			1	3			1
Young married			1	1			3
Young married and middle aged	3		2	2	2	2	2
Middle aged							
From young to middle aged		4		3		1	

Source : (1) Tokyo Style Co., Ltd. (2000); (2) Yano Keizai Kenkyu-jo (1980)
Note: 'Limited brand' includes single items and specific sizes. 'General brand' includes multiple items and sizes. 'High end' goods are those with average prices of over 30,000 yen

1984).[25] World gave 'Only Shops' incentives to promote sales of their own brands and provided guidance about sales floor allotments, product display and sales methods. These strategies helped guide unstable and ambiguous consumers and manage appropriate prices, corresponding to the rapid deterioration of product value and diversification of consumers.

The sales floor management of World Co. was taken over by Designer's & Character's (DC) brand makers such as Bigi (established in 1970), Five Fox (established 1976) and others. DC brand makers later promoted direct management or franchise stores. Old specialty stores also expanded their branch store networks and sought to improve their interior decoration and their selection of goods in

[25] The sales of World Co. stood at 4.9 billion yen in FY1970, 42.3 billion yen in FY1975 and 90.5 billion yen in FY1980. The ratio of ordinary profit to sales was over 10 % through 1970s, except for FY1973, when it was 8.5 %.

harmony with the location of store.[26] Around 1980, DC brand makers' shops were introduced in department stores, with sales spaces managed by the makers themselves (Akihiro Kinoshita 1997; Choi Yonghoon 1999).

As stated above, the pursuit of 'consumer value' began to influence the competitiveness of the firms in the apparel industry after the early 1970s. Advanced sales techniques, including various approaches to consumers and appropriate responses to the deterioration of goods, were developed through competition among firms.

5 Conclusions and Prospects

Previous research argued that apparel makers developed though consignment buying and the system of dispatched salesclerks. This paper has shown that: In the 1950s, the price of raw fabric fluctuated intensely and the production of apparel goods remained underdeveloped. By around the 1960s, conditions in the purchase of raw fabric had improved through coordination among firms, increased production and industrial policy. These changes gave makers strong incentive to improve their product. In the 1960s, the cooperation between makers and retailers and the competition among both for improvements in production progressed. Two types of markets had been formed: one was the high-class and quality oriented department-store type outlet, and the other was the specialty-store oriented to uniqueness and design. Japanese apparel makers and the apparel industry developed within this historical process. In the 1970s, they began to throw themselves into pursuing 'consumer value'.

I referred at the beginning of this paper to three phases in economic development, each characterized by a particular type of profit incentive based on differences in price.

Incentive 1: the differences in market prices in different times and/or places (market value)

Incentive 2: the differences between the price of input goods and the marginal cost of production (production value)

Incentive 3: the difference between the marginal cost of production and the consumer's reservation price (consumer value)

These three incentives always coexist with capitalist economic systems that locate profit in any gap in value (Katsuhito Iwai 1985). It is noteworthy, however, that the particular operating incentive in question strongly directs the way firms compete and that an industry's development depends on historical timing. Incentive 2 is one of the conditions of sustainable economic growth. It requires that

[26] Suzuya opened only 15 stores from the end of Second World War until 1969. It then not only opened as many as 23 new stores during the first half of 1970s but also enlarged and renovated its existing stores.

manufacturers be highly organized, for grouping enterprises or enhancing corporate governance, in order not only to exploit the market but also to repress or absorb fluctuations in market prices. Firms formed various organizations in Japan in the 1920s and 1930s, which functioned effectively (Juro Hashimoto and Haruhito Takeda 1985). This highly organized economy, however, was destroyed and reorganized under wartime controls, the damage of the war and Occupation reforms. These shocks continued to cause distortions in the economy and fluctuations in the price of basic materials, such as fiber and iron, until the mid-1950s. Manufacturers couldn't help but respond to Incentive 1. Industrial policies, post-war corporate governance and long-term relationships between firms improved the situation and brought Incentive 2 into play. The Japanese apparel industry developed within this overall economic environment. Incentive 3 began figuring prominently in the early 1970s based on the development of the apparel industry itself, social and economic changes, and the rise in income. The spread of Incentive 3 after Incentive 2 was already functioning represents a process of refinement in capitalism.

Economic theories of imperialism saw the free economy as pure capitalism and intervention by organizations or governments as altered capitalism. A free economy in which booms and panics alternate, interrupting the pursuit of 'production value,' is understood as immature capitalism. In this case, both Incentive 2 and 3 are underdeveloped. It is the modern economy that responds to all 3 incentives that is called an example of pure capitalism.

The competition stimulated by incentive 3 starts by generating rents through product differentiation, in accord with consumer diversification and the absorption of the consumer surplus. Firms begin to try to generate and absorb unstable rents as part of their marketing strategies. How far the strategy permeates the industrial world depends on industry characteristics and consumer behavior. After the 1970s, consumer goods industries other than apparel saw an increase in product choice and in the main properties on which consumers based their selections. Consumers acquired exposure to information on all kinds of goods. As a result, Japanese consumers became more diversified, unstable and ambiguous. Competition in pursuit of both 'production value' (for example, globalization of production) and 'consumer value' became more intense as income rose. In this sense, the age of consumer society had come to Japan.

This approach to studying consumer society suggested an analytical methodology viz. Japan's post-war economy, which experienced three phases of rapid change. In the high-growth period from the 1950s to the early 1970s, incentives for 'market value' dominated the economy, which justified government intervention in the economy to a certain extent, including improvement of industrial infrastructure and administrative guidance directing firms in the pursuit of 'production value'. Government intervention became less suitable in the post-1970s consumer society because the consumer's surplus, which is unstable and unpredictable, became more important as a source of profit.

The psychological background of consumer societies can be based not only on consumer diversity, which encourages ego-identity, but also on consumer instability and ambiguity, which threatens ego-identity.[27] In other words, the instability of ego-identity could conceivably be a source of profit in consumer society. At the same time, the individuals' will becomes more ambiguous. As a result, the consensus-building process regarding the supply of public goods, for example, might become unclear.

The 'consumer society' after the 1970s appeared to be enjoying a period of splendid expansion. Government intervention in the economy, meanwhile, was becoming ineffectual, and the very basis of democratic decision-making was being questioned. It is conceivable that people tend to comply silently with opaque government decisions in a consumer society.

Primary Sources

Nihon Sen'i Keizai Kenkyu-jo (Japan Research Institute of Textile Economies) (1974) *Nihon no Senmon-ten Chain, 1975 (Chain Specialty Stores in Japan, 1975).*

Tokyo-to Keizaikyoku (Tokyo Metropolitan Government Economic Affairs Bureau) (1957) *Kiseifuku fujin kodomofuku no jittai bunseki (The analysis of actual conditions of ready-to-wear clothes and clothes for women and children).*

Tokyo-to Keizaikyoku (Economic Affairs Bureau of the Tokyo Metropolitan Government) (1965) *Kanda Nihonbashi chiku no kiseifuku fujinnkodomofuku seizo-oroshi-gyo no chii to kino (The position and function of makers and wholesalers of ready-to-wear clothes for women and children in the Kanda and Nihonbashi districts).*

Tsusho Sangyo-Sho Kigyokyoku (Enterprise Bureau of the Ministry of International Trade and Industry) (1964) *Shohizai no ryutsu kikou (Distribution system of consumer products).*

Tsusho Sangyo-sho (Ministry of International Trade and Industry) (1978) *Apparel Sangyo Seisan Ryutsu Jittai Chosa (Investigation of the Production and Distribution of the Apparel Industry).*

Yano Keizai Kenkyu-jo (Yano Research Institute) (1977) *Fujin-fuku Sangyo Hakusho (Whitepaper on the Women's Clothing Industry)*

Yano Keizai Kenkyu-jo (Yano Research Institute) (1979) *Tokyo Fujin-fuku maker no tettei bunseki No.1 (A comprehensive analysis of women's-wear makers in Tokyo NO.1)*

Yano Keizai Kenkyu-jo (Yano Research Institute) (1980) Tokyo Fujin-fuku maker no tettei bunseki (*A comprehensive analysis of women's-wear makers in Tokyo*).

Yano Keizai Kenkyu-jo (Yano Research Institute) (1982) *Shinko Mansion Maker no Jittai (Actual Conditions of Emergent Mansion Makers).*

Yano Keizai Kenkyu-jo (Yano Research Institute) (1983), *Tokyo Yuryoku Depart Fujin-fuku uriba no tettei bunseki (A comprehensive Analysis of Women's Wear Shop Floors in Metropolitan Area Department Stores).*

References

Across Henshubu (Editorial Department of Across) (1995) *Street fashion.*

[27] This understanding draws on David Riesman's concept of the 'other-directed' and Erik Erikson's 'identity diffusion syndrome' (David Riesman 1961; Erik Erikson 1968).

Akihiro Kinoshita (1997) "Kashiyama no brand kochiku to channel kanri no hatten (Brand building and Kashiyama's development of channel management)" in Fumio Kondo & Yasushi Nakano eds. *Nichibei no ryutsu innovation (Distribution innovations in Japan and the US)*, Tokyo, Chuo-Keizai-sha

Akihiro Kinoshita (2001) "Ifuku seizo-oroshi gyo no nihon-teki tenkai to marketing (Japanese development of apparel wholesalers and makers and their marketing)" in Marketing-shi Kenkyu Kai (Society for the history of marketing) *Nihon ryutsu sangyo shi (History of the Japanese distribution industry)* Tokyo, Dobunkan

Alvaro Rodriguez and Luis Locay (2002) "Two models of inter-temporal price discrimination" in *Journal of Economics* Vol.76 No.3

Bernard Van Praag and Ben Bode (1992) "Retail pricing and the costs of clearance sales" in *European Economic Review*, Vol.36

Choi Yonghoon (1999), "Onward Kashiyama ni okeru itakutorihiki hoshiki to tsuika seisan hoshiki no senryaku-teki hokansei (Strategic complements of consignment buying and additional production in Onward Kashiyama)" in Fumio Kondo and Yasunaga Wakabayashi eds. *Nihon kigyo no mass marketing shi (History of Mass marketing in Japanese Firms)*. Tokyo, Dobunkan

David Riesman (1961) *The Lonely Crowd*. New Haven, Yale University Press

Edward P. Lazear (1986) "Retail pricing and clearance sales" in *American Economic Review* Vol. 76 No.1

Erik Erikson (1968) *Identity: Youth and Crisis*. New York, W.W. Norton

Fusako Kumon (1958) "Fujin kisei-fuku no saikentou (Review of ready-to-wear apparel for women)" in *Fujin Koron*, Jul. 1958.

Herbert Blumer (1969) "Fashion: from class differentiation to collective selection" in *Sociological Quarterly*, 10

Hiroshi Ejiri (1979) *Henpin-sei (Return-goods system)*. Tokyo, Nikkei Publishing Inc.

Hiroshi Ejiri (2003) *Hyakkaten henpin-sei no kenkyu (A study of the department store's return-goods system)*. Tokyo, Chuo Keizai Sha

Ichida Co., Ltd. (1974) *ICHIDA: Create 100. Tokyo.* Toyo Keizai Shimpo-sha

Isamu Kanai (1954), "Hyakkaten no torihiki jittai to sono mondaiten (Actual conditions of department stores and their problems)" in *Kosei Torihiki (Fair Trade)*, No. 50

Isetan Co. Ltd., (1990) *Isetan Hyakunen-shi (100-year History of Isetan).*

Jean Baudrillard (1970) *La Société de consummation*. Paris, Gallimard

John Payne, James Bettman and Eric Johnson (1993) *The adaptive decision maker*. Cambridge, Cambridge University Press.

Junko Ouchi & Yuriko Tajima (1996) *20 seiki nihon no fashion (Japanese fashion in the 20th century)*. Tokyo, Genryu-sha

Junzo Kashiyama (1998) *Hashire Onward (Run Onward)*. Tokyo, Nihon Tosho Center

Juro Hashimoto and Haruhito Takeda eds. (1985) *Ryo-taisen-kan ki Nihon no Cartel (Cartels in Japan's Interwar Period)*. Tokyo, Ochanomizu Shobo

Katsuhito Iwai (1985) *Venice no shonin no shihon-ron (The Merchant of Venice and the Theory of Capital)*. Tokyo, Chikuma Shobo

Kazutoshi Maeda (1991) "Ryutsu (Distribution)" in Shinichi Yonekawa, Koichi Shimokawa and Hiroaki Yamazaki eds. *Sengo Nihon keieishi (Business History in Postwar Japan) Vol.3*. Tokyo, Toyo-Keizai Shimpo-sha

Konomi Tomizawa (1995) "Apparel sangyo (The apparel industry)" in *Sangyo-Gakkai ed Sengo nihon sangyo-shi (Industrial history in Post-war Japan)*. Tokyo, Toyo Keizai shimpo sha

Kunio Hayashi (1987) *Sengo fashion seisui-shi (History of the rise and fall of post-war fashion)*. Tokyo, Genryu-sha

Masayo Murata (1988) "Nihon no gendai iseikatsu ni okeru kisei-ifuku teichaku-ka ni kansuru ichi-kosatsu (A study of the spread of ready-to-wear clothes in modern Japanese clothing)" in *Nihon Fukushoku Gakkai Zasshi (Journal of the Japanese Costume Institute)*, No.7

Mika Takaoka (1997) "Sengo fukko-ki no nihon no hyakkaten to itaku-shiire (Department stores and consignment buying in Japan's postwar reconstruction period)" in *Keiei shigaku* (Japan Business History Review), Vol.32 No.1

Mika Takaoka (2000) "Apparel sangyo (Apparel industry)", in Masaru Udagawa, Takeo Kikkawa and Junjiro Shintaku eds, *Nihon no kigyokan kyoso (Competition among firms in Japan).* Tokyo, Yuhikaku

Peter Pashigian (1988), "Demand uncertainty and sales: a study of fashion and markdown pricing" in *American Economic Review*, Vol.78, No.5.

Peter Pashigian and Brian Bowen (1991) "Why are products sold on sale?" in *Quarterly Journal of Economics* Vol.106 No.4

Ryuzo Uchida (1987) *Shohi shakai to kenryoku (Consumer society and Power).* Tokyo, Iwanami shoten

Shozo Nakagomi (1975) *Nihon no ifuku sangyo (The Garment Industry in Japan).* Tokyo, Toyo keiai shimpo sha.

Susan Kaiser (1985) *The Social Psychology of Clothing and Personal Adornment.* London, Macmillan

Susumu Ishii (2004) "Tenkanki no Apparel sangyo: 1970–80 nendai no rekishi (The Japanese Apparel Industry in Transition: 1970s–80s)" in *Keisi-shigaku (Japan Business History Review)*, Vol.39, No.2

Susumu Kamiyama eds. (1999) *Hifuku Kodo no Shakai Shinrigaku (The social psychology of clothing).* Kyoto, Kita-Oji Shobo

Suzuya Co., Ltd. (1975) *Suzuya 65 nen shi (65 year history of Suzuya).*

Takashimaya Co., Ltd. (1982) *Takashimaya 150-nen shi (150 year history of Takashimaya).*

Takeo Kikkawa and Mika Takaoka (1997), "Sengo nihon no sekatsu yoshiki no henka to ryutsu no impact (Changes in lifestyle and the impact of the distribution system in postwar Japan)" in *Shakai kagaku kenkyu (Journal of Social Science)*, Vol.48 No.5, University of Tokyo

Takihyo Co., Ltd. (2002) *So (Creation) Dream 250.*

Tatsuya Nakamura (1992) *Yutaka-sa no kodoku (Loneliness in affluence).* Tokyo, Iwanami Shoten

Teruko Inoue and Josei Zasshi Kenkyu-kai (1989) *Josei zasshi wo kaidoku-suru (Understanding women's magazines).* Tokyo, Kakiuchi Shuppan

Testuo Sugimoto eds (1997) *Shouhisha Rikai no tameno Shinrigaku (Psychology for understanding consumer behavior).* Tokyo, Fukumura-Shuppan

Tokai Sen'i Keizai Shimbun-sha (1975) *Gifu kiseifuku sangyo hattatsu-shi (History of the development of the ready-to-wear apparel industry in Gifu).*

Tokyo Fujin Kodomo-fuku Seizo Oroshi Kyodo Kumiai (TFKSOK: Tokyo Women's and Children's Clothing Producers' & Wholesalers' Cooperative) (1960) *Tokyo fujin kodomo-fuku gyokai sanjunen-shi (Thirty-year history of Tokyo women's and children's clothing trade)*

Tokyo Fujin-Kodomo-fuku Kogyo Kumiai (Tokyo Women's and Children's Wear Manufacturers' Association (1982) *Tokyo Pret-a-porter goju-nen shi (Fifty-year history of Tokyo Pret-a-porter).*

Tokyo Style Co., Ltd. (2000) *Tokyo Style gojunen-shi (50-year history of Tokyo Style), 2000.*

Tokyojuki Kogyo Co., Ltd. (1979) *Tokyojuki Kogyo 40 nenshi (40-year history of Tokyojuki Kogyo).*

Tsunehiko Yui eds (1991) *Saison no Rekishi, Jo-kan (History of Saison, volume 1).* Tokyo, Libroport

Tsusho Sangyo-Sho Seikatsu Sangyo-kyoku (Consumer Goods Industries Bureau in the Ministry of International Trade and Industry) (1984) *Atarashii Jidai no Sen'i Vision (Textile Vision for a new age).* Tokyo, Toyo Hoki Shuppan

Wacoal Co., Ltd. (1999) *Wacoal gojunen-shi (50-year history of Wacoal).*

Yasuji Yamakawa (1984) *World Kyu-seicho no Kiseki: Hatasaki Hirotoshi no Hito to Keiei (World Co.'s Rapid Growth: Hirotoshi Hatasaki, Personality and Management).* Tokyo, Shogyo-kai

Yoko Yanagi (1985) *Fashion-ka shakai-shi Gendai-hen (Social history of fashion: the contemporary age)*. Tokyo, Gyosei

Yoshiaki Ogikubo & Hideyuki Negishi (2003), *Gifu apparel sanchi no keisei (The Development of the Gifu Apparel Industrial District)*. Tokyo, Seibun-do

Yoshikazu Hiraishi (1974) *Fujin kodomo fuku sangyo hatten-shi (The development of the women's and children's clothing)*. Tokyo, Fukushoku Tsushin-sha

Yoshiro Miwa (1990) *Nihon no Torihiki Kanko (Japanese trade practices)*. Tokyo, Yuhikaku

Chapter 2
The Legislative Process of Automobile Exhaust Emissions Control in Japan—The 1966 Regulation and the Role of the Ministry of Transport

Akira Itagaki

Abstract This paper examines the process and significance of the enactment of exhaust emission control in Japan. In the 1960s, the health hazards caused by exhaust emissions became a serious social problem. The Ministry of Transport's existing regulations had been based on insufficient research, and emissions were not regulated by numeric values. The Ministry therefore undertook another study and surveyed the effect of exhaust emissions on air pollution. It also took into account the views of automobile companies in drafting new regulations.

The resulting regulations proved only transitional, however. Because the study of exhaust emissions was not thorough enough, controls were imposed only on CO, in effect reflecting the technical capabilities of the automobile companies and having only a limited effect on air pollution. But it did have some significance as it served as the foundation for subsequent exhaust emission control and reduced the CO emissions of individual cars. The regulation led automobile companies to question air pollution in Japan and improve their products. This was a typical case in which national opinion spurred the Ministry to take the initiative in issuing regulations.

Keywords Exhaust emission control • The Ministry of Transport • Social regulation • The Ministry of International Trade and Industry • Air pollution • The Road Transport Vehicle Act • The Safety Standard • The long-term plan for the prevention of poisonous automobile exhaust emissions • Carbon monoxide • The Ship Research Institute • The four-testing method • The Japan Automobile Manufacturers Association • The non-dispersive infrared gas analysis meters • Horiba Ltd • Nissan • Toyota • Tōyō Kōgyō • Fuji Heavy Industries

---

A. Itagaki (✉)
Hokkai-Gakuen University, 1-40 Asahimachi 4-chome, Toyohira-ku, Sapporo, Hokkaido 062-8605, Japan
e-mail: akitoro@ga3.so-net.ne.jp

H. Takeda (ed.), *Micro-Performance During Postwar Japan's High-Growth Era*,
Monograph Series of the Socio-Economic History Society, Japan,
DOI 10.1007/978-981-10-0709-5_2

1 Introduction

Air pollution due to automobile exhaust emissions has been an important issue ever since people began to view environmental pollution as a serious social problem.

This study aims to clarify the historical significance of Japan's first regulations based on specific numerical targets for automobile exhaust emissions: that is, the so-called 1966 Regulations. Its focus is the legislative process that resulted in these regulations.

The best-known exhaust emission regulations in Japan are those of 1976 and 1978. These regulations not only contributed to environmental conservation but also enabled Japanese automobile manufacturers to improve their international competitiveness in terms of quality, and ultimately to expand into overseas markets, especially in the United States. This is already well established in the historiography (Mutō 1984).

However, little attention has been drawn to the 1966 regulation on account of its transitional character and the relatively small impact it had on the Japanese automobile industry. It is nevertheless worth examination for the following reasons.

First, this examination is worthwhile from the point of view of environmental policy history. As Table 2.1 indicates, the 1966 regulation was the starting point of automobile exhaust emissions control in Japan, and the basic framework of subsequent regulations was devised in the process of legislating this regulation. Examination of this legislative process elucidates not only the contents of the first controls but also how the basic framework of Japan's environmental policy was constructed in its initial stage.

The 1966 regulation is also worth examining from the viewpoint of industrial policy history. Doing so enables us to assess the regulation in terms of both 'policy subject' and 'social regulation.'[1]

The study of social regulations such as exhaust emissions controls focuses on how central government ministries and agencies implement the controls and how the industries involved respond to them. From this perspective, Ei Shu elucidates the process by which 'Three-Way Catalysts' were put to practical use, highlighting how Honda Motor Co., Ltd.'s developed the CVCC engine in the socio-political context of the time (Shu 2002). The main theme of Shu's research is the factors that enabled the advent of the new, prevailing technology. His study also succeeds in explaining the social context of the exhaust emissions controls.

Though the analysis of the policy subject's activities is indispensable for the examination of exhaust emissions control, however, this study pays little attention

[1] Masu Uekusa defines 'economic regulations' as 'those on prices, the entry and withdrawal from the market and companies' financial states, mainly concerning the public utility, telecommunications and Broadcasting industries, as well as the finance, insurance and securities sectors. He also defines 'social regulations' as those on 'environment, security, health and so forth.' (Uekusa 1997 p.9 and Uekusa 1981) The definitions of economic and social regulations adopted in this study are based on those of Uekusa.

Table 2.1 Regulations on exhaust gases emitted by gasoline-fueled automobiles

Year		1966–1968	1969	1970	1971	1972	1973–1974	1975	1976–1977	1978
Method of regulation		Regulation of emission concentration					Regulation of amount			
Method of testing		4 modes					10 modes			
Gasoline-fueled automobile (4 stroke engine)	CO g/km	3 % ※1	2.5 % ※1	→ ※2	→ (1.7 %) ※2	→	26 (18.4)	2.7 (2.1)	→	→
	HC g/km						3.8 (2.94)	0.39 (0.25)	→	→
	NOx g/km						3 (2.18)	1.6 (1.2)	1.2	0.48
Gasoline-fueled automobile (2 stroke engine)	CO g/km			3 %	→ (2.2 %)	→	26 (18.3)	2.7 (2.1)		
	HC g/km						22.5 (16.6)	0.39 (0.25)		
	NOx g/km						0.5 (0.3)	0.5 (0.3)		
Idling	CO %			New cars 4.5 % Used cars 5.5 % ※3	→	4.50 %	→			
Supervisory authority	The Ministry of Transport							The Environment Agency		

Sources: Nihon Jidōsha Kaigisho [The Japan Automobile Business Association] and Nikkan Jidōsha Shinbunsha [The Nikkan Jidōsha Shinbun Newspaper Co.] (eds.), Jidōsha Nenkan [The automobile yearbook], the 1976 issue, p.152: 152 and the 1977 issue, p.126

Note: The figures are the maximum rates or amounts allowed. Figures in parentheses are the averages

※1 Light cars were exempted from the regulation

※2 Light cars were treated equally with two stroke engine vehicles

※3 In the case of used cars, light cars were exempted

to the roles of the central government ministries and agencies. The present study provides a case study of the government ministries' and agencies' activities with regard to the first social regulation for the automobile industry.

The focus is particularly on the Ministry of Transport. Hiromichi Mutō defines the role of the Ministry of Transport as a 'condition setter', citing the example of the exhaust emission regulations (Mutō 1984, p.281). Conventionally, research on industrial policy regarding automobiles has largely dealt with Ministry of International Trade and Industry (MITI) economic regulations, with little attention accorded to Ministry of Transport social regulation. By examining the measures implemented by the Ministry of Transport, this study sheds a new light on automobile-related industrial policy.

In assessing the social regulations, Mutō points out that the proportion of total environmental pollution and petitions that concerned air pollution decreased,[2] arguing that this was the result less of government policies than of the extensive efforts of 'Japanese automobile manufacturers and the very severe competition among them (Mutō 1984, p.289)'.

It is true that manufacturer efforts and the competition principle contributed to the reduction of automobile exhaust emissions. However, if exhaust emissions control is regarded as social, instead of economic, regulation, the assessment will be somewhat different.[3] Automobile manufacturer efforts persisted throughout the course of the exhaust emissions reduction process, the government placing regulations on the industry meanwhile. This case thus allows for separate evaluations of manufacturer efforts and the government's role.

Shigemichi Kadowaki assessed the Ministry of Transport's exhaust emissions control policies rather negatively, regarding them as too dependent on United States policies and too pro-industry (Kadowaki 1990). By contrast, this study highlights positive aspects of the role of the Ministry of Transport, which always had the initiative in the preparation and implementation of control policies.

This study consists of seven sections. The second section takes up the Ministry of Transport's first regulation, which did not have numerical targets. The third section examines the Ministry's attempts to enact regulation with numerical targets. The fourth and fifth sections analyze, through Diet deliberations, the opinions of automobile manufacturers and the Ministry of International Trade and Industry about the Transport Ministry's plan. The sixth section considers the historical significance of the 1966 regulation is discussed, and summaries and conclusions are offered in the seventh section.[4]

---

[2] Here, Mutō is arguing about the effects of the 1978 regulation.

[3] Researchers who regard exhaust emissions control as economic regulation have repeatedly raised the question of whether the government's protective policies or manufacturers' efforts and competition contributed more to the development of the Japanese automobile industry.

[4] The content of this study has been confirmed by Hisashi Kageyama, then Division Director of the Maintenance Division of the Maintenance Department, in the Automobile Bureau of the Ministry of Transport.

2 The Ministry of Transport's First Regulation

It is generally said that the public began to recognize exhaust emissions as an environmental issue of pollution between May and July of 1970. A team of doctors of the Bunkyō Health Co-operative reported that residents of the Ushigomeyanagi-chō district in Tokyo had accumulated at least seven or eight times the average amount of lead in their bodies.[5] In July of the same year, a number of female students felt dizzy and fainted at a high school in Suginami, Tokyo, and the cause of the incident was believed to have been photochemical smog. These incidents shocked society, and drew attention to automobile exhaust emissions as a form of industrial pollution and a serious social issue. (Tsūshōsangyō-shō Kikaijōhōsangyō-kyoku Jidōsha-ka 1976).

As a matter of fact, however, the problem of automobile exhaust emissions as a cause of air pollution had by that time already been addressed in the Diet.

The Act Concerning Regulation of Soot and Smoke Emissions was enacted in 1962. While setting controls on 'soot and other dust' as well as 'sulfurous acid gas or sulfuric acid anhydride,' the Act left automobile exhaust emissions out of the scope of regulation. The Diet deliberations concerning this Act, however, had addressed the issue of automobile exhaust emissions and their exemption from regulation had been criticized (Dai 40-kai Kokkai Sangiin Shōkōiinkai Gijiroku 1962). Sachio Urano of the Liberal Democratic Party (LDP) made a motion to add a supplementary resolution that 'the government should strongly promote technological researches and try to take countermeasures against environmental problems such as exhaust gases, noises, vibrations and offensive odors of motor vehicles.' This resolution was ultimately adopted (Dai 40-kai Kokkai Shūgiin Shakairōdōiinkai Gijiroku 1962), and Health Minister Hirokichi Nadao of the LDP promised that the government would tackle this matter (Dai 40-kai Kokkai Shūgiin Shakairōdōiinkai Gijiroku 1962).

In other words, the connection between automobile exhaust emissions and air pollution had already been discussed in the Diet since the early 1960s and the government was ready to take countermeasures. The central role in exhaust-emissions control was played by the Ministry of Transport, which was in charge of the registration and inspection of motor vehicles.

The Ministry of Transport's involvement goes back to the early 1950s. When the Road Transport Vehicle Act [Dōro Unsō Sharyō Hō] was enacted in 1951, the Ministry issued a Safety Standard[6] that made it impossible for cars to pass inspection unless they were equipped with devices to prevent the emission of soot and

[5] It should be noted that there are some questions about the credibility of this report.

[6] The 'Safety Standard' was a ministerial ordinance based on Chapter 3 of the Road Transport Vehicle Act. It prescribed in detail not only technological standards but also standards for the inspection of vehicles.

poisonous gases. This measure was taken on the basis of Article 41, item (xii)[7] of the Road Transport Vehicle Act, the provision for 'the prevention of the emission of soot, smoke and poisonous gases from motor vehicles.'

In addition, the Road Traffic Act [Dōro Kōtsū Hō] of 1960 had a provision prohibiting the use of cars that were not, or not properly, equipped with the devices stipulated in Chapter Three of the Road Transport Vehicle Act. This means that cars without equipment to prevent the emission of soot, smoke, fetid or poisonous gases were banned from the road.

The Ministry of Transport, moreover, revised the Road Transport Vehicle Act in July 1953, and Article 48 of the Act obliged all car owners to have their vehicles inspected regularly. Before this revision, regular automobile inspection had not been a legal obligation. All car owners were obligated to have their vehicles (with the exception of small-sized special motor vehicles) inspected, and repaired if necessary, either every 6 months in the case of private cars or every month otherwise.[8] This revision also required that the colors of exhaust gases should be checked at the ordinary initial check-ups and that the condition of the exhaust system should be checked at the 6-month (or monthly) inspections.

As has been explained above, the Ministry of Transport sought to curb exhaust emissions by means of inspection and maintenance. However, these regulations were without numerical targets. It was a matter of course that a call for regulations with concrete numerical targets would emerge.

In December 1963, the Administrative Management Agency made a recommendation to the Ministry of Transport. In a document titled 'Recommendation Based on the Administrative Observations Concerning Pollution Control,' the Management Agency urged the Transport Ministry to introduce more effective regulations with numerical targets, maintaining that:

> Currently, automobile exhaust emissions are regulated by the Road Transport Vehicle Act and the Road Traffic Act. Neither of these has concrete targets, however, and they therefore cannot be expected to bring about sufficent results. Concrete and specific standards are needed in order to restrict the emission of exhaust gases, in addition to the reinforcement of inspection and supervision (Un'yu-shō Jidōsha-kyoku 1968, p.10–13).

Concrete and effective measures to restrict exhaust emissions were also demanded at both the Liaison Conference for the Promotion of Anti-pollution

---

[7] Article 41 of the Road Transport Vehicle Act stipulated that no motor vehicle devices should be allowed to be used unless they met security standards specified in Ministry of Transport's ordinances. Item (xii) of the same Article necessitated the installation of a device to prevent the emission of soot, smoke, fetid or poisonous gases and so forth.

[8] The consideration for air pollution was not the only reason this revision was made. Among other reasons were: the increase in the number of car accidents due to defective devices, the alleviation of traffic congestion, the maintenance of security during high speed driving and so forth. However, during the Diet deliberations, the problem of automobile exhaust emissions was addressed, and it was demanded that the Ministry of Transport should take some action(Dai 43-kai Kokkai Shūgiin Un'yuiinkai Gijiroku no. 37 1963). It can be said therefore that the air pollution problem was a major reason for this revision.

Measures established within the Prime Minister's Office and the Liaison Conference for the Joint Promotion of Research on Air Pollution Control established within the Science and Technology Agency (Kageyama and Seki 1965).

The limitations of regulations depending solely on inspection and maintenance were also raised in Diet deliberations. On 19 March 1964, Hajime Yamada of the Social Democratic Party of Japan criticized the Ministry of Transport's existing regulations as follows: '[Even people in the Ministry of Transport][9] know that measures such as the car inspection, the visual observation and the revision of the Road Transport Vehicle Act are not the countermeasures essential for exhaust gases (Dai 46-kai Kokkai Shūgiin Shakairōdōiinkai Gijiroku no.22 1964)'.

Around 1962, moreover, the impact of exhaust gases on police officers working at heavy traffic crossroads such as the Ōhara intersection in Tokyo began to attract public attention.[10]

Eventually, in September 1964, the Ministry of Transport drew up the Long-Term Plan for the Prevention of Poisonous Automobile Exhaust Emissions. This plan, put into practice in fiscal 1964, concerned 'the clarification of environmental standards, measures for poor car maintenance, the inspection of new types of cars, the development of air cleaning devices and measures for fuel and engine problems' (Nihon Jidōsha Kōgyōkai 1968, p.81).

However, it still took a long time to introduce concrete regulations with numerical targets.

3 Towards New Standards: Ministry of Transport Research and Considerations

The Ministry of Transport could not introduce concrete regulations for two reasons. First, although automobile exhaust emissions were assumed to cause of air pollution, the exact relation between them had not been examined objectively. The situation at the time was as follows:

> The connection between automobile exhaust gases and air pollution is not yet clearly understood. Only at a few places are carbon monoxide, hydrocarbons, and nitrogen oxides detected regularly, even in Tokyo. When air pollution is discussed in relation to automobile exhaust emissions, the arguments are not necessarily based on reliable results of experiments or observations. In some cases, they based on figures from Los Angeles, where climatic conditions are totally different (Eguma 1964, p.18).

The Ministry of Transport shared the view that basic research was indispensable for the introduction of concrete regulations. In reply to the above-mentioned

[9] The author's insertion.

[10] Hisashi Kageyama told the author in an interview that police officers' experience of nausea at heavy traffic crossroads was the direct impetus for the Ministry of Transport to take on the exhaust gases problem.

recommendation by the Administrative Management Agency, the Ministry of Transport maintained that 'before the introduction of concrete regulatory targets, more basic problems should be cleared up such as the maximum permissible limit of air pollution, the real conditions of air pollution caused by automobile exhaust emissions and the influence of exhaust emissions on the human body (Un'yu-shō Jidōsha-kyoku 1968, pp.10–11).'

Another reason was that machines and devices used to analyze exhaust emissions were still underdeveloped. Numerical targets were meaningless without measurement equipment able to examine the amounts of exhaust emissions' components. Without such equipment, research on exhaust emissions themselves was impossible. The development of the measurement equipment was crucial for the introduction of concrete regulations.

At the same time, the Ministry of Transport was also concerned about delays in the research and development of devices to curb the emission of poisonous exhaust gases. At the 10th Road Safety Countermeasures Headquarters Conference held on 11 June 1963, Yasuhisa Miyata, Director of the Maintenance Department, the Automobile Bureau of the Ministry of Transport, reported that: (1) there were no proper devices to prevent the emission of exhaust gases; (2) therefore there were no proper means to prevent air pollution other than to maintain motor vehicles perfectly and to drive appropriately (Nikkan Jidōsha Shinbunsha 13 June 1963).

In order to set numerical targets for exhaust emissions control, research on exhaust emissions, on the equipment to analyze exhaust emissions and on the devices to reduce poisonous emissions were all indispensable. In Japan, however, such research lagged far behind.

The following sections examine how the Ministry of Transport solved these problems and determined numerical targets.

3.1 Research on Exhaust Emissions and Air Pollution

Even before the adoption of the Long-Term Plan for the Prevention of Poisonous Automobile Exhaust Emissions mentioned above, the Ministry of Transport had already decided that fiscal 1963 should be the 'first year in the studies' (Eguma 1964, p.19) of exhaust emissions and granted subsidies for related research and experiments. The introduction of the Long-Term Plan prompted the Ministry of Transport to intensify its efforts to comprehend empirically the real situation of exhaust emissions. In fact, the Ministry stated that the promotion of 'research and experiments necessary for the comprehension of the reality of exhaust emissions problem and for the implementation of effective countermeasures against it' (Kageyama 1965, p.6) was the immediate objective.

Within the Ministry of Transport, the Ship Research Institute, in particular, played the central role in the research on automobile exhaust emissions. The following will explain how the Ministry of Transport, and the Ship Research Institute in particular, conducted the research.

The Transport Engineering Department of the Ship Research Institute was, from its outset, tasked with the implementation of experiments required for transport administration. In 1963 when criticism against automobile exhaust emissions gained momentum, the Ship Research Institute 'was granted 7345 thousand yen of special research subsidies by the Science and Technology Agency, and installed the experiment equipment' necessary for research on exhaust emissions. In the recognition that 'the Automobile Bureau's top priority' was this problem, the Institute was 'fully ready to commence the research.' (Un'yu-shō Senpakugijutsu Kenkyūjo 1964, p.95) Thus, as the new fiscal year started in April 1964, the Ship Research Institute began to implement its experiments.

The Ship Research Institute's research on exhaust emissions was incorporated in the Long-Term Plan for the Prevention of Poisonous Automobile Exhaust Emissions that was adopted in September 1964, and helped propel its efforts (Un'yu-shō Senpakugijutsu Kenkyūjo 1965).

The Ship Research Institute's studies during this period yielded two major outcomes of historical importance: (1) the four-mode testing method was established, which later became the standard method to measure exhaust emissions; (2) reliable data were collected concerning a number of motor vehicles, both domestic and imported.

During the latter half of 1964, the Institute conducted experiments with both new and used cars irrespective of where they were manufactured. During the process, the four-mode method was consolidated as the basis of the testing. The four-mode testing method was devised by adapting the seven-mode method used in California to driving patterns in and around Tokyo. Carbon monoxide concentration rates were measured with a car situated on the Chassis Dynamometer testing facilities. The measurements were made with regard to the four modes of driving: 'idling,' 'acceleration from 0 to 40 km/h,' 'driving at 40 km/h,' and 'deceleration from 40 km/h.' Then, the weighted average of the concentration rates was calculated with weight factors set in proportion to the driving distances corresponding to each driving mode. The establishment of the testing standards was a significant advancement. Standard driving patterns differ from country to country. It is only by discerning the standard driving pattern of a given country that workable regulations can be designed. As Table 2.1 indicates, the four-mode method established in this period remained the measuring framework until 1971.

With the establishment of the four-mode testing method, the Ministry of Transport held a briefing session concerning exhaust emission regulations in April 1965, gathering member companies of the Japan Automobile Manufacturers Association and the Midget Motor Manufacturers' Association of Japan. While explaining the long-term regulatory prospects and the methods being used to measure exhaust emissions, the Ministry of Transport also required car manufacturers to have new models of cars tested for exhaust emissions at the Ship Research Institute from June 1965 onwards. In the same year, new Chassis Dynamometer testing facilities were installed, so that the Institute became able to test the types of vehicles whose exhaust emissions had been, until then, difficult to detect.

Table 2.2 Experiments concerning exhaust emissions conducted by the Ship Research Institute in Fiscal 1965

Period	April 1965–April 1966
Purpose	Experiments examining the emission of poisonous gases of cars currently used in Japan, in assorted driving and maintenance conditions, were conducted for the purpose of collecting basic data necessary for the establishment of effective countermeasures, such as rational regulations on exhaust emissions.
Outline	Both new car models and ordinary cars including used cars were put on the Chassis Dynamometer and given loads similar to the actual load of road travel.
	Under various driving conditions, carbon monoxide and hydrocarbon contained in the exhaust emissions were analyzed by the non-dispersive infrared gas analysis meter.
	While these experiments were being conducted, the testing method itself was improved. In addition to engine exhaust, the air-fuel ratio, the boost pressure and the exhaust gas temperature were measured.
Results	54 vehicles were tested, including newly produced cars, used cars and imported cars. While the concentration of carbon monoxide is highest during idling, that of hydrocarbon is highest during deceleration. Concentrations of both substances tended to be lower, the higher the speed, in cars driven at various constant speeds. Even in such cases, however, used cars emit more of these substances than new cars, and light cars (360 cm^3 class) emit more than small-sized cars. There are remarkable differences in concentration even among the same model of cars. This means that the inspection and maintenance of engines would significantly improve the situation. As for the testing method, the testing and assessment methods based on the use of Chassis Dynamometer and the non-dispersive infrared gas analysis meter were put together into 'the Automobile Exhaust Gases Testing Method,' which is now being studied by the Transport Ministry and the Japan Automobile Manufacturers' Association. According to this testing method, the average concentration of the 54 vehicles is 3.06 % for carbon monoxide and 459 ppm for hydrocarbon.

Source: Un'yu-shō Senpakugijutsu Kenkyūjo [The Ministry of Transport, the Ship Research Institute], *Senpaku Gijutsu Kenkyūjo Nenpō* [The Ship Research Institute Year Book], the 1965 issue(1966, P. 115)

Because of these measures, more data became available to the Ministry of Transport and the Ship Research Institute for investigation.

As summarized in Table 2.2, the result of this is obvious. With more data available, the Ship Research Institute gained more detailed knowledge about real conditions in automobile exhaust emissions. In addition, while implementing these experiments, the Institute tried and improved various testing methods, which led to the establishment of the standard exhaust measurement methods. These efforts by the Ship Research Institute provided a basis for Ministry of Transport, as well as the Japan Automobile Manufacturers Association, decision-making on this matter.

As has been shown, the Ship Research Institute's research on exhaust emissions, which started in earnest in 1963, had already produced substantial results by March 1966. The 1966 regulation was drawn up on the basis of those results.

3.2 Research on Devices to Measure Exhaust Emissions

As mentioned, the Ministry of Transport was aware of the need to develop devices for measuring exhaust emissions. In fact, Hisashi Kageyama, then Division Director (Kachō) of the Maintenance Division of the Maintenance Department in the Automobile Bureau of the Ministry of Transport, pointed out that in order to strengthen countermeasures for exhaust emissions it was imperative 'to develop an effective component analyzer for poisonous gases and to establish a system for testing and maintenance' (Kageyama 1965, p.9).

The Ministry of Transport strongly promoted the development of measurement devices. Eventually, the Ship Research Institute succeeded, for the first time in Japan, in making the infrared automobile exhaust gas analyzer. The analyzer is an apparatus for measuring gas concentration by utilizing the characteristic of gases that they absorb certain wavelengths of infrared light. It was shown to the public at the Briefing Session Concerning Researches on Countermeasures for Poisonous Automobile Exhaust Emissions held on 19 June 1964 (Nikkan Jidōsha Shinbunsha 19 June 1964).

The infrared analyzer had four characteristics: (1) it was able to distinguish one component from among many; (2) it was able to analyze the components in an instant and continuously and also to record the change in concentration rates automatically; (3) gas concentration ranges to be measured could be altered freely; (4) it functioned even at low concentration. (Arai 1965) The second characteristic was the most important, because automobile exhaust emissions had to be measured under ever-changing conditions. Among infrared analyzers, the non-dispersive infrared gas analysis meter, in particular, was highly reliable.

At the briefing session held in April 1965, the Ministry of Transport issued the requirement that the Japan Automobile Manufacturers Association and Midget Motor Manufacturers' Association of Japan purchase the non-dispersive infrared gas analysis meters by the middle of fiscal 1966. In order to promote the circulation of the gas analysis meters, the Ministry of Transport granted 'applied research subsidies' to private companies. Horiba, Ltd. [Horiba Seisakujo] is a particularly good example of such manufacturers. The company started as a pH meter manufacturer in 1945. During the 1960s, it expanded its business into the production of medical infrared analysis meters.[11] When it embarked on the manufacturing of exhaust gas analysis meters, the Ministry of Transport supported its efforts by granting 2237 thousand yen of 'experiment and research subsidies' between 1965 and 1967 (Horiba Seisakujo 1978).

The company's subsidized research is summarized in the 1967 publication, *Research on Analysis Meters for Carbon Monoxide in Automobile Exhaust Emissions* (Un'yu-shō November 1967). According to that, the difference in measurements between the Horiba's MEXE-15 m and the Ministry of Transport's standard meter was less than 0.3 %. Thus, within a relatively short period of time, Horiba

[11] The original name of the company at the time of its establishment was Horiba Radio Laboratory [Horiba Musen Kenkyūjo].

succeeded in producing an analysis meter that was inexpensive, easy to handle and almost equal to the standard meter in quality.

At the same time, the Ministry of Transport also sought to develop a low-priced, simple measurement apparatus for car maintenance shops.

The Ship Research Institute commissioned the Japan Automobile Service Promotion Association to make such an apparatus, and the Association in turn commissioned Yokohama National University to do so. Subsequently, the Ministry of Transport, the Ship Research Institute, the Japan Automobile Service Promotion Association and Yokohama National University carried out a joint research program. In September 1965, they completed the prototype for a simple measurement apparatus (Nikkan Jidōsha Shinbun 13, 17 and 31 January 1964 and Nihon Keizai Shinbunsha 5 September 1965).

3.3 Research on Devices to Curb Exhaust Emissions

With regard to exhaust emission control devices, the Ministry of Transport carried out experiments to examine the purifying effect of such devices developed by both domestic and foreign companies. For instance, from January through February of 1965, the Ministry examined the purifying effect of a gas-clearing device using the gas–liquid contact method (the manufacturer is unknown). In addition, from April 1965 through March 1966, the Ministry examined the effect of exhaust emission control devices made by Ishikawajima-Harima Heavy Industries Co., Ltd., by Japan Exhaust Gas Laboratory and by Norris-Thermador Corporation. From January through March of 1966, it also tested the effect of the Chrysler's CAP method and its adaptability to Japanese automobiles. The same was then done with the General Motor's air injection method from April through June of 1966 (Un'yu-shō Senpakugijutsu Kenkyūjo 1965 and 1966 and 1967). The Ministry of Transport also granted subsidies for the development of exhaust emission control devices. For instance, the Kyōwa Kōgyō Co., Ltd. received 1250 thousand yen in subsidies between April 1965 and March 1966 (Un'yu-shō March 1967).

4 The Ministry of Transport's Regulation Plan and Automobile Manufacturers' Response

On the basis of the research results elucidated in the previous section, the Ministry of Transport in 1966 made the first concrete proposal on automobile exhaust emissions standards.[12] The following traces the process of developing the

[12] So far as diesel-powered vehicles were concerned, the Safety Standard based on the Road Transport Vehicle Act had already prescribed that exhaust gas concentration should be below the level of Munsell N7.

proposals, which formed the framework for the 1966 Regulation. (The following account is based on Nihon Jidōsha Kōgyōkai (1968) and Tsūshōsangyō Kenkyūsha (1967).)

As mentioned earlier, the Ship Research Institute collected data concerning exhaust gases of new models of cars from June 1965 onwards.[13] The Ministry of Transport referred to this database when it drew up the regulation plan. At the same time, it also collected information on automobile manufacturers. Around the end of 1965, it started hearings with individual manufacturers (Nihon Kogatajidōsha Kōgyōkai 1966a). In addition, experts in the Ministry gathered information at academic conferences or through their personal connections.

Automobile manufacturers, for their part, presented their requests to the Ministry of Transport. At the 97th Technology Committee Meeting (the First Subcommittee meeting) of the Midget Motor Manufacturers' Association of Japan held on 2 February 1966, the Ministry of Transport explained the pending regulation as follows: (1) the new regulation would be introduced in the fall of 1966; (2) it was not yet decided whether light cars and motorcycles would be included in the regulation; (3) it was not yet determined whether hydrocarbons should be regulated before carbon monoxide or vice versa; (4) exhaust gases were to be measured according to the Ship Research Institute's testing method and the standard concentration rate for carbon monoxide would be set at around 2 % (Nihon Kogatajidōsha Kōgyōkai 1966a). The member companies of Midget Motor Manufacturers' Association of Japan responded that they would request that light cars be exempt from the regulation because they had not been tested at the Ship Research Institutes due to the lack of proper facilities (Nihon Kogatajidōsha Kōgyōkai 1966a).

Taking this request into consideration, the Ministry of Transport drew up its regulation plan. The plan strongly reflected expert opinion. In addition, because there was no advisory council on automobile exhaust emissions at the time, the principles and contents of the regulation plan were discussed and decided within the Ministry of Transport itself (Interview with Hisashi Kageyama 2005).

The gist of the regulation plan was as follows: (1) All three- and four-wheeled motor vehicles produced in and after September 1966 should be equipped with blow-by gas control devices; (2) the concentration rate of carbon monoxide should be less than 3 % in all three- and four-wheeled motor vehicles produced in and after September 1966 (when measured in the Ship Research Institute's four-mode testing method); (3) the concentration rate of carbon monoxide would be less than 2.5 %, in all automobiles produced in and after 1967, and less than 2 % in those produced in and after 1968,; (4) hydrocarbons would be regulated from September 1968

[13] In this relation, the Division Director of the Vehicle Division of the Transport Ministry's Automobile Bureau sent a document titled 'Concerning the Promotion of the Measurement of Automobile Exhaust Gases' (dated 28 May 1965) to the Japan Automobile Manufacturers Association and the Midget Motor Manufacturers' Association of Japan.

Table 2.3 Implementation schedule of regulations on exhaust emissions

	1966 (September)	1967 (September)	1968 (September)
Blow-by Gases	Installation of Blow-by Gas Venturi All Three- and Four-wheeled Vehicles		
	——————→	——————→	——————→
CO	3 % All New Models of Three- and Four-wheeled Vehicles		
	——→	——————→	——————→
	2.5 % All Three- and Four-wheeled Vehicles		
		————→	——————→
	2 % All Three- and Four-wheeled Vehicles		
			——————→
HC	(International Standard) All Three- and Four-wheeled Vehicles		
			——————→

Source: Tsūshōsangyō Kenkyūsha (ed.), Nihon no Jidōshakōgyō [The Japanese Automobile Industry], 1966–1967 issue (1967, p.235)

onwards for all three- and four-wheeled motor vehicles according to the international standard.[14] (Table 2.3)

The Ministry of Transport explained this plan at the Technology Committee meeting of the Japan Automobile Manufacturers Association and also at the Technology Committee meeting of the Midget Motor Manufacturers' Association of Japan in February and March of 1966, respectively. The Japan Automobile Manufacturers Association made such counterproposals as: (1) blow-by gas control devices would be installed in multiple models of cars produced in and after September 1966, and from September 1967 onwards, on all models of cars; (2) the carbon monoxide concentration limit should be 3 % for new models of cars produced in and after September 1966, 3 % for cars newly produced in and after September 1967 and 2.5 % for cars produced in and after September 1968; (3) the Association would present its opinion on hydrocarbons when the limit was announced; (4) some exceptions should be made. While the Midget Motor Manufacturers' Association of Japan took the same stance, it stressed that the particular character of light cars should be taken into consideration (Nihon Kogatajidōsha Kōgyōkai, 1966b).

Prior to the announcement of the regulation plan (in December 1965), the Japan Automobile Manufacturers Association conveyed its intentions to the Ministry of Transport as follows: (1) the development of blow-by gas control devices would be completed by the end of fiscal 1966; (2) the development of devices to restrain exhaust emissions would be completed by the end of fiscal 1967. Therefore, when the regulation plan was announced, both Associations demanded its postponement and relaxation.

In February 1966, incidentally, the Ministry of Health and Welfare publicized the Report of the Investigation into the Influence of Automobile Exhaust Emissions

[14] Although the regulation rates were eased from the original plan of February, the reason for this is unknown. As for the timing to tighten the regulation rate of carbon monoxide to 2 %, the Transport Ministry's original intention cannot be known due to the lack of evidence. However, there is a possibility that it had been thinking about this timing from the beginning.

on the Human Body. Unlike the Ministry's previous investigations, this one was conducted to collect basic data 'in preparation for the establishment of the regulatory standards concerning exhaust emissions.' (Sugiyama 1966, p.31)

The investigation's results highlighted the harm caused by automobile exhaust gases, which until then had only been vaguely assumed. 'Distinct differences were discerned' between places with high and low exhaust gas concentrations.[15] (Sugiyama 1966, p.32) The average carbon monoxide concentration was 4.1 ppm and the maximum was 22 ppm at the Ōhara intersection, whereas it was not detected at all in Tamagawayōga-chō.

The content of this Report was disseminated through the mass media, inflaming public calls for effective exhaust emission regulations. This precipitated deliberations on the Transport Ministry's regulation plan in the Special Committee on Countermeasures for Industrial Pollution[16] of the 51st Session of the National Diet, which was underway at the time.

The following section examines the Special Committee's deliberations. During the deliberations, differences in opinions between the Ministry of Transport and the Ministry of International Trade and Industry became apparent. One of the main objectives of the following discussion is the clarification of these differences. The claims and requests of the automobile manufacturers representatives who were summoned to the Special Committee as witnesses are also examined.

4.1 Automobile Manufacturers' Contentions

I will begin with an analysis of automobile manufacturers' contentions. Most of the automobile manufacturers were of the same opinion, and an analysis of their viewpoint will help us understand the differences in the views of the two Ministries.

On 13 April 1966, the House of Representatives' Special Committee on Countermeasures for Industrial Pollution summoned four witnesses: Riichi Maeda, Managing Director of Nissan Motor Co., Ltd.; Hanji Umehara, Managing Director of Toyota Motor Co., Ltd.; Yoshio Kōno, Managing Director of Tōyō Kōgyō Co., Ltd.; and Masaru Iino, Managing Director of Fuji Heavy Industries Ltd.

According to Maeda of Nissan, it was 'very difficult' for Japanese automobile manufacturers to comply with the proposed regulation for the following reasons: (1) because Japanese cars' engines were small-sized, it was very difficult to suppress the emission of carbon monoxide; (2) the suppression of poisonous exhaust emissions depended on carburetor makers' efforts, but they could not be

[15] The former is Ōharakōsaten 1-chōme, Setagaya Ward, Tokyo, and the latter is Tamagawayōga-chō, Setagaya Ward, Tokyo. When the measurement was conducted, other sources of air pollution such as factories and the heating of buildings had to be avoided as much as possible in order to isolate the effect of automobile exhaust emissions. It was for this reason that these two places were chosen for the measurement.

[16] It was set up in January 1965.

expected to make rapid improvements; (3) the Japanese automobile industry was already too busy dealing with the regulations in the U.S. to spare time for the domestic market. Maeda then asked to postpone implementation of the regulation, maintaining as follows:

> First, the test-driving method, the method for analyzing exhaust gases and the calculation method need to be decided. Next, the standard concentration rates of exhaust gases have to be determined. After that, we should be given time for research and development. It is only when we get promising results that the new regulation should be introduced. (Dai 51-kai Kokkai Shūgiin Kōgaitaisaku Tokubetsuiinkai Gijiroku 1966d)

Umehara of Toyota, by contrast, did not ask for postponement of the implementation of the regulation or leniency with regard to the standard concentration rates of exhaust gases. Moreover, when Chiyozō Noma of the Social Democratic Party of Japan asked if the Japanese automobile industry was ready for the new regulation, Maeda of Nissan replied that best efforts would be made even if results could not be guaranteed, but Toyota's Umehara replied that it would be possible to meet the requirements because there had been discussions and negotiations with the relevant authorities on this issue. (Dai 51-kai Kokkai Shūgiin Kōgaitaisaku Tokubetsuiinkai Gijiroku 1966d)

Maeda's statements need to be taken with care. He cited technical difficulties as a reason to oppose the Ministry of Transport's regulation plan. However, it should not be assumed by this alone that Nissan opposed the regulation because of its failure to meet the required standards. Considering that President of the Nissan, Katsuji Kawamata, was also President of the Japan Automobile Manufacturers Association at the time, it is likely that Maeda was speaking not so much for Nissan as for the industry as a whole.

In other words, manufacturers of ordinary-sized motor vehicles such as Toyota and the Nissan were ready to accept the Ministry of Transport's regulation plan.

As for compact car manufacturers, both Kōno of Tōyō Kōgyō and Iino of Fuji Heavy Industries requested revisions in the regulation plan. Kōno claimed that engine displacements should be taken into consideration and that regulation rates should be graded accordingly. (Dai 51-kai Kokkai Shūgiin Kōgaitaisaku Tokubetsuiinkai Gijiroku 1966d) Stressing technological difficulties, Iino also requested that the rates should be graded according to engine displacements. (Dai 51-kai Kokkai Shūgiin Kōgaitaisaku Tokubetsuiinkai Gijiroku 1966d)

Also, with regard to the implementation schedule, Iino asked to put off the introduction of the regulation for technological reasons. (Dai 51-kai Kokkai Shūgiin Kōgaitaisaku Tokubetsuiinkai Gijiroku 1966d)

In short, the automobile industry's response to the regulation plan was two-sided. Manufacturers of ordinary-sized cars were ready to accept the Ministry of Transport's regulation plan, whereas manufacturers of compact cars requested postponement of the implementation of the regulation on the basis of technological difficulties while demanding graded regulation rates for engine displacements.

The next section will examine the views of the supervisory authorities.

4.2 *The Opinions of the Ministry of Transport and the Ministry of International Trade and Industry*

On 6 and 7 April 1966, Yasuhisa Miyata, Director of the Maintenance Department of the Automobile Bureau of the Ministry of Transport, attended the House of Representatives' Special Committee on Countermeasures for Industrial Pollution and clarified the ideas in the Ministry's regulation plan, answering questions posed by Diet members.

On the implementation schedule, he made clear that the Ministry would introduce the new regulation in the fall of 1966 with regard to new models of cars and that all newly produced cars would be subject to the regulation 'without exception' by the fall of 1967. (Dai 51-kai Kokkai Shūgiin Kōgaitaisaku Tokubetsuiinkai Gijiroku 1966a and 1966b) On regulation standards, he remarked that the Ministry was planning to set the regulation rate at around 3 %, but that a final determination had not yet been made and consultation with private companies was still under way. (Dai 51-kai Kokkai Shūgiin Kōgaitaisaku Tokubetsuiinkai Gijiroku 1966b)

Table 2.4 compares the contents of various regulation plans leading up to the regulation that was eventually implemented. *Ministry of Transport Plan 1* refers to the plan proposed by the Ministry to the Japan Automobile Manufacturers Association. *Ministry of Transport Plan 2* refers to the plan introduced by Miyata in the Special Committee of the Diet. As is evident, the two plans are almost identical except for the regulation rate for 1967, which was eased from 2.5 to 3 %.

At the same Special Committee, the Ministry of International Trade and Industry was also asked about its opinion on the regulation of exhaust emissions. It was at this point that the difference of opinion between the two Ministries became apparent. The largest difference concerned the timing of the introduction of the carbon monoxide regulation of all manufactured automobiles.

Shōichi Akazawa, Deputy Director of the Bureau of Heavy Industries in the Ministry of International Trade and Industry (MITI), remarked at the Special Committee that the Ministry was planning to introduce regulation that 'the situation of this country could tolerate' by March 1968. (Dai 51-kai Kokkai Shūgiin Kōgaitaisaku Tokubetsuiinkai Gijiroku 1966b)

The *International Trade and Industry Ministry's Plan 1* in Table 2.4 is based on Akazawa's statement to in the Special Committee.

With regard to the timing of the introduction of the regulation, MITI was considering the spring of 1968,[17] whereas the Ministry of Transport was considering the fall of 1966 for new models of cars and the fall of 1967 for all newly produced cars. MITI not present a numerical target, whereas Miyata of the Ministry of Transport did mention a concrete target of 3 % though with reservations.

[17] Akazawa also talked about those automobile manufacturers that were exporting their products to the United States. He was of the opinion that cars produced by such manufacturers should meet a certain regulatory standard. He remarked that he was trying to make sure that all cars newly produced by such manufactures would be subject to regulation by about the fall of 1967.

Table 2.4 Regulation plans of the ministry of transport and the ministry of international trade and industry

	Transport Ministry's Plan (1)	Transport Ministry's Plan (2)	Transport Ministry's Plan (3)	International Trade and Industry Ministry's Plan (1)	International Trade and Industry Ministry Plan (2)	Diet resolution	1966 regulation
Vehicles subject to regulation	All three and four-wheeled vehicles	All three and four-wheeled vehicles	All ordinary cars except for some special types	All three and four-wheeled vehicles	All cars except for some special types	All cars except for some specified types	Ordinary and compact four-wheeled cars
Regulation rates and schedule	1966: new models of cars 3 %	1966: new models of cars 3 %	1966: new models of cars 3 %	1968: all types of cars	1966: new models of cars	1966: new models of cars	1966: new models of cars
	1967: newly produced cars 2.5 %	1967: newly produced cars 3 %	1967: newly produced cars 3 %		1967: newly produced cars	1967: newly produced cars	1967: newly produced cars
	1968: newly produced cars 2.0						
Notes		Both rate 3 % the rate to be tightened gradually	Both rate 3 % the rate to be tightened gradually	Regulation rates not specified	Regulation rates to be graded in accordance with engine displacement	1966: new models of cars 3 %	Both rate 3 %
						1967: new models of cars 2.5 %	
						Newly produced cars 3 %	

Note: This table was made by the author

These differences can be explained as follows. The Ministry of Transport drew up its regulation plans basically by itself on the basis of the data collected at the Ship Research Institute, although it heard the opinions of automobile manufacturers. As Chiyozō Noma of the Social Democratic Party pointed out, the Ministry of Transport 'set the regulation standard on the basis of its own technological developments' (Dai 51-kai Kokkai Shūgiin Kōgaitaisaku Tokubetsuiinkai Gijiroku 1966b).

MITI, on the other hand, set the implementation schedule for the regulation in accordance with the opinion of automobile manufacturers. Akazawa spoke at the Special Committee about the discussions between automobile manufacturers and the Ministry at meetings of the Technology Committee of the Japan Automobile Manufacturers Association. According to Akazawa, the Committee had been discussion methods of eliminating carbon monoxide and the timing of the introduction of the regulation since 1965, and had ultimately decided that measures to eliminate carbon monoxide would be introduced in the spring of 1968. He stated that MITI did not see a need to move up the regulation schedule (Dai 51-kai Kokkai Shūgiin Kōgaitaisaku Tokubetsuiinkai Gijiroku 1966b).

Noma argued that MITI should accept the Ministry of Transport plan because the Transport Ministry, as the competent authority primarily responsible for the matter, was taking pains to move up the schedule. Akazawa, however, insisted that it was difficult to move up the schedule due to technological problems (Dai 51-kai Kokkai Shūgiin Kōgaitaisaku Tokubetsuiinkai Gijiroku 1966b).

In short, the Ministry of Transport took the stance of 'pushing auto manufacturers into a corner' on the basis of its authority and the scientific information it had collected through the Ship Research Institute studies. MITI's regulation plan, by contrast, was based on the opinions the of automobile manufacturers. This difference in their stances led to a situation in which: (1) automobile manufacturers, while basically accepting the Ministry of Transport's plan, demanded exceptions; (2) the Ministry of Transport made its own regulation plan; and (3) MITI developed its implementation schedule n accordance with the opinion of automobile manufacturers presented at the Technological Committee of the Japan Automobile Manufacturers Association.

This difference in opinion, however, was shortly to be resolved. On 12 April 1966, Isamu Fukui (LDP), Parliamentary Vice-Minister of the Ministry of Transport, and Kazuma Shindō (LDP), Parliamentary Vice-Minister of MITI, attended the Special Committee and expressed their views. Fukui noted the following three points as the Transport Ministry's basic policy: (1) new models of cars produced in and after September 1966 would not pass inspection unless they met a certain standard; (2) cars that had already been produced should meet the same standard and be able to pass re-inspection by the fall of 1967; and (3) in ordinary cars, the carbon monoxide concentration should be less than 3 % and the regulation rate would be tightened gradually in the years to come (Dai 51-kai Kokkai Shūgiin Kōgaitaisaku Tokubetsuiinkai Gijiroku 1966c).

Shindō, on the other hand, announced MITI's changes to the plan. He stated that it would be possible to reduce carbon monoxide emissions in new models of cars sold from the fall of 1966 forward and in all cars sold beginning in the fall of 1967, provided that 'automobile manufacturers and parts makers made their utmost efforts' (Dai 51-kai Kokkai Shūgiin Kōgaitaisaku Tokubetsuiinkai Gijiroku 1966c).

Ministry of Transport Plan 3 in Table 2.4 refers to Fukui's statement at the Special Committee, and *MITI Plan 2* to Shindō's. Attention should be drawn to the *MITI Plan 2:* MITI made concessions to the Ministry of Transport on the timing of the introduction of the regulation, although it insisted that graded standards should be set according to engine displacements, and that a small number of exceptions should be made. In any event, MITI changed its policy and sided with the Ministry of Transport.

The author, Hisashi Kageyama, then Division Director of the Maintenance Division of the Maintenance Department in the Transport Ministry's Automobile Bureau, said in an interview that there was no serious confrontation between the two Ministries over the regulation of exhaust emissions. This statement can be corroborated by the fact that the differences in their plans were resolved so speedily. We must consider why their differences were readily resolved in line with the Ministry of Transport's plan.

One of the reasons was that the general public had an abhorrence of automobile exhaust emissions and politicians wanted to introduce regulations as soon as possible.

Table 2.5 shows the result of a public opinion poll conducted in August 1966 concerning images of environmental pollution. As can be seen, one in four people on average (one in three in Tokyo) associated environmental pollution with automobile exhaust emissions. In addition, the media urged the early implementation of exhaust emissions control. Regardless of party affiliation, therefore, politicians put effort into introducing regulations.

Public opinions and politicians' aims were strong factors in the policy-making process. Michio Muramatsu surveyed more than 250 bureaucrats in posts higher than Division Director, from all Ministries. The subject was policy-making under the so-called '1955 political system.' The survey revealed that politicians had the

Table 2.5 Public images of environmental pollution (Unit: %)

	Soot and smoke from factories	Bad smell from factories	Automobile exhaust gases	Smog	Filthy river	Car noise	Others	Total
Central Tokyo	36.3	12.3	33.7	25.6	12.4	31	49.3	151.3
Six largest cities	41.4	21.3	23.4	27.7	8.2	30.1	49.9	152.1
Other cities	29.9	13.1	18.9	19.3	13.3	17.2	44.6	111.7
Total	38	16.8	25.9	25.3	13.5	25.9	52.6	197.8

Note: 1. Multiple answers were allowed
2. 'Others' includes the following items in the original document: 'Electromagnetic interference caused by buildings,' 'Factory noise,' 'Construction noise,' 'Airplane noise,' 'Soot and smoke from incineration plant,' 'Commercial noise,' 'Traffic congestion,' 'Land subsidence,' 'Others' and 'Unknown'

upper hand in their relationship with bureaucrats, and that bureaucrats could not disregard Diet deliberations. (Muramatsu 1981) According to Muramatsu, bureaucrats were also well aware of the media's influence. (Muramatsu 1981) It can be assumed, therefore, that the Ministry of Transport's preferred schedule was boosted by the demand of public opinion, the media, and politicians for the early introduction of regulations.

The second reason for the ultimate adoption of the Ministry of Transport's plan was that it was largely based on the opinions of Ministry experts. Kageyama told the author in an interview that the timing of the introduction of the regulation was basically a 'technological issue.' (Interview with Hisashi Kageyama 2005) In other words, the implementation schedule depended primarily on whether or not it was technologically possible. As long as it was technologically possible, timing was not a serious issue.

4.3 The Diet Resolution and the Introduction of the Regulation

After the above-mentioned deliberations, Seisuke Okuno of the Liberal Democratic Party proposed a resolution titled 'Concerning the Regulation of Automobile Exhaust Emissions' at the House of Representatives' Special Committee on Countermeasures for Industrial Pollution on 21 April 1966. It was jointly endorsed by the LDP, the Social Democratic Party and the Democratic Socialist Party. The resolution consisted of the following: (1) a carbon monoxide concentration limit of 3 % in new models of cars produced from September 1966 onwards, (2) a carbon monoxide concentration limit of 2.5 % in new models of cars and of 3 % in newly produced cars produced from September 1967 onwards (with a continued reduction of the standard rate thereafter until it fell below 2 %); (3) from September 1967 onwards, regular car inspection confirmation that the car's carbon monoxide concentration would not be more than 1.3 times as much as the original rate; (4) exemptions from these requirements for certain types of cars; (5) (a) guidance for the technical guidance system, the production of gas analysis meters and the development of blow-by gas control devices, (b) financial support for the companies of auto parts in the development of exhaust control devices and (c) promotion of such comprehensive measures as engine development, road improvement and grade separation (Dai 51-kai Kokkai Shūgiin Kōgaitaisaku Tokubetsuiinkai Gijiroku 1966e).

'The Diet Resolution' in Table 2.4 refers to this plan. As can be seen, it was an eclectic mix of the two Ministries' plans.

After the resolution was adopted, the Ministry of Transport worked out the details. Although the regulation rates had been determined, testing methods had not. The Ministry of Transport therefore established a Testing Method Committee made up of governmental research institutions including the Ship Research Institute, Vehicle Division of the Automobile Bureau (the Ministry of Transport) and automobile manufacturers. (Nikkan Jidōsha Shinbunsha 25 May 1966 On 26 April and 19 May, the Japan Automobile Manufacturers Association, the Midget Motor Manufacturers' Association of Japan and the Ministry of Transport held a joint meeting, discussing the four-mode testing method developed at the Ship Research Institute. Thus, finally, the testing method was determined, the details of which are shown in Tables 2.6 and 2.7 (Sumida 1966).

On 14 July 1966, the Director of the Transport Ministry's Automobile Bureau sent the Japan Automobile Manufacturers Association and the Midget Motor Manufacturers' Association of Japan a notification titled 'RE the Standards for Poisonous Automobile Exhaust Gases'. It can be summarized as follows: (1) from

Table 2.6 Testing method adopted in the 1966 regulation

Outline of the test	A car is fixed on a Chassis Dynamometer, and the concentration of carbon monoxide emitted in the standard driving condition is measured and analyzed in the method prescribed below.
	The average concentration is calculated.
Chassis Dynamometer	The car is loaded to its maximum loading capacity. Under this condition, the same load is placed on the car as the running resistance it receives when running on a flat paved road.
	In this case, the running resistance is determined by the boost pressure.
Driving condition	1. Idling.
	2. Acceleration: The car is accelerated at the rate of 0.1 g until it reaches 40 km/h. Then, it is shifted into top gear.
	3. Constant Speed: Driving at 40 km/h.
	4. Deceleration: The car is decelerated from 40 km/h by engine braking. The clutch is disengaged at 20 km/h. If the deceleration rate does not reach 0.06 g, use of the foot brake is allowed.
Measurement device	Non-dispersive Infrared Gas Analysis Meter
Analysis	The carbon monoxide concentration during idling: the average concentration between 12 and 4 s before the end of idling.
	The carbon monoxide concentration during acceleration: the average concentration during the period of acceleration.
	The carbon monoxide concentration during constant speed driving: the average concentration between 12 and 4 s before the end of constant speed driving.
	The carbon monoxide concentration during deceleration: the average concentration during the period of acceleration..
The final calculation of the concentration	The weighted average of the concentration during idling, the concentration during acceleration, the concentration during constant driving and the concentration during deceleration, which are gained through the method explained above, is calculated by using the coefficients shown in Table 2.7.

Source: Yutaka Sumida, "Haikigasu Kisei ni Tsuite – Un'yu-shō Tsūtatsu: Jidōsha no Yūgai na Haikigasu no Haisyutsu Kijun no Kaisetsu [About the Regulation on Exhaust Gases – the Explanation of the Transport Ministry's Notification Titled 'The emission standard of poisonous automobile exhaust gases'']," in Nihon Jidōsha Kōgyōkai [The Japan Automobile Manufacturers' Association], Jidōsha Kōgyō [The Japanese Automobile Industry], vol. 1 no. 2 (1966, P.27)

Table 2.7 Coefficients used for the calculation of the carbon oxide concentration

Driving condition	Exhaust gas coefficient
Idling	0.11
Acceleration	0.35
Constant speed	0.52
Deceleration	0.02

Source: Yutaka Sumida, "Haikigasu Kisei ni Tsuite – Un'yu-shō Tsūtatsu: Jidōsha no Yūgai na Haikigasu no Haisyutsu Kijun no Kaisetsu [On the regulation on exhaust gases – The explanation of the transport ministry's notification titled 'The emission standard of poisonous automobile exhaust gases'], in Nihon Jidōsha Kōgyōkai [The Japan Automobile Manufacturers' Association], Jidōsha Kōgyō [The Japanese Automobile Industry], vol. 1 no. 2 (1966, P.27)

September 1966 onwards, the carbon monoxide concentration of new models of cars would be less than 3 %; (2) from September 1967 onwards, the carbon monoxide concentration of newly produced cars would be less than 3 %; (3) light cars and motorcycles would be exempt from the regulation; (4) the regulation standard would gradually be tightened in the future. (Nihon Jidōsha Kōgyōkai 1968) This marked the first implementation of the 1966 regulation on automobile exhaust emissions. It was 'the world's first nationwide regulation.'[18]

As can be seen in Table 2.4, the Diet resolution and the 1966 regulation were almost identical. However, there were some differences between them. The most important difference regarded the future reinforcement of the regulation standard. Although the Diet resolution had required that the regulation rate of carbon monoxide concentration be tightened to 2.5 % in September 1967, the 1966 regulation did not specify the rate and date of future strengthening of the regulation. It should be noted in this connection that on 21 April 1966, just before the opening of the House of Representatives' Special Committee on Countermeasures for Industrial Pollution, automobile manufacturers filed a petition asking that the regulation rate not be tightened to 2.5 % in the following year, 1967. In addition, they demanded that the final target rate should be 2.5 instead of 2 %. The petition did not affect the Diet resolution. However, it can be assumed that the Ministry of Transport responded to the automobile manufacturers' request by not specifying the details of the tightening to come.

5 The Significance of the 1966 Regulation

The following will consider the consequences and significance of the 1966 regulation.

[18] Remark by Keitarō Nakajima, Director of the Fourth Technology Department, Toyota Motor Co., Ltd. (Nihon Jidōsha Kōgyōkai 1969 p.4)

First, the basis for research on exhaust emissions control was established and a testing method developed during the preparatory process leading up to the introduction of the regulation. As shown in Table 2.1, the four-mode testing method devised during the preparatory process remained in use until the regulatory framework was altered in 1973. In the test, the maximum speed at which exhaust emissions were measured was set at 40 km an hour. This condition remained unchanged even in the 1978 regulation. Moreover, the non-dispersive infrared gas analysis meters developed during the preparatory period are still in use even today as a measuring device for carbon monoxide.

Next, the 1966 regulation did reduce the amounts of exhaust gases emitted by individual cars to a certain extent. According to a follow-up survey conducted by the Ministry of Transport, the 1966 regulation had the effect of curtailing the amount of carbon monoxide emitted by an ordinary car by 40 % (Nanto 1977).

In addition, the 1966 regulation changed the viewpoint of Japanese automobile manufacturers. Even before the introduction of the regulation, exporters to the United States such as Toyota and Nissan had already conducted preliminary research and development on exhaust emissions in order to adapt to its regulations. At the time, however, Nissan did not particularly intend to develop engines for domestic cars with the specific purpose of restricting exhaust emissions such as carbon monoxide, as the following remarks by Nissan's Riichi Maeda show: "[Since] the regulation will be implemented in the United States in 1968, [. . .] we are now working very hard to develop cars to export there. [. . .] If a new regulation is introduced for domestic cars at this crucial time, our burden will be enormous, because there are too many domestic car models. [. . .] We will be forced to make a difficult choice. Which should be given priority, exports or the domestic market?" (Dai 51-kai Kokkai Shūgiin Kōgaitaisaku Tokubetsuiinkai Gijiroku 1966d) Regarding Toyota's situation, remarks at a round-table conference by Keitarō Nakajima, Director of the Fourth Technology Department, are noteworthy. Asked why the Toyota had not tried voluntarily to control exhaust emissions before the Ministry of Transport introduced its regulations, he replied that although the company had begun to deal with the exhaust emissions issue around 1964, it had not been especially keen on controlling carbon monoxide until the regulation was introduced (Nihon Jidōsha Kōgyōkai 1969).

In this sense, the 1966 regulation gave Japanese automobile manufacturers an opportunity to address Japan's air pollution problem. In this sense, the regulation was a significant one for both the regulators and the regulated.

It should be stressed, however, that the 1966 regulation controlled only carbon monoxide and therefore had limited effect as a countermeasure for air pollution as a whole. Many cases were reported concerning the harm carbon monoxide caused and the research on it was relatively advanced. However, results of scientific research on other poisonous gases such as hydrocarbon and nitrogen oxide were still scarce despite doubts about their toxicity. As a corollary, only carbon monoxide was made subject to the regulation. However, as the above-mentioned photochemical smog incident in Suginami indicates, the exhaust emissions problem could not be handled by regulating carbon monoxide alone.

Table 2.8 Changes in average carbon monoxide concentration

Year	1964	1965	1966	1967	1968
Carbon monoxide concentration	3.2	4.1	4.4	4.9	5.1

Sources: Nihon Jidōsha Kōgyōkai [The Japan Automobile Manufacturers' Association], Jidōsha to Taikiosen ni Kansuru Chōsahōkokusho [The research report on automobiles and air pollution] (Tokyo: Nihon Jidōsha Kōgyōkai, 1968, P.10) and Un'yu-shō Gijutsushingikai [The Ministry of Transport, the Technology Commission], Jidōsha Haishutsugasu Taisaku Kihonkeikaku [The basic countermeasure plan against exhaust gases] (1970, P.18)

In, the observed amounts of carbon monoxide kept increasing even after the introduction of the 1966 regulation. Table 2.8 shows the changes in the average amount of carbon monoxide measured at three places in central Tokyo. It is clear that the amount of carbon monoxide continued to rise after 1966.[19] However, simple conclusions should not be drawn from this result, because it is very difficult to measure numerically the exact effects of exhaust emissions regulation. The changes in the amount of carbon monoxide at a certain place can be caused by an increase in the number of cars, the installation of traffic lights and so on. In fact, traffic volumes were increasing at the time. It is almost impossible to distinguish the effects of the regulation from those of other factors. However, it can at least be said that the 1966 regulation was unable to make up for the increase in the amount of carbon monoxide caused by traffic growth.

In that case, how should we interpret the significance of the carbon monoxide concentrate rate's being set specifically at 3 %?

The 3 % regulation rate was set out of consideration for the technological abilities of Japanese automobile manufacturers. Yutaka Sumida, then Division Director of the Vehicle Division in the Automobile Bureau of the Ministry of Transport, admits in his paper that the rate was set at 3 % not because it was environmentally necessary but because 'it was the maximum rate technologically possible in September 1965.'[20] (Sumida 1967, p.77)

Moreover, Hisashi Kageyama acknowledged in an interview with the author of this paper that when deciding the regulation rate, the Ministry of Transport took into consideration automobile manufacturers' opinions and that if the Ministry had judged that the regulation standard was technologically impracticable, it might have eased the standard (Interview with Hisashi Kageyama 2005).

According to the 1966 experiment by the Ship Research Institute, carbon monoxide concentration averaged at 3.06 % in all cars put to the test, and at 2.38 % in newly produced cars. Considering these figures, it is clear that the 3 % regulation rate corresponded to the technological level that Japanese automobile manufacturers were expected to reach with relative ease. In fact, all new cars sold in and after December 1965 had carbon monoxide concentration values below 3 %,

[19] It was only after 1973 that the observed values of carbon monoxide began to decline.

[20] It can be conjectured from the context that the correct year is 1966.

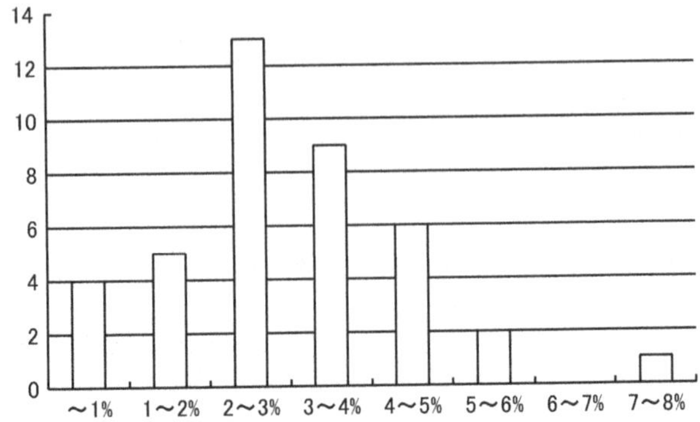

Fig. 2.1 Average concentration of carbon monoxide emitted from automobile (*Source*: Un'yu-shō Senpakugijutsu Kenkyūjo [The Ministry of Transport, the Ship Research Institute], Senpaku Gijutsu Kenkyūjo Kenkyūhappyokai Kōengaiyō [The Ship Research Institute Research Presentation Meeting: The outline] (1966))

most of them being 2.6–2.7 % (Nikkan Jidōsha Shinbunsha 1966 1 September 1966).

However, this does not necessarily mean that the Ministry of Transport simply approved the status quo. As Fig. 2.1 indicates, values of carbon monoxide concentration as measured at the Ship Research Institute ranged rather widely, even though the average concentration was 3.06 %. Sumida points out in this relation that among the cars sold before the introduction of the 1966 regulation, there were some types of cars whose carbon monoxide concentration values were over 6 %. (Sumida 1967) When deciding the regulation rate, the Ministry of Transport was chiefly concerned about the cars already in use and sought to set a rather strict standard for them.

In sum, one of the characteristics of the Ministry of Transport's regulation policy was that it looked carefully into the technological abilities of Japanese automobile manufacturers in order to set a practical and workable standard.[21] This is indicated by the fact that the Ministry set the regulation rate at 3 % and adopted a more flexible approach to future regulations than to the Diet resolution.

6 Concluding Remarks

As has been shown, the world's first nationwide regulation on automobile exhaust emissions was drawn up and introduced by the Ministry of Transport. Even before the introduction of the 1966 regulation, the Ministry had already made attempts to restrict exhaust gases with the Road Transport Vehicle Act. However, research on automobile exhaust emissions was still in its preliminary stage and the exact relation between exhaust emissions and air pollution was not yet clearly understood. The Ministry of Transport's regulation therefore still remained rather 'abstract.' Then, the Ministry and the Ship Research Institute advanced their

[21] During the interview with the author, Kageyama repeatedly remarked, "It is no use doing what is impossible." This remark is indicative of the situation at the time.

research on automobile exhaust emissions. On the basis of such research, the Ministry of Transport drew up a concrete regulation plan with numerical targets.

In the meantime, arguments for the introduction of effective regulations intensified both in public opinion and in Diet deliberations. In fact, when the Act Concerning Regulation of Soot and Smoke Emissions was enacted, the supplementary resolution demanding restrictions on automobile exhaust emissions was adopted. Eventually, during the 51st Session of the National Diet, the resolution based mostly on the Ministry of Transport's plan was adopted at the Special Committee on Countermeasures for Industrial Pollution. The Ministry of Transport worked out the details and, on 14 July 1966, isent a notification titled 'Concerning the Standard Concerning Poisonous Automobile Exhaust Gases' to the Japan Automobile Manufacturers Association and the Midget Motor Manufacturers' Association of Japan under the name of Director of the Automobile Bureau.

The 1966 regulation was of a transitional nature and was both significant and limited. Since scientific research on the components of automobile exhaust emissions was still in its early stages, only carbon monoxide was made subject to the regulation. In addition, the regulation rates were determined out of consideration for the technological abilities of Japanese automobile manufacturers. The 1966 regulation therefore did not bring about the remarkable numerical results that had been expected.

Despite these limitations, however, it did serve as a foundation for subsequent regulations. It also had the effect of reducing the amount of carbon monoxide emitted by individual cars.

Moreover, the 1966 regulation provided an opportunity for Japanese automobile manufacturers to take note of the air pollution problem and spurred them to change their attitude. As mentioned earlier, Mutō argues that the eventual reduction of exhaust gasses resulted not from government policy but from the efforts of Japanese automobile manufacturers and the competition among them. It is true that these factors contributed greatly to the reduction of exhaust gases. Had it not been for the 1966 regulation, however, the introduction of low-emission vehicles into the domestic market by Japanese automobile manufacturers would have been delayed. By implementing the regulation on exhaust emissions, the Ministry of Transport put pressure on Japanese automobile manufacturers to develop the necessary technology. In this sense, the Ministry of Transport should be regarded as having made a definite contribution to the reduction of exhaust gases.

In terms of policy assessment, it should be noted that the Ministry of Transport established, without recourse to the regulations of the United States, an original regulatory system consisting of testing methods and regulation standards designed specifically to address realities in Japan. As has been shown, the Ministry of Transport prepared steadily for the introduction of its regulatory plan and ultimately accomplished its objective.

This positive assessment of the Ministry of Transport's role is at odds with the assessment by Kadowaki mentioned above. His more negative assessment is likely due to the view that the Ministry, by setting regulation rates in line with the technological abilities of Japanese automobile manufacturers, had in effect compromised with the manufacturers and produced loose regulations as a result.

Finally, the 1966 regulation exemplifies one of the typical behavioral patterns of regulators (Ministries) and the regulated (industries). Where social regulation is supported by strong social demand, regulators have the upper hand in introducing that regulation and easily realize their aims. With the public demanding immediate action, the regulated have little chance of blocking the introduction of regulations. All the regulated can hope is, at best, to slow the introduction process or to ease the regulation standard. The process by which the 1966 regulation was introduced was a typical example of this pattern.

Primary Sources

Dai 40-kai Kokkai Sangiin Shōkōiinkai Gijiroku [The 40th Session of the Diet, the House of Councilors, the Commerce and Industry Committee, Minutes], no. 28 (1962)

Dai 40-kai Kokkai Shūgiin Shakairōdōiinkai Gijiroku [The 40th Session of the Diet, the House of Representatives, the Labor and Welfare Committee, Minutes], no. 32 (1962)

Dai 43-kai Kokkai Shūgiin Un'yuiinkai Gijiroku [The 43rd Session of the Diet, the House of Representatives, the Transport Committee, Minutes], no. 37 (1963)

Dai 46-kai Kokkai Shūgiin Shakairōdōiinkai Gijiroku [The 46th Session of the Diet, the House of Representatives, the Labor and Welfare Committee, Minutes], no. 22 (1964)

Dai 51-kai Kokkai Shūgiin Kōgaitaisaku Tokubetsuiinkai Gijiroku [The 51st Session of the Diet, the House of Representatives, Special Committee on Countermeasures for Industrial Pollution, Minutes], no. 8 (1966a)

Dai 51-kai Kokkai Shūgiin Kōgaitaisaku Tokubetsuiinkai Gijiroku [The 51st Session of the Diet, the House of Representatives, Special Committee on Countermeasures for Industrial Pollution, Minutes], no. 9 (1966b)

Dai 51-kai Kokkai Shūgiin Kōgaitaisaku Tokubetsuiinkai Gijiiroku [The 51st Session of the Diet, the House of Representatives, Special Committee on Countermeasures for Industrial Pollution, Minutes], no. 10 (1966c)

Dai 51-kai Kokkai Shūgiin Kōgaitaisaku Tokubetsuiinkai Gijiroku [The 51st Session of the Diet, the House of Representatives, Special Committee on Countermeasures for Industrial Pollution, Minutes], no. 11 (1966d)

Dai 51-kai Kokkai Shūgiin Kōgaitaisaku Tokubetsuiinkai Gijiroku [The 51st Session of the Diet, the House of Representatives, Special Committee on Countermeasures for Industrial Pollution, Minutes], no. 13 (1966e)

Interview with Hisashi Kageyama conducted by the author on 25 August 2005.

Un'yu-shō Jidōsha-kyoku [The Ministry of Transport, the Automobile Bureau], *Jidōshagyōsei ni Kansuru Gyōseikanri-chō no Kankoku ni tsuite* [On the Recommendation by the Administrative Management Agency Concerning Automobile Regulations] (Library of the Ministry of Land, Infrastructure and Transport, 1968)

References

Ei Shu, "Jidōsha Haikijōkagijutsu no Taishōbunseki – CVCC to Sangenshokubai [The Analysis of the Development of the Exhaust Emissions Purification Technology – CVCC and the Three-

Way Catalysts],” in *Akamon Manejimento Rebyū* [Akamon Management Review], vol. 1 no. 2 (May 2002)

Hisashi Kageyama, “Jidōsha niyoru Taikiosen no Bōshitaisaku [Preventive Measures for Air Pollution Caused by Automobiles],” in Un'yu Daijin Kanbō Bunsho-ka [The Archives and Documents Section, Secretariat of the Minister of Transport], *Un'yu* [Transport], vol. 15 no. 12 (December 1965)

Hisashi Kageyama and Yasuhiko Seki, “Jidōsha Haikigasu niyoru Taikiosen Bōshi ni Kansuru Hōkisei ni tsuite [Legislative Control of Air Pollution Caused by Automobile Exhaust Gases],” in Jidōsha Gijutsukai [The Automobile Technology Association] (ed.), *Jidōshagijutsu* [The Journal of Automobile Technology], vol. 19 no. 3 (March 1965)

Hiromichi Mutō, “Jidōsha Sangyō [the Automobile Industry],” in Ryūtarō Komiya et al. (eds.), *Nihon no Sangyō Seisaku* [Japan's Industrial Policies] (Tokyo: the University of Tokyo Press, 1984)

Horiba Seisakujo, *Omoshiro Okashiku Nijūgonen: Kabusikikaisha Horiba Seisakujo Nijūgonen no Ayumi* [25 Years of Fun and Joy: the 25-year History of Horiba, Ltd.] (Kyoto: Horiba Seisakujo, 1978)

Masayoshi Arai, “Osenbutsu no Bunseki oyobi Sokuteihō [Determination and Analysis of Contaminants of the Atmosphere],” in *Jidōshagijutsu* [The Journal of Automobile Technology], vol. 19 no. 3 (March 1965)

Masu Uekusa, “Beikoku Sangyōkai wo Osou Kiseikanwa no Arashi [The Deregulatory Storm Attacking Industry in the United States],” in *Ekonomisuto* [Economist], 15 December 1981

Masu Uekusa (ed.), *Shakaitekikisei no Keizaigaku* [Economics of Social Regulation] (Tokyo: NTT Shuppan, 1997)

Michio Muramatsu, *Sengo Nihon no Kanryōsei* [The Bureaucracy in Post-war Japan] (Tokyo: Tōyōkeizai Shinpōsha, 1981)

Nihon Jidōsha Kōgyōkai [The Japan Automobile Manufacturers Association], *Jidōsha to Taikiosen ni Kansuru Chōsahōkokusho* [Research Report on Automobiles and Air Pollution] (Tokyo: Nihon Jidōsha Kōgyōkai, 1968)

Nihon Jidōsha Kōgyōkai, “*Zadankai: Kōgaimondai ni Torikumu* [Round-table Conference on Industrial Pollution],” in Nihon Jidōsha Kōgyōkai *Jidōsha Kōgyō* [The Japanese Automobile Industry], vol. 3 no. 7 (August 1969)

Nihon Keizai Shinbunsha [Nikkei Inc.] Nihon Keizai Shinbun [The Nihon Keizai Shinbun Newspaper] dated 5 September 1965.

Nikkan Jidōsha Shinbunsha [The Daily Automobile Newspaper Company], *Nikkan Jidōsha Shinbun* [The Daily Automobile Newspaper] dated 13 June 1963.

Nikkan Jidōsha Shinbunsha [The Daily Automobile Newspaper Company], *Nikkan Jidōsha Shinbun* [The Daily Automobile Newspaper] dated 13, January 1964

Nikkan Jidōsha Shinbunsha [The Daily Automobile Newspaper Company], *Nikkan Jidōsha Shinbun* [The Daily Automobile Newspaper] dated 17 January 1964

Nikkan Jidōsha Shinbunsha [The Daily Automobile Newspaper Company], *Nikkan Jidōsha Shinbun* [The Daily Automobile Newspaper] dated 31 January 1964.

Nikkan Jidōsha Shinbunsha [The Daily Automobile Newspaper Company], *Nikkan Jidōsha Shinbun* [The Daily Automobile Newspaper] dated 19 June 1964.

Nikkan Jidōsha Shinbunsha [The Daily Automobile Newspaper Company], *Nikkan Jidōsha Shinbun* [The Daily Automobile Newspaper] dated 1 September 1966.

Nikkan Jidōsha Shinbunsha [The Daily Automobile Newspaper Company], *Nikkan Jidōsha Shinbun* [The Daily Automobile Newspaper] dated 25 May 1966.

Nihon Kogatajidōsha Kōgyōkai [The Midget Motor Manufacturers' Association of Japan], *Kogata Jōhō* [Information on Compact Cars], vol. 80 (1966a)

Nihon Kogatajidōsha Kōgyōkai [The Midget Motor Manufacturers' Association of Japan], *Kogata Jōhō* [Information on Compact Cars], vol. 81 (1966b)

Shigemichi Kadowaki, *Kurumashakai to Kankyōosen* [The Motorized Society and Environmental Pollution] (Hiroshima: Keisuisha, 1990)

Takamoto Sugiyama, “Jidōsha Haikigasu Jintaieikyō Chōsahōkoku [Report on Research on the Influence of Automobile Exhaust Gases on the Human Body],” in Zaidanhōjin Kōsei Tōkei

Kyōkai [The Health and Welfare Statistics Association] (ed.), *Kōsei no Shihyō* [Journal of Health and Welfare Statistics], vol. 13 no. 7 (July 1966)

Tsūshōsangyō-shō Kikaijōhōsangyō-kyoku Jidōsha-ka [The Ministry of International Trade and Industry, the Machinery and Information Industries Bureau, the Automobile Division] (ed.), *Tenkanki no Jidōshasangyō* [Turning Point for The Japanese Automobile Industry] (Tokyo: Nikkan Jidōsha Sinbunsha, 1976)

Tsūshōsangyō Kenkyūsha (ed.), *Nihon no Jidōshakōgyō* [The Japanese Automobile Industry], 1966-1967 issue (1967)

Un'yu-shō [The Ministry of Transport], *Kagakugijutsu Sikenkenkyū Hojokin niyoru Sikenkenkyū Seikashū* [Collected Papers of Tests and Research Supported by the Grants for Science and Technology Research], vol. 13 (November 1967)

Un'yu-shō [The Ministry of Transport], *Kagakugijutsu Sikenkenkyū Hojokin niyoru Sikenkenkyū Seikashū* [Collected Papers of Tests and Research Supported by the Grants for Science and Technology Research], vol. 12 (March 1967)

Un'yu-shō Senpakugijutsu Kenkyūjo [Ministry of Transport, the Ship Research Institute], *Senpaku Gijutsu Kenkyūjo Nenpō* [The Ship Research Institute Year Book], the 1963 issue, (1964)

Un'yu-shō Senpakugijutsu Kenkyūjo [Ministry of Transport, the Ship Research Institute], *Senpaku Gijutsu Kenkyūjo Nenpō* [The Ship Research Institute Year Book], the 1964 issue, (1965)

Un'yu-shō Senpakugijutsu Kenkyūjo [Ministry of Transport, the Ship Research Institute], *Senpaku Gijutsu Kenkyūjo Nenpō* [The Ship Research Institute Year Book], the 1965 issue, (1966)

Un'yu-shō Senpakugijutsu Kenkyūjo [Ministry of Transport, the Ship Research Institute], *Senpaku Gijutsu Kenkyūjo Nenpō* [The Ship Research Institute Year Book], the 1966 issue, (1967)

Yasuhiro Eguma, "Jidōsha ni yoru Kōgai no Bōshi [The Prevention of Environmental Pollution Caused by Automobiles]," in Un'yu Daijin Kanbō Bunsho-ka [The Archives and Documents Section, Secretariat of the Minister of Transport], *Un'yu* [Transport], vol. 14 no. 10 (October 1964)

Yoshihiro Nanto, "Teikōgai Jōyōsha Haishutsugasu Tsuisekichōsa no Gaiyō [Outline of the Follow-up Survey on Exhaust Gases Emitted by Low-pollution Cars]," in Un'yu-shō Daijin Kanbō [The Ministry of Transport, Minister's Secretariat], *Toransupōto* [Transport], vol. 27 no. 9 (September 1977)

Yutaka Sumida, "Haikigasu Kisei ni Tsuite – Un'yu-shō Tsūtatsu: Jidōsha no Yūgai na Haikigasu no Haisyutsu Kijun no Kaisetsu [On the Regulation on Exhaust Gases – the Explanation of the Ministry of Transport's Notification Titled 'The Emission Standard of Poisonous Automobile Exhaust Gases']," in Nihon Jidōsha Kōgyōkai [The Japan Automobile Manufacturers Association], *Jidōsha Kōgyō* [The Japanese Automobile Industry], vol. 1 no. 2 (1966)

Yutaka Sumida, "Jidōsha no Haikigasu Taisaku to Sono Kisei ni tsuite [On Automobile Exhaust Gas Countermeasures and Regulation]," in *Toki no Hōrei* [Today's Law], nos. 592 and 593, combined issue (January 1967)

Chapter 3
Adjustment Policies in the Japanese Coal Mining Industry During the Period of High Economic Growth – Production Volume Maintenance and Adjustments in Employment

Jin Sung Chung

Abstract The Japanese coal-mining industry underwent adjustment around 1958 with the commencement of a full-scale energy revolution. Government coal policies, which greatly influenced the adjustment process, affected production and employment differently. On the one hand, coal production was maintained at an output level of 55 million tons per year until 1966. This output level was considered a form of 'social insurance' to ensure energy security. On the other hand, the number of employees in the coal mining industry decreased by 58 % between 1959 and 1965. This drastic step was unavoidable: to overcome the problems posed by high coal prices, the coal industry needed a rapid increase in productivity. While the adjustment in employment practices contributed positively toward a shift in labor from this declining industry to growth industries, it also had negative consequences including the unemployment of miners and decline of mining districts.

Keywords Adjustment policies • Coal-mining industry • Energy revolution • Energy security

1 Introduction

This study examines the roles and characteristics of the government's policy on the Japanese coal mining industry during its adjustment period. The volume of coal production decreased gradually after peaking in 1961, and then, in and after 1967, began dropping fairly sharply before hitting the trough at just under 20 million tons around 1973 (Fig. 3.1). Coal production values, by contrast, declined steadily from

J.S. Chung (✉)
Korea National Open University, Seoul 03087, South Korea
e-mail: jins@knou.ac.kr

H. Takeda (ed.), *Micro-Performance During Postwar Japan's High-Growth Era*, Monograph Series of the Socio-Economic History Society, Japan,
DOI 10.1007/978-981-10-0709-5_3

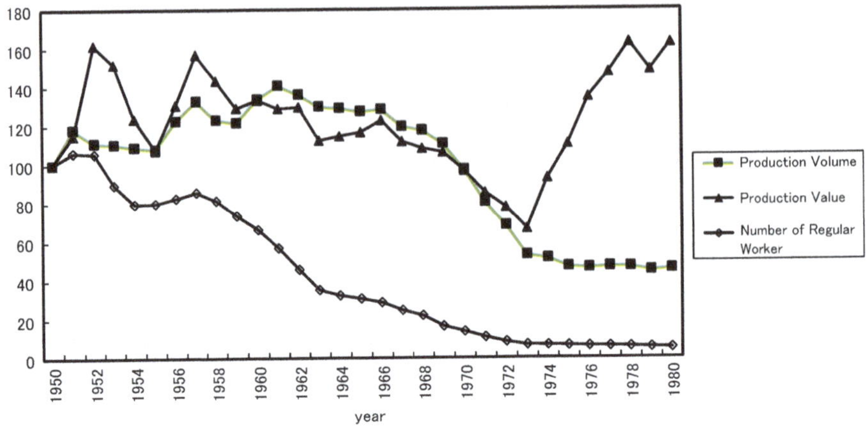

Fig. 3.1 Production of coal: volume, value and number of workers (Indices: 1950 = 100)
Source: For production volumes and the numbers of regular workers, see Tsusho Sangyosyo, *Sekitan Kōkusu Tōkeinenpō* [The Annual Report on Coal and Coke]. For production values, see Tsusho Sangyosho, *Honpo Kogyo no Susei* [The Trend of the Japanese Mining Industry]
Note: The years indicated for production volumes and numbers of regular workers are fiscal years. *Years* indicated for production values are calendar years

1957 and 1973.[1] The number of coal miners also fell after the 1957 peak, sinking to the 20,000 level around 1973. These figures indicate that the Japanese coal-mining industry entered its adjustment period in earnest around 1958 and reached a new equilibrium around 1973, the year of the first oil crisis. Between 1957 and 1973, production volumes dropped by more than 60 % (from 55.4 to 20.9 million tons) and the number of coal miners by more than 90 % (from 218,190 to 23,515).

The main cause of the industry's sharp contraction was the 'energy revolution' -- the rapid shift in energy sources from solid to liquid fuel. The price of heavy oil, an alternative to coal, began to fall in 1957 after the Suez Crisis, and the unit price of C fuel oil fell lower than that of coal in the third quarter of 1958 (Sekitan Keizai Kenkyūjo, 1962, p. 327).[2] The October 1962 liberalization of oil imports further accelerated the use of oil.[3] The supply of primary energy increased by 5.2 times in Japan between 1957 and 1973, and domestic coal's proportion of the total primary energy supply dropped from 42.7 to 3.8 %, while that of oil rose from 23.6 to 77.4 %.

[1] The production value of coal rose sharply in and after 1974 because of the sudden rise in coal prices due to the oil crisis.

[2] In terms of 'merit (the comparison between the per calorie prices of heavy oil and coal),' heavy oil had already been more economical since 1952 in the Tokyo-Yokohama area (since the first quarter of 1957 in the Osaka-Kōbe area).

[3] 'The Foreign Exchange and Foreign Trade Liberalization Program Outline' drawn up in June 1960 stated that the liberalization of oil imports would be implemented in April 1963. However, 'The Foreign Exchange and Foreign Trade Liberalization Promotion Plan' of September 1961 moved implementation up implementation by 6 months.

Faced with the rapid contraction of the coal-mining industry, the Japanese government was forced to take measures for a stable energy supply, displaced coal miners, and so forth. Thus far, however, historical research has not taken sufficient account of the government's intention, as evident in a series of coal policies, of implementing structural adjustments in the industry. Although coal policies received frequent mention in prior studies, they have mostly been considered a failure because of the eventual decline, or collapse, of the coal-mining industry (Sonoda, Minoru, 1970, Akiba, Satoshi 1975–1976, Yada, Toshifumi, 1975, 1977, Senba, Tsunenori, 1977–1978). This assessment, however, is based on the assumption that the government's aim was to maintain the coal-mining industry as it was. Previous studies have failed to recognize that the government's coal policies were in fact structural adjustment policies. Even *Tsūshō Sangyō Seisakushi* (*The History of Industrial Policies*), which is the most detailed research in this area, pays little attention to the 'adjustment' aspect of the policies, though its close analysis of the Act on Temporary Measures Concerning Displaced Coal Miners is instructive (Tsūshō Sangyōshō, 1991, pp. 416–420).

The coal policies only began to be evaluated as adjustment policies when the need for structural adjustment surged globally after the oil crisis.[4] While some studies evaluated the 'adjustment' effects of the coal policies positively (Namiki Yoshinobu, 1973, Ono, Gorō 1999, p. 219), others did not (Sekiguchi Sueo, 1973, 1975, Sekiguchi and Horiuchi, 1988).[5] Whatever their views, they were not entirely persuasive because of a lack of sufficient empirical analysis.

This study is based on the recognition that the government's coal policies were aimed at the structural adjustment of the coal-mining industry. It begins by examining the levels of production and employment set by the government as its policy targets, because these targets reflected the government's view on the coal-mining industry in relation to the national economy.

Initially, the government sought to maintain the industry's production levels while rapidly reducing employment. As Fig. 3.1 shows, production volume and employment did not change in parallel during the adjustment period. Employment dropped drastically from the very outset of the adjustment period, while production volumes held up until the mid-1960s and did not show notable declines until around 1967. As it happened, Europe's coal-mining industries entered their adjustment phase at around the same time. As seen in Fig. 3.2a, b, production volumes and employment followed different trajectories in the Japanese coal-mining industry, in contrast with the case in Europe. In Belgium, for example, which underwent the most drastic adjustment process in Europe, production volumes and the number of miners fell by 32 % and 46 %, respectively, from 1957 to 1965, while in Japan, the number of underground workers dropped by 58 % but production volumes by only 4 % during the same period.

[4] 'Industrial adjustment' designates the shift of production factors such as capital and labor from declining industries to more competitive industries. Industrial adjustment policies aim for the smooth implementation of this shift.

[5] Sekiguchi and Horiuchi regarded the coal policies as policies of adjustment and aid, emphasizing the importance of revitalizing policies for coal-producing regions. However, they did not present concrete analysis (Sekiguchi and Horiuchi 1988).

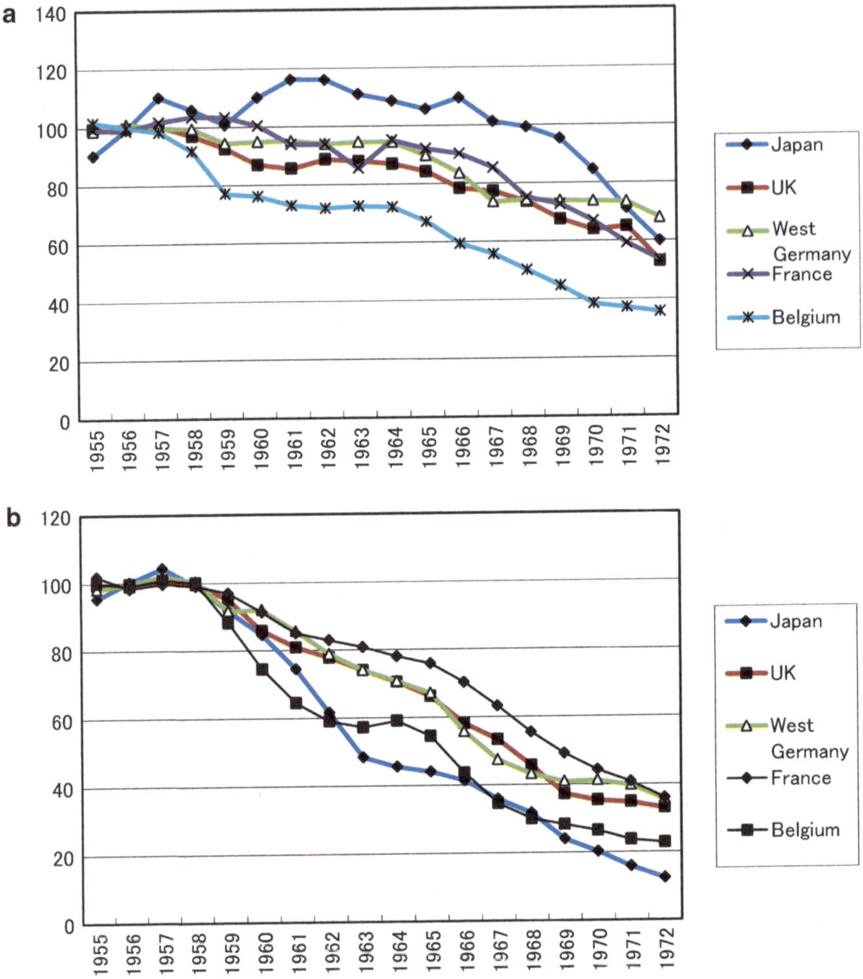

Fig. 3.2 Volume of coal production and number of undergound coal workers – international comparison. (**a**) Production volume (Average of 1955–1957 = 100). (**b**) Number of underground coal workers

Sources: (a) Tsusho Sangyosho, *Sekitan Kokusu Tokeinenpo* [The Annual Report on Coal and Coke]. *The original source* is Kokuren Tōkei Nenkan [The United Nations Statistical Yearbook] (b) United Nations, Quarterly Bulletin of Coal Statistics for Europe. *Source on Japan*: Sekitan Kōkusu Tōkeinenpō

These numbers raise a question: Why did the Japanese coal-mining industry maintain production levels until the mid-1960s, in spite of the ongoing energy revolution? To answer this question, we must analyze Japan's coal policies in the context of Japan's energy policy as a whole. High economic growth in those years was based on the stable supply of cheap energy. Therefore, the question can be rephrased: How was Japan's coal policy, which until the mid-1960s sought the maintenance of conventional production levels, compatible with the so-called 'oil first, coal second' national energy policy? In this connection, we must also investigate the grounds on which the government determined the 'proper' level of coal production.

The next question is: What enabled the rapid adjustment in employment? Employment adjustment naturally incurs strong opposition from workers and local communities. It is therefore important to examine the factors that contributed to the successful implementation of drastic employment adjustment.

Two points need to be stressed in this regard. First, we must note the political measures taken by the government to alleviate the social friction caused by employment adjustment, because these measures will be assumed to have mitigated the harm of unemployment and other regional problems and thereby to have forwarded the employment adjustment effort. Next, we need to take into consideration the influence of rapid economic growth on the employment adjustment process. It is possible that workers displaced from the coal-mining industry were absorbed by other growing industries, and that this may have helped enable rapid employment adjustment. Coal miners did not necessarily constitute a mobile or malleable labor force, however, because many of them were middle-aged men providing for their families. Careful examination is therefore required as to the influence of high economic growth on the employment adjustment of coal miners.

This study is structured as follows. Section 2 outlines the process towards full-scale implementation of structural adjustment policies for the coal-mining industry. Section 3 examines the background of the establishment of the so-called '55 million-ton production system.' Section 4 investigates the process of, and reasons for, the collapse of the '55 million-ton production system.' Section 5 examines the process of employment adjustment and evaluates the measures taken by the government for displaced coal miners. In the Conclusion, this study's findings are summarized and subjects for future research presented.

2 The Introduction of Adjustment Policies in the Coal-Mining Industry

2.1 The Enactment of the Act on Temporary Measures Concerning Coal Industry Rationalization

As mentioned above, the Japanese coal-mining industry entered its adjustment phase around 1958, and the government implemented a series of coal policies. The basic framework of these policies was provided by the Act on Temporary Measures Concerning Coal Industry Rationalization (hereafter, the Rationalization Act) enacted in August 1955.

The Rationalization Act was a response to growing criticism by coal consumers against high coal prices. The 'high coal-price problem' was first addressed by the steel industry in December 1949, immediately after the removal of controls on coal production. It was raised again around 1952, at the peak of the Korean War's special procurement boom (Tsūshō Sangyōshō Sekitankyoku, 1953). Japan's economy at the time was tightly constrained by the balance of international payments; export industry development therefore had to be encouraged for 'economic independence.' In these circumstances, high coal prices were harmful to the competitiveness of such industries as steel, cement, ammonium sulfate and soda ash industries, in which coal constituted a large proportion of total production costs. In an attempt to deal with the 'high coal-price problem,' the Ministry of International Trade and Industry drew up the 5 Year Shaft Excavation Plan in October 1952.[6] Ministry of Finance opposition and the lukewarm response of the coal-mining industry prevented the plan from being brought to fruition, however. Furthermore, as the economy entered recession around 1953 and the 'coal crisis' became a public concern, new coal mine development projects became infeasible. It was during this recession that plans were laid for the Rationalization Act. In addition to conventional development plans for shaft excavation, the rationalization plan included government purchase of inefficient coal mines (Nakamura, Takafusa, 1961, p. 252). The contents of the Rationalization Act can be summed up as follows. (1) Enhancement of productivity by the scrap and build method: The closure of inefficient mines was encouraged, and financial support was given to investment in, for instance, shaft excavation. This was the first time that a rationalization plan included the 'scrap' method.[7] (2) Approval of cartels: Cartel activities such as production controls and price fixing were exempted from the application of the Anti-Monopoly Law in the case of the coal-mining industry. (3) Measures to secure demand: The Oil Boiler Restriction Act (valid for 5 years) was enacted in order to curb demand for fuel oil and to secure demand for coal. In addition, tariffs were imposed on B and C fuel oil. (4) The establishment of the Coal Mining Maintenance Corporation and the Coal Industry Advisory Council: The Coal Mining Maintenance Corporation was established as an organization to purchase inefficient coal mines. At the same time, the Coal Industry Advisory Council, comprised of academic experts, was established within the Ministry of International Trade and Industry as an advisory body on the rationalization of the coal-mining industry.

National energy policy at the time espoused a 'coal first, oil second' principle, on the basis of which the Rationalization Act restricted oil consumption in order to maintain demand for coal. At the same time, it tried to cope with the sluggishness of the industry and the 'high coal price problem' by cost-cutting through rationalization. The measures set forth in the Rationalization Act were reiterated consistently in subsequent coal policies. In this sense, the basic framework of the government's coal policies was established in the 1955 Rationalization Act.

[6] There had already been two coal industry rationalization plans that were eventually called off: the 3 year rationalization plan submitted by the Industrial Rationalization Committee in June 1950 and the 3 year plan submitted by the Coal Subcommittee of the Industrial Rationalization Committee in March 1952. The Industrial Rationalization Committee was established as an affiliate of the Ministry of International Trade and Industry in December 1949.

[7] The coal-mine rationalization of 1944 and the saltpan rationalization prior to that are precedents of the government's purchase of inefficient coal mines (Sekitankōgyō Gōrika Jigyōdan, 1965).

However, this Act did not include institutional measures for social problems such as unemployment and the decline of regional economies that were expected to arise in the course of rationalization. It was not that the government ignored such problems. On the contrary, it was fully aware that the coal industry was in a slump and that unemployment was becoming a serious problem. Unemployment relief was in fact among the Act's basic objectives. Nevertheless, the Act included provisions – that is, Articles 33 and 34 – to support only those miners who were forced to leave their jobs due to the government's purchase of coal mines. No comprehensive institutional measures were taken for unemployed coal miners in general.[8]

The enactment of the Rationalization Act was accompanied by the Basic Plan for Rationalization of the Coal Industry Rationalization. The Plan was not implemented as designed, however. The so-called 'Jimmu Boom' intervened, generating large demand for coal, and the coal industry was therefore required to increase production. When the Basic Plan was revised in May 1957, the 1957 production target was set at 57 million tons, 7.5 million tons higher than in the original Plan. Then, in December 1957, the Cabinet approved the New Long-Term Economic Plan based on the 'coal first, oil second' principle, according to which the domestic coal industry was expected to supply 72 million tons of coal in fiscal 1975. In line with this Plan, the Rationalization Act was revised in April 1958, raising production targets to as much as 69 million tons for fiscal 1967, the final year of the rationalization plan. The underlying concept of the 1955 Rationalization Act had been the 'stable supply of cheap coal through rationalization.' As the supply–demand balance of coal tightened, however, the priority shifted to 'rationalization through production increases' (Tsūshō Sangyōshō, 1991, p. 369).

2.2 *Structural Recession in the Coal-Mining Industry and the Full-Scale Implementation of the Adjustment Policies*

Although the policies to increase coal production were implemented in accordance with the New Long-Term Economic Plan, the coal industry entered a serious

[8] Since the government was concerned about the problem of unemployment among coal miners, a cabinet decision (May 1955) and cabinet approval (October 1956) were issued on 'countermeasures for unemployment caused by the rationalization of the coal industry.' A policy was thus established to implement public works and unemployment relief projects mainly in coal-mining regions. The 1956 cabinet approval, in particular, can be regarded as the first progressive attempt to support regions plagued by unemployment through countermeasures such as 'wide-ranging job placement' and 'industrial development projects' (Koyōsokushin Jigyōdan, 1971, p.21). However, the government's aid for displaced miners was confined to the traditional framework of unemployment relief programs. The government did not try, for instance, to establish specific organizations or systems designed to support unemployed coal miners.

recession in 1958. The economy as a whole recovered from the recession by the end of the year, but demand for coal remained slack, showing no sign of recovery. Meanwhile, the price of fuel oil fell below that of coal and kept dropping. It became evident that the existing coal policy based on the 'coal first, oil second' principle could no longer be sustained.

The gist of the new coal policy can be seen in the Interim Report of the Basic Issue Committee (chaired by Hiromi Arisawa) established by the Coal Industry Advisory Council. The Report, made public on 19 December, 1959, stated that the government's new coal policy should aim for the structural adjustment of the coal-mining industry. It attributed the industry's weakness not to temporary factors related to the business cycle, but to structural factors responding to economic rationality, namely the preference for liquid- over solid-energy sources. The Report accordingly emphasized the need to create a business environment in which coal was able to compete with other energy sources. It addressed two concrete policy objectives. First, the per-ton price of coal was to be cut by 1200 yen by the end of fiscal 1963. Second, the coal production target for fiscal 1963 was to be set between 50 and 55 million tons. In other words, the New Long-Term Economic Plan, which aimed at domestic coal production of 72 million tons for fiscal 1975, was totally abandoned. Additionally, the Interim Report raised concerns about social problems entailing the structural adjustment of the industry. Stressing the need to take immediate action to support displaced miners and regional communities, the Report asked for the cooperation of all the parties involved. In 1960, the measures proposed in this Interim Report were put into effect in the form of the so-called '1200 Yen Price-Cut Policy.' (Table 3.1)

As the unemployment situation deteriorated due to the protracted downturn of the industry, the government intensified its efforts to support displaced miners, especially after February of 1959. It became obvious, however, that the situation could no longer be handled by administrative measures alone, and that legislative measures were required. The Act on Temporary Measures Concerning Displaced Coal Miners was enacted the day before the release of the Interim Report. It provided for the establishment of the Relief Association for Displaced Coal Miners to furnish institutional support for unemployed miners in general.

As discussed, full-scale implementation of the adjustment policy, including structural adjustments and the relief program for displaced miners, began at the end of 1959. This change in coal policies was reflected in budgets.

As Table 3.2 shows, budget amounts related to coal policies increased rapidly from fiscal 1960 onwards. The coal-related budget for fiscal 1960 was 5.8 billion yen, 6.4 times the previous year's budget. In 1960, the budget for 'Rationalization,' which constituted about half the total coal budget, jumped from 177 million to 2.6 billion yen. Moreover, budget items related to 'social policy' – namely, the 'Relief Project for Displaced Miners' and 'Local Revitalization Project' – were newly added in 1960 and 1961, respectively. These 'social policy budgets' constituted a large proportion of the total coal budget. In 1961, for example, the 'Relief Project for Displaced Miners,' 'Local Revitalization Project' and 'Countermeasures for Mining Pollution' together amounted to 3.5 billion yen, more than half the total coal budget.

Table 3.1 The outline of major coal policies

Coal policy	Date of report	Gist of report	Policy target proposed in report	Measures implemented after the first countermeasure policy
The 1200 Yen price-cut policy	19 December, 1959 Interim Report of the Basic Issue Committee in the Coal Industry Advisory Council	1. The current recession of the coal industry results from structural problems such as the superiority of liquid over solid energy and from prevailing economic rationality	Cuts to the unit price of coal of 1200 yen by fiscal 1963. Annual production targets of 50 and 55 million tons	1. Reorganization of the Coal-Mining Maintenance Corporation into the Coal-Mining Rationalization Corporation
		2. Specific conditions and methods must be suggested in which coal can compete with its alternatives		2. Provision of interest-free loans for the modernization of coal-mining facilities
		3. There is an urgent need for countermeasures for displaced workers and revitalization projects for coal-mining regions		3. Establishment of the Coal-Mining Adjustment Subsidy and Coal-Mining Adjustment Facilitation Subsidy systems. Establishment of the Coal-Mining Adjustment Fund. Provision of loans by the Coal-Mining Rationalization Corporation for the restructuring of the coal-mining industry
				4. Conclusion of the Long-term Coal Trade Agreement

(continued)

Table 3.1 (continued)

Coal policy	Date of report	Gist of report	Policy target proposed in report	Measures implemented after the first countermeasure policy
The first counter-measure policy (starting in fiscal 1963)	13 October, 1962 First Report of the Coal Inquiry Commission	1. It is a national imperative to take preventive measures lest the collapse of the coa- mining industry does serious damage to local communities and to the national economy	Establishment of a secure and independent energy supply system by fiscal 1967. Establishment of the 55 million-ton production system	1. Raising of the long-term demand for coal by building coal-fired power generating stations
				2. Attempts to rationalize of distribution by, for example, building bulk coal carriers
		2. The coal production system needs to be restructured In accordance with the changes in the demand structure caused by the energy revolution		3. Establishment of the Steam Coal Payment Clearing Co. Ltd
				4. Modernization of efficient coal mines and closure of inefficient mines were closed (he so-called 'scrap and build' policy)
				5. Establishment of the 'Job-Hunting Notebook' system for displaced coal workers
				6. Imposition of financial regulations on the coal-mining industry
The second counter-measure policy (starting in fiscal 1965)	16 December, 1964 The Second Report of the Coal Inquiry Commission	The collapse of the coal mining industry would bring grave social and economic outcomes. In addition, to increase dependence on imported energy should be avoided in terms of not only international payments but energy security. It is	Maintenance of production at the 55 million-ton level. Consolidation of the management basis of coal-mining companies by around 1967	1. Raising of the unit price of coal was raised (300 yen a ton for general coal; 200 yen a ton for coking coal)
				2. Reorganization of the Steam Coal Payment Clearing Co. Ltd. into the Steam Coal Sales Co. Ltd., so that steam

		a national imperative to secure the supply of coal as an important domestic energy source		coal was purchased and sold exclusively by this company at official prices
				3. Establishment of the interest subsidy scheme for loans to support coal-mining companies
The third countermeasure policy (starting in fiscal 1967)	25 July, 1966 The Coal Industry Advisory Council's Report on the Fundamental Countermeasure Policy	If the government takes measures to secure demand for domestic coal and shoulders 100 billion yen of coal mining companies' debts to help rebuild their management base, it is possible to maintain the 50 million-ton level of domestic coal production. It can be expected that with the implementation of these countermeasures the financial status of coal mining companies will return to the black by fiscal 1970	Maintenance of production levels at around 50 million tons. (Establishment of the basic framework of countermeasures for the period up to fiscal 1970)	1. Granting of around 100 billion yen in subsidies for coal-mining companies in order for them to repay their interest-bearing debts (the so-called First Debt-Shouldering Policy)
				2. Establishment of the Management Stabilization Subsidy system.
				3. Establishment of the subsidy system for coal-seam exploration and the excavation of tunnels (from fiscal 1966 onwards). Raising of the unit subsidy amount for the closure of a coal mine
				4. Stimulus to the demand for coal by, for instance, granting subsidies to companies which increased their purchases of coal
				5. Establishment of the special budgetary account for countermeasures for coal problems (until fiscal 1970)

(continued)

Table 3.1 (continued)

Coal policy	Date of report	Gist of report	Policy target proposed in report	Measures implemented after the first countermeasure policy
The fourth countermeasure policy (starting in fiscal 1969)	25 December, 1968 The Report of the Coal Industry Advisory Council	1. The revitalization of the coal mining industry needs to be pursued in order to establish a secure energy supply system for the national economy	(No expression of a clear production target. Postponment of the termination of important countermeasures until fiscal 1973)	1. Granting of around 85 billion yen of subsidies for coal mining companies to rebuild their management basis (the so-called Second Debt-Shouldering Policy). Reinforcement of the Management Stabilization Subsidy system. Expansion of the Coal Mining Rationalization Corporation's interest-free loan system
		2. However, if the financial situation of coal-mining companies is not improved by the government's countermeasures, drastic decisions including a complete withdrawl from the coal-mining industry will have to be taken. Reductions in the scale of production and closures of mines need to be implemented deliberately and smoothly		2. Establishment of the special subsidy system for companies which carried out a complete withdrawal from the coal-mining industry (the so-called 'special subsidies,' granted until fiscal 1971). Raising of the unit amount of the general subsidy for the closure of coal mines
				3. Postponement of the termination of the special budgetary account for countermeasures for coal problems until fiscal 1973

The fifth counter-measure policy (starting in fiscal 1973)	29 June, 1972 The Report of the Coal Industry Advisory Council	1. In consideration of the possibility that a sudden reduction in coal production would lead to social turmoil, the coal production target for fiscal 1975 needs to be set at no less than 20 million tons. In order to realize this scale of production, measures have to be taken to raise demand for domestic coal	Setting the production target for fiscal 1975 at no less than 20 million tons	1. Granting of around 70 billion yen of subsidies for coal-mining companies to rebuild their management basis (the so-called Third Debt-Shouldering Policy.) Shortening of the period of government assumption of a portion of the existing debts
		2. Provided that more comprehensive support is given to the coal-mining industryin Japan than in any other country in the world, coal-mining companies and their employees have to unite and give their best effort		

Note: This table is made by the author

Table 3.2 Budget amounts related to coal policies (Unit: 1 Million Yen)

Fiscal year	Measures for rationalization					Relief projects for displaced miners	Revitalization projects for mining regions	Countermeasures for mining pollution	Total
	Total	Proportion (%)	Capital investment	Implementation of closure	Improvement of financial situation				
1955	14							376	390
1956	15							350	365
1957	98							566	664
1958	137							510	647
1959	177							734	911
1960	2640	45.4	2140	400		2330		850	5820
1961	3039	46.4	2800	400		2607	30	880	6556
1962	7654	52.1	3790	4062		5077	680	977	14,688
1963	9957	52.2	4376	5266		6172	1330	1633	19,092
1964	9199	46.8	4892	3985		6591	2048	1800	19,637
1965	12,341	54	5712	4312		5762	1810	2941	22,854
1966	18,324	60.1	7511	5427	5032	4633	2836	4679	30,472
1967	41,613	74.1	10,045	10,586	14,532	5030	3046	6334	56,193
1968	41,354	69.3	11,269	4888	14,708	5091	3294	7796	59,638
1969	62,057	70.2	14,763	10,536	26,919	7637	5691	10,640	88,454
1970	66,544	68.5	14,410	16,270	30,030	8553	6483	12,312	97,114
1971	67,995	64.1	15,050	18,070	27,890	9539	7990	13,994	106,078
1972	60,436	60.3	15,420	11,100	26,800	9941	8007	15,160	100,151
1973	62,294	57	13,670	12,450	27,600	10,947	8232	17,092	109,228

Note: The amount listed under ‘Capital Investment’ is the sum of those in ‘Improvement of Production Systems’ and ‘Investment by the Coal-Mining Rationalization Corporation.’

Source: (Sekitankōgyō Gōrika Jigyōdan 1965): 374–375

After the '1200 Yen Price-Cut Policy,' a series of coal policies (from the First to Fifth Countermeasure Policies) followed, all of them implemented by the end of fiscal 1973. All of these coal policies in essence functioned as structural adjustment policies, even though their concrete targets and measures varied. The contents of the policies are summarized in Table 3.1. The next section presents an analysis of two major aspects of these policies: production adjustment and employment adjustment.

3 The Maintenance of the 55 Million-ton Production System

3.1 Reasons for the Annual Coal Production Target of 55 Million Tons

As mentioned above, the Interim Report by the Coal Industry Advisory Council held that annual coal production should be between 50 and 55 million tons. On the basis of this Report, the Basic Plan for the Coal Industry Rationalization, which was revised in September 1960, set the fiscal 1963 production target at 55 million tons. This annual production target of 55 million tons was thereafter maintained consistently from the '1200 Yen Price-Cut Policy' through the 'First Countermeasure Policy' to the 'Second Countermeasure Policy,' but its significance changed with the adoption of the 'First Countermeasure Policy'. The '1200 Yen Price-Cut Policy' had been coupled with the 55 million-ton annual production target in order to maintain coal's competitiveness against other energy sources. The 'First Countermeasure Policy,' by contrast, was designed not so much for economic as for social security purposes.

When the '1200 Yen Price-Cut Policy' was instituted, the estimated price of heavy oil was an important factor for the determination of an appropriate level of coal production, although it is not known what estimate was used in the making of the Interim Report.[9] The Report does say, however, that an annual production level of 40 million tons was considered too low for coal to realize the economies of scale necessary to compete with other energy sources. It also says that the 40 million-ton level was not enough to sustain employment and reduce the international payments imbalance caused by the import of heavy oil. It can be assumed, therefore, that factors such as employment and the international balance of payments, along with competitiveness, were taken into consideration in determining the appropriate coal production level.

[9] In July 1959, the Fourth Subcommittee of the Energy Committee set up within the Industrial Rationalization Council estimated the price of C fuel oil for fiscal 1967 at 0.84 yen per thousand kilo calories. In October 1959, the Japan Coal Association in its 'New Long-term Plan' estimated the price of C fuel oil for fiscal 1963 at 0.83 yen per thousand kilo calories.

The intent of the 'annual production level of 55 million tons' can be assessed by analyzing how the long-term coal targets were determined at the Economic Council's Energy Subcommittee of the Government Sector Committee (the Economic Council dealt with energy problems related to the so-called 'Income Doubling Plan' approved by the Cabinet on 27 December 1960).

The report of the Energy Subcommittee advocated a shift in the basic energy policy from 'coal first, oil second' to 'oil first, coal second' in view of "the recent global tendency towards consumers' free choice regarding energy sources." The report posed three principles on which to build energy policy: the supply of cheap energy (the economic principle); minimization of the burden of international payments without compromising the economic principle; and the establishment of a secure energy supply system.

The annual coal production target of 55 million tons was compatible with these energy policy principles for the following two reasons. First, at the 55 million-ton scale, the Japanese coal industry was able to compete with heavy oil importation. Second, this production level was in line with the 'oil first, coal second' policy.

The Energy Subcommittee's view reflected that of the Economic Council's Energy Committee.[10] The Energy Committee's view on long-term energy prospects explains why 55 million tons was set as the desired production level to enable domestic coal to compete with imported heavy oil. The Energy Committee's report dated 25 July 1960 concluded that annual coal production could be maintained in the future at the conventional level of 55 million tons on condition that the price of heavy oil remained 0.75 yen a thousand kilocalories and the price of imported semi-caking coal remained 4700 yen a ton (NIRA, 2000, pp. 381–384). This conclusion also presupposed the successful implementation of the '1200 Yen Price-Cut Policy' and the expected cost-cutting effects of the rationalization plan ending in fiscal 1970. Energy Committee calculations noted, however, that the correct level of coal production would be just 37.7 million tons if economic factors were the only ones taken into consideration.[11] It was because of employment and international balance of payments considerations that the annual coal production target was set at 55 instead of 37.7 million tons.

Given that the production volume target had been increased deliberately, it was imperative that the government secure sufficient demand for domestic coal. The

[10] In April 1959, the Economic Planning Agency set up the Energy Committee within the Economic Council in order to discuss a new long-term energy plan. In November 1959, however, the Economic Council was called on by the government to consult about the Income Doubling Plan. Therefore, it was decided that the energy problem would be discussed at both the Energy Committee and the Energy Subcommittee of the Government Sector Committee. The members of the Subcommittee were chosen from among the members of the Energy Committee. The Subcommittee drew up the energy plan on the basis of discussions in the Energy Committee.

[11] The Energy Committee calculated the minimum necessary production level of domestic coal required to compete with imported oil. Three cases were examined to determine the necessary production level for fiscal 1970. If the price of C fuel oil was 0.8 yen a thousand kilo calorie, the necessary coal production level was 46.3 million tons. If the price was 0.75 yen, the necessary production level was 37.7 million tons. If the price was 0.7 yen, the necessary production level was 31.3 million tons (NIRA, 2000, p.367).

Long-Term Coal Trade Agreement was accordingly struck between the coal industry and large coal consumers (the electric power, steel, gas and cement industries) in June 1961. This agreement obliged the latter to purchase certain amounts of domestic coal, even if it was relatively expensive, in order to enable the maintenance of annual coal production at 55 million tons.

What was the proportion of 55 million tons of domestic coal in the total energy supply? According to the long-term energy projections on which the 'Income Doubling Plan' was based, total energy demand was expected to increase by 2.1 times and the proportion of imported energy was expected to rise from 34 to 59 % between 1959 and 1970. The proportion of domestic coal was expected to decline from 32 to 18 % during the same period. The government's plan was obviously to cater to the growing energy demand with imported energy while maintaining the conventional 55 million-ton level of domestic coal production. The liberalization of oil imports implemented in October 1962 was a preliminary step for this plan. To set an annual coal production target of 55 million tons did not conflict, after all, with the shift to the 'oil first, coal second' energy policy.

3.2 *The 55 Million-Ton Coal Production System as 'Security Insurance'*

The price of heavy oil fell more drastically than the Energy Committee had expected, with the C fuel oil price sinking to 0.72 yen a thousand kilocalories in fiscal 1962. Nevertheless, the First Report of the Coal Inquiry Commission[12] dated 13 October 1962, maintained the annual coal production target at 55 million tons. This Report, however, plainly stated that 'coal was no longer able to compete with heavy oil.' No longer able to justify the 55 million-ton coal production system as necessary for sustaining coal's competitiveness, the Report shifted its emphasis to concerns about the 'economic and social ramifications of the collapse of the coal industry.' Therefore, the Report concluded that the maintenance of the 55 million-ton coal production system was imperative 'in terms both of the balance between energy sources and of energy security.' In addition to the Heavy Oil Regulation Act's being extended, other political measures were taken in order to secure sufficient demand for domestic coal. As mentioned above, the 'Long-Term Coal Trade Agreement,' designed to increase demand for coal, was already in force. In addition, the government requested that electric power and steel industries purchase more coal than stipulated in the agreement, assuring that the extra costs imposed on

[12] Because of the drop in oil prices and the Japan Coal Miners Union's 'Struggle for Policy Change,' the government was forced to reconsider the '1200 Yen Price-Cut Policy.' The extraordinary Cabinet meeting accordingly decided on 6 April 1962 to organize the Coal Inquiry Commission (led by Hiromi Arisawa) to investigate the modernization of the coal mining industry and the employment situation.

both industries would be reimbursed through a special refund system (the import duty refund system for heavy crude oil).[13]

In any event, the Coal Inquiry Commission Report maintained the annual coal production target at 55 million tons in consideration of 'economic and social ramifications of the collapse of the coal industry.' This represented the addition of a new emphasis on the issue of 'energy security,' alongside the already familiar issues of 'employment' and 'the balance of international payments.'

The issue of 'energy security' had initially been raised in reports of the European Energy Policy Commission (the interim report submitted in April 1961 and the final report released on 17 July 1961). The Ministry of International Trade and Industry dispatched the Commission to Europe in February 1961 to investigate the energy policies of European countries hit by coal crises. The Commission leader was Kiyoshi Tsuchiya and the sub-leader, Hidezō Inaba, both of them members of the Coal Industry Advisory Council.

The Commission's reports raised three issues to be addressed: national energy security, social problems and stable labor relations. The emphasis on energy security had an especially significant effect on the direction of energy policy. The coal industry, in particular, was greatly encouraged by the argument for national energy security presented in the Commission's reports, 'regarding it as an expression of the industry's long-cherished wish and making it a basis for its countermeasure actions against its business predicament' (Daidō Tsūshinsha 1961, p. 61).

The argument for energy security was most clearly expressed in the report of the Energy Task Force[14] set up within the Industrial Structure Investigation Council. This report was publicized in December 1963, a year after the release of the Coal Inquiry Commission's First Report.

The Energy Task Force set the following three points as principles for a comprehensive energy policy: the supply of cheap energy, the establishment of a secure energy supply system and the importance of addressing these in coordination with other economic and social problems such as the balance of international payments and social friction. With regard to the establishment of a secure energy supply system, two types

[13] With regard to the extra costs imposed on large coal consumers by the existing 'Long-Term Coal Trade,' the equivalent value from the increase in the tariff on crude oil made in April 1962 was reimbursed through the tax refund system (general refund system).

[14] In the 40th ordinary session of the Diet of 1962, both Houses of the Diet passed the resolution that 'a comprehensive energy policy should be established immediately and the role of oil and other energy sources should be clarified.' Following this resolution, the Energy Task Force was set up within the Industrial Structure Investigation Council in May 1962. The Industrial Structure Investigation Council had been established as an affiliate organization of the Ministry of International Trade and Industry in April 1961 for the purpose of 'investigating and discussing important issues concerning the industrial structure.' The Energy Task Force was to function for 3 years until the end of March 1964. In April 1964, its role was taken on by the Industrial Structure Council, which was newly set up as an affiliate of the Ministry of International Trade and Industry. The Industrial Rationalization Council's role was simultaneously assumed by the Industrial Structure Council. This marked the end of the historical role of the Industrial Rationalization Council, which had contributed significantly to the formation of industrial policy in postwar Japan.

of risks were considered: the disruption of the supply of oil due to non-economic causes such as political instability in oil-producing countries and the rigging of oil prices. The former was considered an issue of energy supply security, while the latter was understood to be linked to the nature of oil as an international commodity and the relationship between international oil majors and domestic oil refining companies. The Energy Task Force expected that coal production would remain at the 55 million-ton level from 1968 onwards. At the same time, however, the Task Force commented as follows: 'If national energy security were the only issue taken into consideration, it would be desirable to expand domestic coal production in proportion to the growth in total energy demand. It is true that this contradicts the principle of cheap energy. Nevertheless, the maintenance of a certain level of domestic coal production is imperative in order to retain an independent coal industry as a secure provider of energy.' Shifting between the contradictory principles of cheap energy and energy security, the Energy Task Force eventually concluded that the production level of 55 million tons was 'within the acceptable limit in terms of *security insurance* against energy security risks.' At this time, the Energy Task Force estimated that the compositional proportion of domestic coal viz. total primary energy supplies would fall from 25.7 to 11.4 % between 1962 and 1972.

Although the principle of energy security was a persuasive reason for the maintenance of domestic coal production, the phrase 'acceptable limit' left room for debate. Each party involved naturally sought to interpret it to its own advantage, and it was practically impossible to calculate the insurance premium objectively. The ambiguity of the notion of 'security insurance' was highlighted when the Third Report of the Coal Inquiry Commission, publicized in July 1966, concluded that the appropriate level of coal production should be 50, instead of 55, million tons a year, even though the Commission and the Energy Task Force, too, espoused the principle of 'security insurance.'

4 The Collapse of the Annual 55 Million-Ton Coal Production System

4.1 The Reduction of Production Levels to 50 Million Tons

Although the content of the Coal Inquiry Commission's First Report was immediately turned into concrete policy and implemented as the First Countermeasure Policy, the industry showed no sign of recovery and it therefore became apparent that the policy required reconsideration. As Fig. 3.3 shows, despite the improvement in production efficiency brought about by the rationalization measures, reductions in production coasts were still held back by rising wages and material costs such that selling prices remained below production costs. Taishō Mining Company, one of the major coal mining companies, went bankrupt in October 1964. The coal industry was in a serious financial situation.

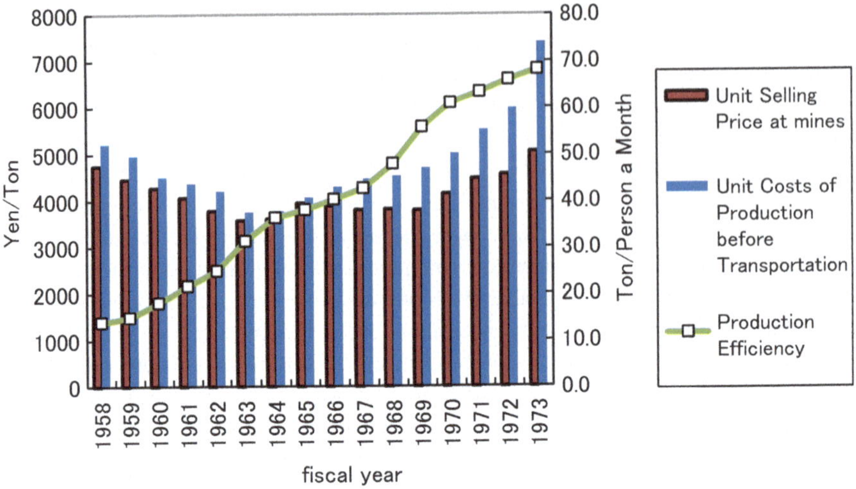

Fig. 3.3 Unit selling price, unit costs of production and production efficiency
Source: (Sekitankōgyō Gōrika Jigyōdan 1976)

The Second Countermeasure Policy was drawn up and implemented on the basis of the Coal Inquiry Commission's Second Report[15] released on 16 December 1964. The 1200 Yen Price-Cut Policy was abandoned and the prices of general coal and coking coal were raised by 300 and 200 yen, respectively. An interest subsidy scheme was also introduced at the same time. Such measures were not enough, however, to save the industry from its worsening financial situation and more drastic measures were required. Thus the Coal Inquiry Commission submitted its Third Report, the so-called 'Report on the Fundamental Countermeasure Policy' publicized on 25 July 1966. Its most important proposal was to urge the government to shoulder coal-mining companies' debts up to 100 billion yen so that they could restructure themselves.

Since this was a policy requiring the use of a large amount of taxpayers' money for the bailout of private companies, the government had to explain the need for the policy to the public. This job was left to the Energy Problem Investigation Council,[16] and the coal mining industry waited anxiously for its report to come out. Before submitting the final report in February 1967, the Council released an interim report on 20 July 1966

[15] Faced with the aggravation of the coal problem, the government decided in the Cabinet meeting of 11 August 1964 to organize the Second Coal Inquiry Commission (led by Hiromi Arisawa).

[16] The Energy Task Force was set up as a section of the Industrial Structure Investigation Council. Although the latter was abolished, the former continued to function within the Industrial Structure Council. However, when the Energy Problem Investigation Council was newly established as an advisory body to the Ministry of International Trade and Industry in August 1965, the organization and roles of the Energy Task Force, together with those of the Nuclear Industry Task Force, were transferred to the Energy Problem Investigation Council. This Council was established to deal comprehensively with the following problems: the deepening dependence on energy imports, the utilization of nuclear power generation, environmental pollution and so forth.

Table 3.3 Production scales of coal and corresponding social costs (Unit: 100 Million Yen)

	Plan A	Plan B	Plan C
Production scale	52.8 Million ton	31.3 Million ton	11.8 Million ton
Costs for continuation of coal production	206	129	0
Additional costs for purchasers	275	87	0
Increase in costs for closure of mines	0	2643	4681
Increase in costs for revitalization projects	0	1640	2920
Total	481	4480	7601
Amount of deficit covering for continuation of mining	1621	1063	222

Source: Tsūshō Sangyōshō Sekitankyoku 1968): 89–90
For the 'Amount of Deficit Covering the Continuation of Mining,' see "Shōwa 41-nen Sekiyugyōkai no Suii [The Oil Industry of 1966]: 120."

regarding 'the roles of the coal mining industry' and set the desired annual coal production level at 50 million tons. The Coal Inquiry Commission accepted this view in its Third Report and decided to lower the production target from 55 to 50 million tons.

The Energy Problem Investigation Council stated in its report that it was 'appropriate to keep the annual coal production at the 50 million-ton level,' considering that 'the secure supply of cheap energy' had to be pursued in connection with other policy objectives such as the balance of international payments and the stabilization of employment. In making this report, the Investigation Council calculated the social costs based on simulations of three case scenarios: Case A in which domestic coal was produced at full capacity; Case B in which coking coal and hard coal were produced domestically, while steam coal was procured through the free market; Case C in which all kinds of coal were procured through the free market. In each case, estimates were made of the attendant 'social costs,' including 'maintenance costs,' 'additional costs for consumers,' 'costs for the closure of mines' and 'costs for regional revitalization.' Other factors such as the balance of international payments and the security of the energy supply were also taken into consideration. The Energy Problem Investigation Council concluded from this that the 50 million-ton production level was an appropriate aim (Tsūshō Sangyōshō Sekitankyoku, 1968, pp. 86–93). The results of the simulations are shown in Table 3.3. The Investigation Council found Cases B and C impractical, because the social costs imposed by them on the public would be too enormous.

This explanation, however, still does not seem fully objective. The Investigation Council calculated that domestic coal production for fiscal 1970 would be 52.8 million tons and that the unit production cost per ton would be around 4100 yen. However, the Council did not fully elucidate the premises on which its calculation was based, such as the rate of increase of wages and prices.[17] There was therefore room for the

[17] This estimate of unit production cost was based on the premise that the annual rates of increase of wages and prices were 7 and 1 %, respectively. Increases in productivity and economies of scale were also taken into consideration. However, these assumptions about the rates of wage and price

Investigation Council to interpose political judgments. As a matter of fact, domestic coal production continued to stagnate at a little over 50 million tons from fiscal 1964 onwards. It can be assumed, therefore, that the Investigation Council was seeking to maintain the status quo in the industry, using 'social insurance' as a pretext.

4.2 *The Abandonment of the 50 Million-Ton Coal Production System*

Despite the implementation of the Third Countermeasure Policy, which included the government's shouldering of coal companies' enormous debts, the government was frustrated in its aim of maintaining traditional production targets. First, the domestic coal industry was unable to maintain production at 50 million ton because of a severe labor shortage. In fiscal 1963, 1 year after the release of the First Report, domestic coal production was just 51.1 million tons, far short of the target of 55.3 million tons. Between fiscal 1964 and 1966, the industry managed to produce a little over 50 million tons. However, in fiscal 1967, the year the Third Countermeasure Policy was introduced, only around 47 million tons was produced, more than 3 million tons short of the 50.3 million-ton target. The decline in the number and quality of coal miners was considered the crucial factor in the failure to meet the target. Already by the end of 1963 it was noted that there were 'labor shortages and a deterioration of labor quality deriving from workforce reductions' (Daidō Tsūshinsha 1965, p. 122). It was observed that while the coal industry was 'busy taking care of those who left their jobs, labor shortages [were] becoming a serious problem, especially in newly developed, large-scale coal mines' (Fukuoka-ken, 1964a). The urgent need to acquire a younger labor force was addressed, but in practice, it proved difficult to prevent outflows of labor, and the number of coal miners dropped below the 100-thousand level in fiscal 1967. It was no longer possible for the industry to 'keep a sufficient number of workers required to maintain the so-called proper production level of 50 million tons (Daidō Tsūshinsha 1968, p. 22).'

Another reason for the failure to maintain the 55 million-ton production system was the financial situation in which coal-mining companies found themselves. Although the Third Report expected that coal companies would return to profitability by the end of fiscal 1970, their financial difficulties in fact kept deteriorating.[18] As Fig. 3.3 shows, production costs continued to rise despite productivity improvements, due to rising prices and production cutbacks caused by the labor

---

rises were unrealistic. Between 1966 and 1970, wages and prices in fact increased at the average annual rates of 12.4 and 1.9 %, respectively. This calculation by the author takes regular wages of coal miners from a survey by the Japan Coal Association. Price increase calculations are based on the 'overall wholesale price index' presented in Kazushi Ōkawa et al. (1966).

[18] Although the relief plan had estimated the loss of major coal mining companies for fiscal 1967 at 9.9 billion yen, it actually came to 16.9 billion yen.

shortage. As shown in Table 3.3, the Energy Problem Investigation Council estimated that 162.1 billion yen would be needed to make up for coal company losses. Although the government did assume 100 billion yen of their debts under the Third Countermeasure Policy, the coal industry was still in serious financial condition and needed additional financial support.[19]

As has been shown, it became obvious by around 1967 that the annual 50 million-ton production system was no longer economically sustainable. At the same time, other reasons or pretexts for maintaining the system, such as energy security, the balance of international payments, and social friction, were becoming less significant issues.

The balance of international payments stayed in the black in the latter half of the 1960s. Although Japan recorded a trade deficit of around 15 million dollars in 1968, that constituted only 0.1 % of total exports amounting to 12,972 million dollars. As Kiyoshi Tsuchiya pointed out in 1966, even if the entire 50 million tons of domestic coal were replaced by imported oil, it was unlikely to cause a serious balance of payments problem (Tsuchiya Kiyoshi, 1966, p. 207).

A more flexible approach emerged on the issue of energy security as well. For instance, in its introduction of European and U.S. energy policies, the Overseas Energy Situation Investigation Commission[20] reported that 'the idea of national energy security based solely on coal' was becoming 'more diversified, based on: energy development both at home and abroad; the diversification of energy supply sources; energy reserves; the notion of collective security and so forth.' This new approach to energy security was reflected in the 1967 report of the Energy Problem Investigation Council. The report proposed diversified energy security measures, including the development of nuclear power; the encouragement of overseas oil development; oil reserves; and making the oil refining industry more independent.

The problem of displaced miners, which was the most crucial social friction issue, was also becoming less pressing. By the mid-1960s, the annual decrease in the number of regular coal miners fell to the 10-thousand level. Although the number of displaced coal miners seeking employment totaled almost 60 thousand at peak, it declined to the 10 ~ 20-thousand level in the latter half of the 1960s (Table 3.4). As will be discussed below, the coal-miner unemployment problem was not completely resolved, but it no longer had a significant effect on energy policy.

Although these changes contributed to a reduction in social insurance costs, or in other words to a lowering of coal production targets, neither the government nor the coal industry was able to find a new rationale for rebuilding the industry. There was

[19] Eventually, the government shouldered the coal companies' debts of 85 billion yen through the Fourth Countermeasure Policy and the debts of 70 billion yen through the Fifth Countermeasure Policy.

[20] The Overseas Energy Situation Investigation Commission (led by Hiromi Arisawa) was dispatched overseas in May 1964. For 2 months, the members of the Commission investigated the energy problems and energy policies of European countries and the United States. They released an interim report on 25 August.

Table 3.4 Reemployment of displaced coal workers (Unit: Person)

	Number of job seekers			Number of those employed through Public Employment Security Offices			Number of others							
Fiscal year	Job seekers at the end of previous year	New job seekers	Total	Wide range (beyond juristiction of local P.E. S.O.)	General (within jurisdiction of local P. E.S.O.	Total	Revitalization projects for coal-mining regions	Companies' job placement	Finding jobs onttheir own, self-employment, return to farming	Total	Number of the reemployed	Number of job seekers at the end of year	Number of the reemployed/ new job seekers (%)	Number of the reemployed/ total job seekers (%)
1962	16,300	32,800	49,100	5800	9100	14,900		7900	7500	15,400	30,300	18,800	92.4	61.7
1963	18,800	41,000	59,800	10,800	9500	20,300	2500	11,600	6200	19,600	39,900	19,900	97.3	66.7
1964	19,900	18,980	38,880	9000	9810	18,810	980	2330	3930	6760	25,570	13,310	134.7	65.8
1965	13,310	12,000	25,310	6980	7040	14,020	360	980	3590	4790	18,810	6500	156.8	74.3
1966	6500	11,200	17,700	1390	5160	6550	690	1220	1900	2150	8700	9000	77.7	49.2
1967	9000	12,380	22,500	3760	6370	10,130	690	2270	3960	4670	14,800	6580	119.5	65.8
1968	6580	4800	11,380	1270	4190	5460	540	720	1240	1710	7170	4210	149.4	63
1969	4210	19,010	23,220	5070	9040	14,110	620	1560	1110	1490	15,600	7620	82.1	67.2
1970	7620	12,980	20,600	5300	6670	11,970	900	910	1010	1540	13,510	7090	104.1	65.6
Total	102,220	165,150	268,490	49,370	66,880	116,250	7280	29,490	30,440	58,110	174,360	93,010		

Note: 'Total' numbers in 'Number of Others' do not include the numbers of those counted in 'Number of Those Employed through Public Employment Security Offices'

Source: Rōdōshō Shokugyō Anteikyoku 1971: 342

in fact a rather heated debate over the restructuring of the coal-mining industry around 1967,[21] but it never brought about significant change. Instead, annual coal production targets were rapidly reduced, and the government finally set the production target at 20 million tons in 1972. This process will be examined in the next section.

4.3 The Reduction of the Annual Coal Production Target to 20 Million Tons

As it became unrealistic to maintain the 50 million-ton production system, the Coal Industry Advisory Council released the Report on Countermeasures for the Coal Problem (Fourth Report) on 25 December 1968, aiming for the gradual contraction of the coal industry.

This Fourth Report was based on the recognition that 'the coal-mining industry [could] no longer revive on its own.' A policy of gradual reduction was advocated under the slogan 'smooth closure.' The Report said as follows: 'The closure of mines has to be carried out smoothly and carefully, because it will incur significant consequences for coal miners and regional economies.' As concrete measures to achieve 'smooth closure,' the Report proposed raising the unit amount of the subsidy for coal-mine closures and to creating a special subsidy system for companies that carried out a complete withdrawal from a coal mine. At the same time, it also emphasized the need to reinforce the 'subsidy system for the rebuilding of the industry' in order to prevent the coal industry from collapsing altogether, proposing a second debt-shouldering scheme, among other measures.

At this point, the policy on coal was clearly shifting towards a diminishing equilibrium. Nevertheless, while the Report admitted that it was 'impossible to maintain the current production level,' it did not specify a new production target to replace the conventional 50 million-ton level.

The Second Energy Problem Investigation Council issued new long-term energy projections in July 1970. It estimated domestic coal production for fiscal 1975 at 38 million tons, a 14 million ton reduction from the estimates of the First Report of the Energy Problem Investigation Council. Then, on 29 June 1972, the Coal Industry Advisory Council released the Report on Remedial Measures for the Coal Mining Industry (Fifth Report) and estimated that domestic coal production

[21] Around 1967, debate surged over the restructuring of the coal-mining industry. Underlying the arguments was the recognition that the industry's revitalization would be impossible unless the 'traditional business system based on individual, private companies' was altered. It was therefore urged that 'coal-mining companies should be owned or administrated by the state, or there should be only one nationwide coal company or three companies corresponding to three regions.' Although the debate became heated at its peak, changes of this kind were not brought to fruition. Regarding the debate on the industry's restructuring, see (Sekitankōgyō Gōrikaseisakushi Kenkyūkai, 1990, pp. 166–187).

in fiscal 1975 would be 'no less than 20 million tons,' representing a further cut in estimates of 18 million tons. The following reasons for the reduced estimates were cited by the Coal Industry Advisory Council: the deterioration of mining conditions, the increase in production costs, the difficulty in the procurement of workers and the serious financial situation of coal mining companies. The 1972 Report of the Coal Industry Advisory Council also pointed out that although the Basic Plan for Coal Industry Rationalization assumed 36 million tons of coal production for fiscal 1973, realistic projections for fiscal 1972 came to 27.5 million tons. Incidentally, the 20 million-ton production level presented as the new standard in the 1972 Report (Fifth Report) remained the standard until November 1986, when the Coal Industry Advisory Council released the Report on the Future of Coal Policies (Eighth Report) and set the proper production level at 10 million tons.

5 Rapid Employment Adjustment and Employment Countermeasures

5.1 Rapid Employment Adjustment

In contrast to the slow pace of coal production adjustment, employment adjustment was carried out rather rapidly. The number of regular coal workers began to decline in 1958 when the industry went into recession. Employment adjustment was intensified in and after fiscal 1960, as the coal policy began to be implemented in earnest. Between fiscal 1960 and 1965, the number of regular coal miners was reduced by 152 thousand. During the 3 years between fiscal 1961 and 1963, in particular, their number dropped by more than 30 thousand each year. From fiscal 1964 onwards, the pace of decline generally slowed except in fiscal 1969 when the number fell by more than 20 thousand. Finally, in 1973, the number of regular coal miners decreased only by 6 thousand (Fig. 3.4).

This rapid employment adjustment was a natural outcome of the coal policy, which aimed to enhance productivity while maintaining production levels. The Japanese coal-mining industry at the time lagged far behind its European counterparts in productivity,[22] and therefore was more susceptible to the pressures of imported oil. It was imperative for the Japanese coal mining industry to improve productivity as quickly as possible. Large-scale reductions in the workforce were therefore inevitable.

The policy for the closure of coal mines functioned as a strong tool for employment adjustment. The number of coal workers who left their jobs because of mine closure soared in fiscal 1962, the year in which the subsidy and loan systems for

[22] In 1960, the labor productivity of a Japanese coal miner was only 52 % that of his German counterpart, 56 % that of his French counterpart and 65 % that of his Belgian counterpart (Tsūshō Sangyōshō 1964).

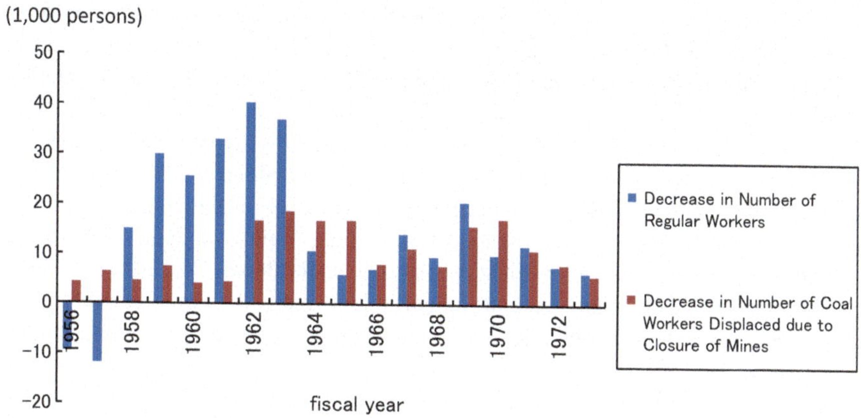

Fig. 3.4 Decrease in Numbers of Regular Coal Workers and Those Displaced due to Closure of Coal Mines
Source: Tsusho Sangyosho, *Sekitan Kokusu Tokeinenpo* [Annual Report on Coal and Coke] and Sekitankōgyō Gōrikaseisakushi Kenkyūkai 1990

mine closures were introduced. Although the number declined in and after fiscal 1966, it rose rapidly again in fiscal 1969 and 1970, because of the establishment of the special subsidy system for the closure of mines. (Fig. 3.4) It is clear that the reduction of regular coal workers was backed and precipitated by government measures regarding the closure of mines.

Another characteristic of the employment adjustment was that the adjustment proceeded faster than policymakers had expected. The number of remaining coal miners not only fell below the estimates set forth in the mid-term (5 year) plans such as the 1200 Yen Price-Cut Policy and the 1962 First Report, but also below the estimates calculated each year based on the Rationalization Plan.[23]

One of the reasons the numbers of remaining coal miners were smaller than expected was that a lot of workers left their jobs voluntarily. Although the Coal Inquiry Commission's First Report of 1962 had the intention of rebuilding the coal mining industry, 'it ironically served to propagate the impression that the industry was on the decline and to create an atmosphere urging workers to leave their jobs (Daidō Tsūshinsha 1964, p.126).' This eventually led to an unexpected increase in voluntarily unemployed workers. Faced with the growing number of workers who voluntarily left their jobs, the Coal Inquiry Commission pointed out in its Second Report released on December 1964 that: 'Although coal miners used to have a strong wish to [earn their livings] in coal mines, many of them are now leaving their jobs voluntarily because of their concern about the future of their companies and the

[23] The 1200 Yen Price-Cut Policy estimated the number of regular coal miners for fiscal 1963 at 175,670. The First Countermeasure Policy estimated the number of regular coal miners for the same year at 147,120. In reality, however, there were only 122,779 regular coal miners in fiscal 1963.

coal mining industry, and [because of] general labor shortages in other industries.' According to the Report, the biggest cause of the business decline of the coal industry was that the unexpected spread among coal miners of the 'inclination to leave.'

Of course, trade unions fiercely opposed the rapid employment adjustment, but with little success. When coal-mining companies intensified their rationalization efforts at the end of the 1950s, trade unions fought back in the Miike Coal Mine Dispute of 1959–1960, the biggest industrial dispute in postwar Japan. After their defeat in this dispute, however, trade unions such as the Japan Coal Miners' Union (Nihon Tankō Rōdōkumiai) were no longer able to resist the employment adjustment trend, even though they continued their struggle in pursuit of a change in the coal policy.

The Japan Coal Miners' Union was in fact losing its industrial power. After the Miike Coal Mine Dispute, those coal miners who opposed the confrontational policy of the Union and the General Council of Trade Unions of Japan (Sōhyō) quit the Union.[24] The proportion of total regular employees who were union members accordingly dropped from 73 to 51 % between fiscal 1960 and 1966 (Nihon Tankō Rōdōkumiai, 1961, 1991).[25] In addition, as competition among coal-mining companies intensified due to the rationalization policy, workers in the industry lost their solidarity, which in turn contributed to the decline of the Japan Coal Miners' Union as an industrial union (Daidō Tsūshinsha 1964, p.131).

5.2 The Government's Countermeasures for the Unemployment Problem and Their Effects

Countermeasures for displaced coal workers began to be implemented in earnest around the end of 1959. By that time, coal-worker unemployment had already become a serious social issue. The 'black feather movement,' a campaign to aid displaced coal workers which spread throughout the country from a small district in Kyūshū, was a symbolic phenomenon. Many contemporary academics were also paying close attention to the seriousness of coal workers' unemployment (Tokita, Yoshihisa, 1958; Yamamoto, Junko, 1959, Tokumoto and Yoda 1963).

According to the Survey on Unemployed Coal Workers in Northern Kyūshū, conducted immediately after the Act on Temporary Measures Concerning Displaced Coal Miners of 1959 went into effect, among 3806 survey subjects, 13 % were completely unemployed, 8 % partially unemployed, 5 % engaged in

[24] In this connection, the New Miike Coal Miners' Union's affiliation with the National Coal Mining Labor Union, which was critical of the General Council of Trade Unions of Japan, was a symbolic event.

[25] Although the rate of membership in the Japan Coal Miners' Union began rising again in 1968, that was long after the severest measures of employment adjustment had been undertaken.

unemployment relief work and 53 % working in other industries. As many as 26 % of displaced coal workers were unemployed, including those who were 'completely unemployed,' 'partially unemployed,' and 'engaged in unemployment relief work' (Naikakusōridaijin Kanbō Shingishitsu, 1960). Another survey of displaced coal workers in the Chikuhō (northern Kyūshū) region concerning the period between 1955 and 1960 found that 16,189 (34.9 %) out of 46,448 displaced coal workers remained in the region, looking for jobs (Fukuoka Ken, 1962).

These surveys indicate that by the end of the 1950s there were already many displaced coal workers who were unemployed without any institutional support, and it should be noted that the government acted too slowly in carrying out countermeasures.

With the 1959 Act on Temporary Measures Concerning Displaced Coal Miners and the establishment of the Relief Association for Displaced Coal Miners, the government began to take on the unemployment problem in earnest, implementing a series of countermeasures. In June 1961, the Act on the Employment Promotion Project Corporation came into effect, and the Employment Promotion Project Corporation succeeded to the roles of the Relief Association for Displaced Coal Miners (Rōdōshō Shokugyō Anteikyoku, 1971, Koyōsokushin Jigyōdan, 1966, 1971). In August 1960, the so-called 'new coal policy' was announced and the decision was made to establish the Council for the Revitalization of Coal Mining Regions. This policy was based on the 1959 Interim Report recommendation that a comprehensive revitalization project was needed for coal-mining regions. Moreover, the Act on Temporary Measures Concerning the Revitalization of Coal Mining Regions came into effect in 1961, establishing the Corporation for Revitalization of Coal-Mining Regions. It supported businesses in coal-mining regions by conducting land-forming operations, for instance, and providing financial services (Santanchiiki Shinkō Jigyōdan, 1972).[26]

These countermeasures for displaced coal workers and revitalization projects for coal mining regions reflected the idea of 'labor mobilization' (Koyōsokushin Jigyōdan, 1971, pp. 2–3) espoused by the government. For example, to the Prime Minister's questions about countermeasures for the unemployment problem, the Employment Council (chaired by Hiromi Arisawa) replied as follows in its report released on 11 October 1960: 'We must make our best efforts have to enable these unemployed coal workers to get jobs in other developing industries in other regions...in other words, labor mobilization must be urged in order to prevent a buildup [in the numbers of] unemployed.' The Acts on the Employment Promotion Project Corporation and on Temporary Measures Concerning the Revitalization of Coal Mining Regions can be described as institutional tools for precipitating 'labor mobilization.'

[26] In addition to the countermeasures for unemployment and the revitalizing projects for coal mining regions, countermeasures for mining pollution were also reinforced. The Act on Security for Compensation for Damages Caused by Mining Pollution was enacted and the Mining Pollution Compensation Fund was established in 1963 (Sekitan Kōgai Jigyōdan, 1971).

Countermeasures to the unemployment problem were reinforced by the First Countermeasure Policy, in that it connected the closure of coal mines with reemployment plans. The Rationalization Act was revised, and the Minister of Labor was obliged to hear the Coal Industry Advisory Council's opinion about the Rationalization Plan and devise a 'reemployment plan for displaced coal workers' every year.

In addition, the government paid severance allowances of up to 100 thousand yen to displaced coal workers who received less than 300 thousand yen in severance payments from their companies. Moreover, 'Job Hunting Notebooks' were provided and 'employment encouragement allowances' granted those unemployed workers who had difficulty in finding new jobs. As a result, the budget for the relief of displaced coal workers amounted to more than 6 billion yen in fiscal 1963. (Table 3.2) Since revitalization measures for coal-mining regions were also expanded, the budget amount for fiscal 1963 was twice as much as that of the previous year.

It should be noted, however, that these attempts by the government to reinforce the countermeasures for the unemployment problem differed from employment security policy, which is what labor was demanding. The 1962 First Report clarified its standpoint as follows: 'Employment security does not mean that all workers in the coal mining industry will maintain their employment within the industry, but [rather] means that workers in the coal mining industry will be provided with modernized working conditions as good as those in other industries, while those who have been displaced will be provided with new, secure workplaces through responsible actions by the government and companies.' Consequently, the Report rejected a proposal by the Social Democratic Party of Japan to enact of a law restricting the dismissal of workers, insisting [instead] that coal-miner employment should be cut by around 70 thousand by fiscal 1967. The Report's standpoint on employment security was in line with the government's employment policy based on the idea of 'labor mobilization.'

According to a survey on the reemployment of displaced coal workers conducted by the Employment Security Bureau of the Ministry of Labor, 60 % of the displaced found their new jobs within 3 months, and 80 % of them within 6 months (Rōdōshō Shokugyō Anteikyoku, 1971, p. 326). Table 3.4 shows that 174,360 unemployed coal workers found their new jobs between fiscal 1962 and 1970. The total number of job seekers over the same period is 181,450. (The sum of 165,150, the total number of 'New Job Seekers,' and 16,300, the number of 'Job Seekers at the End of the Previous Year' for fiscal 1962.) It can be said, therefore, that the reemployment rate of displaced coal workers for this period was 96 %. This rate is consistent with the results of the Employment Security Bureau's survey mentioned above.

According to Table 3.4, 116,250 displaced coal workers found their new jobs through the Public Employment Security Offices between fiscal 1962 and 1970. Table 3.5 is the breakdown by industry and by region of these new jobs. It shows that 97,534 displaced coal workers (83.9 %) found new jobs in secondary industries, 53.0 % moved out of their original prefectures, and 47.0 % were reemployed in the same prefectures. In cases of employment 'Outside Coal-Producing Prefectures,'

Table 3.5 Reemployment of coal miners displaced through rationalization projects – breakdown by industy and by region

	Number (persons)	Proportion (%)
By industry		
Primary industries	232	0.2
Secondary industries	97,534	83.9
Manufacturing industry	84,821	73
Building industry	9184	7.9
Tertiary industries	18,484	15.9
Transportation and telecommunications industries	7440	6.4
Service industries	5115	4.4
Total	116,250	100
By Region		
Within Coal Mining Prefectures	54,638	47
Outside Coal Mining Prefectures	61,612	53
Aichi	15,773	13.6
Osaka	9303	8
Tokyo	6346	5.5
Kanagawa	6223	5.4
Others	23,967	20.6
Total	116,250	100

Source: Rōdōshō Shokugyō Anteikyoku 1971: 341

the proportions of manufacturing regions such as Aichi, Osaka, Tokyo and Kanagawa Prefectures were relatively large. (These four together accounted for 61.1 %.[27]) On the basis of these results, policymakers claimed that the reemployment of displaced coal workers was proceeding smoothly thanks to the large demand for workers created by high economic growth [Koyōsokushin Jigyōdan, p. 174]. Moreover, emphasizing the effects of the nationwide job placement system, they asserted that the mobilization of labor from stagnant industries to developing industries was taking place (Koyōsokushin Jigyōdan, 1971, p.65). In reality, however, the government's countermeasures for the unemployed were not as effective as policymakers claimed.

First, unemployment rates among coal workers remained high, in spite of the countermeasures. Although the exact unemployment rates of coal workers are hard to trace, it is known that unemployment rates in coal mining regions were significantly higher than in other regions. For example, the national average unemployment rates for 1960 and 1965 were 0.8 and 1.4 %, respectively, whereas those of the Chikuhō region in the same years were 3.9 and 8.0 %. It goes without saying that the main reason for this phenomenon was the existence of displaced coal workers.

[27] For case studies of reemployment situations in the Kaijima and Jōban Coal Mines, see Takagawa, Masamichi 2002, Takeda, Ryozō, 1963.

That the unemployment rates of coal workers remained high despite their high reemployment rates can be explained by the growing incidence of the long-term unemployed among displaced workers in coal mining regions. A close look at Table 3.4 shows that the proportion of reemployed to the total number of job seekers including the number carried over from the previous year was only around 60 % each year. This reflects the fact that many displaced coal workers remained in coal-mining regions without employment despite the implementation of the countermeasures by the government. In fact, the Kyūshū Mining Industry Federation reported that 208,000 coal workers were displaced in the Kyūshū district between 1959 and 1963; 63,000 of them, displaced again after reemployment in coal mines, were double-counted; among the remaining 145,000 unemployed workers, 85,000 (60 %) found new jobs in other coal mines or industries through the good offices of their companies and the Public Employment Security Offices; 60,000 of them (40 %) were either completely unemployed or engaged in unemployment relief work as day laborers and their numbers were growing in local communities (Kyūshū Keizai Chōsakyōkai, 1966, p.271).

Most of the long-term unemployed coal workers were middle-aged men. In the case of Fukuoka Prefecture, the proportion of 'Job Hunting Notebook' holders over 40 years of age rose from 55.5 to 74.0 % between December 1963 and July 1964 (Fukuoka Ken, 1964b). In Hokkaidō, among 3394 displaced coal workers who looked for jobs in fiscal 1967, 673 could not get one. 376 of them, more than half, were over fifty. (Incidentally, 187 were in their forties and 61 were in their thirties (Hokkaidō Rōdōbu, 1968, p. 6).) In addition, the average age of coal workers continued to rise throughout the 1960s (from 36.1 to 41.2 years of age between 1960 and 1970). Moreover, while younger coal workers were more inclined to move to other regions for new jobs, the older they were, the more they wanted to work in their local areas.[28] All this indicates the difficulty for middle-aged coal workers of finding new jobs in other industries or regions. They tended to stay in their local areas even after the closure of their mines, and eventually, they were either reemployed by other mines in the area or remained there as the unemployed.

'Labor mobilization,' meaning the effort to press 'unemployed coal workers to get jobs in other developing industries in other regions,' fell short of policymakers' expectations. Table 3.4 shows that 116,250 displaced coal workers found their new jobs through the Public Employment Security Offices between fiscal 1962 and 1970, of whom 49,370 (42 %), or 27 % of the total number of job seekers, moved to other regions. According to the same source, 66,870 displaced coal workers had originally been expected to take new jobs in other regions, but only 49,370 (74 %)

[28] It is based on a survey on the patterns of job-seeking by age conducted among coal workers of the Jōban Coal Mining Co. Ltd. shortly before the closure of the mine (Masaoka ed. 1998, p.203).

ultimately did. At the time, these were considered poor results, and the effectiveness of the job placement system was questioned.[29]

To sum up, the government's countermeasures for displaced coal workers functioned effectively so far as new job seekers were concerned. The strong demand for workers generated by high economic growth enabled a high rate of reemployment. However, the problem of growing numbers of displaced middle-aged coal workers in local communities remained unresolved. Moreover, the job placement system did not yield the expected results in its attempts at 'labor mobilization.' In this sense, the countermeasures for displaced coal workers must be regarded as having had only limited effect.

6 Conclusion

The government's coal policies affected the adjustment process of the Japanese coal-mining industry in crucial ways. However, their effects differed in the areas of production adjustment and employment adjustment. In terms of scale of production, the government aimed for maintenance of the status quo, and annual production targets therefore remained at the 55 million-ton level until the mid-1960s. Employment adjustment, by contrast, proceeded rapidly from the very outset of the adjustment process, and the number of regular workers was reduced by 58 % between 1959 and 1965. The characteristics of the industry's adjustment process were shaped by the strong growth that characterized the Japanese economy at the time.

A secure supply of cheap energy was indispensable for Japan's high economic growth. In this sense, the policy shift from 'coal first, oil second' to 'oil first, coal second' was economically rational. At the time, however, the Japanese economy faced tight constraints in its balance of international payments and national energy security was furthermore an area of grave concern. Those circumstances led the government to seek to maintain the status quo in coal production until the mid-1960s as long as it did not contradict the 'oil first' policy.

At the same time, rationalization policies were implemented forcefully in order to enhance domestic coal's international competitiveness by reducing the cost of

[29] For example, the results of the so-called wide-range job placement system for 1963 were assessed poorly: 'Less than 20 % of the job seekers were reemployed through the wide-range system and the level of labor mobilization beyond the region represents only the tip of the iceberg (Kyūshū Keizai Chōsakyōkai, 1966, p. 271).' It is also observed that 'not many miners [were] responding to the labor mobilization policy (Fukuoka Ken, 1966, p. 101).' The same tendency can be found in Hokkaidō. An investigation into the reemployment of displaced coal workers in the period between 1963 and 1976 revealed that the proportion of displaced coal workers who found new jobs in the regions of their local Public Employment Security Offices remained high. To move out of Hokkaidō, or to move to major cities in Hokkaidō out of local regions was not a major trend (Shirakashi 1982, pp. 783–784).

production. This rationalization process was, in reality, a process of rapid employment adjustment. Employment adjustment was thought to serve national economic growth by precipitating the shift of labor from low-productivity to high-productivity sectors. The government's countermeasure policies for those coal workers displaced in the process of the employment adjustment were not sufficient, however. They were not able to solve the unemployment problem of growing numbers of displaced middle-aged coal workers in local communities. Neither did the job-placement system, wide-ranging as it was, function as expected as a tool for 'labor mobilization.' In this sense, the coal policies had only limited effects with regard to employment adjustment. As a result, an excessive burden was placed on coal workers.

The unemployment of coal workers caused by the industry's adjustment was a negative outcome of Japan's high economic growth, and the problem concerned not only coal workers themselves but also the coal-producing regions as a whole. The decline, or collapse, of coal-producing regions had much wider consequences, which themselves demand careful examination. In order properly to assess the coal policies, we need comprehensive research that addresses not only the coal-mining industry but local communities as well.[30] Such research would shed new light on the historical implications of Japan's high economic growth.

References

Akiba, Satoshi. 1975, 1976. 'Enerugī Kiki' ka no Shinsekitanseisaku ni tsuite, (Jō), (Chū), (3), (4) [The New Coal Policies during 'the Energy Crisis,' (1), (2), (3) and (4)]. In *Keizai* [Economy], nos. 138. 140, 141, 142.

Daidō Tsūshinsha *Sekitan Nenkan* [The Coal Yearbook]. 1961, 1964, 1965, 1968. Tokyo: Daidō Tsūshinsha.

Fukuoka Ken [Fukuoka Prefecture]. 1962. *Fukuoka Ken Santanchiiki Shinkōtaisaku Kihonchōsa Hōkokusho (Chikuhōchiku Shiryōhen)* [Survey on measures for the revitalization of coal-mining regions in Fukuoka Prefecture (Materials concerning the Chikuhō Region)]. Fukuoka: Fukuoka Ken.

Fukuoka Ken [Fukuoka Prefecture]. 1964a. *Tankōrōdōryoku Jusoku Taisaku* [Measures for the improvement of coal-mining labor force]. Fukuoka: Fukuoka Ken.

Fukuoka Ken [Fukuoka Prefecture]. 1964b. *Tanko Risyokusha Taisaku* [Countermeasures for displaced coal miners]. Fukuoka: Fukuoka Ken.

Fukuoka: Fukuoka Ken. Fukuoka Ken [Fukuoka Prefecture]. 1966. *Santanchiiki Shinkō Chōsahōkokusho* [Survey on the revitalization of coal-mining regions in Fukuoka Prefecture]. Fukuoka: Fukuoka Ken.

Hirana, Motonari, Ōhashi, Kaoru, and Utsumi, Yōichi. 1998. *Kyūsantanchi no Toshi Mondai – Chikuhō Iizuka-shi no Baai* [Urban problems of former coal-ining regions – The case of Chikuo Iizuka City]. Tokyo: Taga Shuppan.

Hokkaidō Rōdōbu [Hokkaidō Labour Department]. 1968. *Tankō Rishokusha Taisaku no Gaikyō* [Overview of the countermeasures for displaced coal miners]. Sapporo: Hokkaidō.

[30] Although the revitalization policy for coal mining regions constituted an important part of coal policy, it did not necessarily produce good results (Hirana, Ōhashi and Utsumi, 1998, p. 55–61).

Koyōsokushin Jigyōdan [The Employment Promotion Project Corporation]. 1971. *Koyōsokushin Jigyōdan 10-nenshi* [*Ten-year history of the employment promotion project corporation*]. Tokyo: Koyōsokushin Jigyōdan.

Kyūshū Keizai Chōsakyōkai [Research Association on the Kyūshū Economy]. 1966. *Kyūshū Keizai no 20-nen* [Twenty-year history of the Kyūshū economy]. Fukuoka: Kyūshū Keizai Chōsakyōkai.

Masaoka, Kanzi. ed. 1998. *Tankōrōdōsha no Heizanrishoku to Kyaria no Saikeisei, Part 1* [Displaced coal miners and the rebuilding of careers, Part 1]. Tokyo: Waseda Daigaku Ningen Sogo Kenkyusenta [Waseda University, Advanced Research Center for Human Sciences] and Waseda Daigaku Bungakubu Shakaigaku Kenkyushitsu [Waseda University, Faculty of Letters, Arts and Sciences Research Office].

Naikakusōridaijin Kanbō Shingishitsu [Prime Minister's Secretariat Council Office]. 1960. *Sekitankōgyō no Koyō Shitsugyō Kankeishiryō Sononi* [Materials concerning employment and unemployment in the coal- mining industry, no. 2]. Tokyo: Naikakusōridaijin Kanbō Shingishitsu.

Nakamura, Takafusa. 1961. Sekitansangyō no Shihon Chikuseki [Capital Accumulation in the Coal Industry]. In *Gendai Nihon no Shihon Chikuseki* [Capital accumulation in Present-day Japan], ed. Shigeru Aihara, Tokyo: Tokyo University Press.

Namiki, Yoshinobu. 1973. The Japanese Economy: An introduction to its industrial adjustment problems." In *Structural adjustment in Asian-Pacific trade*, vol. 2, ed. Kiyoshi Kojima. Tokyo: The Japan Economic Research Center.

Nihon Tankō Rōdōkumiai [Japan Coal Miners' Union], ed. 1961. *Tanrō 10-nenshi* [Ten-year history of the Japan Coal Miners' Union]. Tokyo: Rōdōshunbosha.

Nihon Tankō Rōdōkumiai [Japan Coal Miners' Union], ed. 1991. *Tanrō 40-nenshi* [Forty-year history of the Japan Coal Miners' Union]. Tokyo: Nihon Tankō Rōdōkumiai.

NIRA. 2000. *Kokuminshotoku Baizōkeikaku Shiryō Dai 31- kan* [Materials concerning the income doubling plan, vol. 31]. Tokyo: Nihon Keizai Hyoronsha.

Ōkawa, Kazushi, et al. 1966. *Chōki Keizai Tōkei 8 Bukka* [Estimates of long-term economic statistics of Japan since 1868: 8 Prices]. Tokyo: Tōyōkeizai Shinpōsha.

Ono, Gorō. 1999. *Gendai Nihon no Sangyō Seisaku* [The industrial policy of contemporary Japan]. Tokyo: Nihon Keizai Shuppansha.

Rōdōshō Shokugyō Anteikyoku [Ministry of Labor, Employment Security Bureau]. 1971. *Tankō Rishokusha Taisaku 10-nenshi* [Ten-year history of the countermeasure policy for displaced coal miners]. Tokyo: Nikkan Rōdōtsūshinsha.

Santanchiiki Shinkō Jigyōdan [Corporation for the Revitalization of Coal-Mining Regions]. 1972. *Santanchiiki Shinkō Jigyōdan 10-nenshi* [Ten-year history of the corporation for the revitalization of coal-mining regions]. Tokyo: Santanchiiki Shinkō Jigyōdan.

Sekiguchi, Sueo. 1973. Comments and discussion of Namiki's paper. In *Structural adjustment in Asian-Pacific trade*, vol. 2, ed. Kiyoshi Kojima. Tokyo: The Japan Economic Research Center.

Sekiguchi, Sueo. 1975. "Industrial adjustment policies in Japan (I)," in OECD Development Center. In *Adjustment for trade: Studies on industrial adjustment problems and policies*. Paris: OECD.

Sekiguchi, Sueo and Toshihiro Horiuchi. 1988. Bōeki to Chōsei Enjo [Trade, adjustments and aid]. In *Nihon no Sangyō Seisaku* [Japan's Industrial Policies], ed. Ryutarō Komiya, et.al. Tokyo: Tokyo University Press.

Sekitan Kōgai Jigyōdan. 1971. *Sekitan Kōgai Fukkyūshi* [History of the recovery from mining pollution]. Fukuoka: Homansha.

Sekitankeizai Kenkyūjo [Research Center for Coal and Economy]. 1962. *Sekitansangyō no Shomondai* [Problems of the coal industry]. Tokyo: Sekitankeizai Kenkyūjo.

Sekitankogyo Gorika Jigyodan [The coal rationalization corporation]. ed. 1965. *Danshi(Seibihen)* [The history of the coal mining rationalization corporation(maintenance)]. Tokyo: Sekitankogyo Gorika Jigyodan.

Sekitankōgyō Gōrika Jigyōdan [The Coal Mining Rationalization Corporation], ed. 1976. *Danshi (Seibi/Kindaikahen)* [The history of the coal mining rationalization corporation (Maintenance/ *Modernization*)]. Tokyo: Sekitankōgyō Gōrika Jigyōdan.
Sekitankōgyō Gōrikaseisakushi Kenkyūkai [Research Association on the History of Coal-Mining Rationalization Policies]. 1990. *Sekitankōgyō Gōrikaseisakushi* [History of Coal-Mining Rationalization Policies]. Tokyo: Gōrikaseisakushi Kenkyūkai.
Senba, Tsunenori. 1977, 1978. Sengo Sekitanseisaku no Hensen to sono Kiketsu, (1), (2), (3) [Postwar coal policies: Changes and results, (1), (2) and (3)]. In *Refarensu* [Reference], vol. 27 nos.11 and 12 and vol. 28 no.1.
Shirakashi, Hisashi. 1982. Tankō Rishokusha no Seisan・ Rōdō [Production and labor of unemployed coal miners]. In *Chiiki Sangyōhendō to Kaikyū・ Kaisō* [Changes in local industry and class], ed. Tetsuji Fuse. Tokyo: Ochanomizu Shohō.
Sonoda, Minoru. 1970. *Sengo Sekitanshi* [The history of coal in Postwar Japan]. Fukuoka: Sekitantsūshin.
Takagawa, Masamichi. 2002. Kaijima Tankō no Rishokusha Taisaku [Countermeasures for the unemployment problem of the Kaijima Coal Mine]. In *Idōshakai to Seikatsu Nettowāku* [The Mobile Society and Life Networks], ed. Takahashi Shinichi. Osaka: Takasuga Shuppan.
Takeda, Ryozō. 1963. Tankō to Chiikishakai [Coal mines and local communities]. In *Shakaikagaku Tōkyū* [Social Science Research], vol. 8 nos. 2 and 3.
Tokita,Yoshihisa. 1958. Tankō Shitsugyō no Shomondai [Unemployment problems of the coal mining industry]. In *Shakai Seisaku Gakkai Nenpō* [The Bulletin of the Japan Association for Social Policy Studies], vol. 6. Tokyo: Yūhikaku.
Tokumoto, Masahiko, and Seiichi Yoda. 1963. *Sekitan Fukyō to Chiiki Shakai no Henyō* [Depression in the coal- mining industry and the transformation of local communities]. Tokyo: Hōritsubunkasha.
Tsuchiya, Kiyoshi. Tenkanten ni Tatsu Sekitanseisaku [Coal policy at a turning point]. In *Shōwa 41-nen Sekiyugyōkai no Suii* [The Oil Industry of 1966]. Tokyo: Sekiyurenmei.
Tsūshō Sangyōshō [Ministry of International Trade and Industry]. 1964. *Sekitan Kōkusu Tōkeinenpō* [The annual report on coal and coke].Tokyo: Nihon Sekitangyōkai.
Tsūshō Sangyōshō [Ministry of International Trade and Industry], ed. 1991. *Tsūshō Sangyō Seisakushi Dai 7-kan* [The history of industrial policies, vol. 7]. Tokyo: Tsūshō Sangyōshō.
Tsūshō Sangyōshō Sekitankyoku [Ministry of International Trade and Industry, the Coal Bureau], ed. 1953. *Kōtanka Mondai to Gōrika no Hōkō* [The high coal-price problem and rationalization]. Tokyo: Tsūshō Sangyōshō Sekitankyoku.
Tsūshō Sangyōshō Sekitankyoku [Ministry of International Trade and Industry, the Coal Bureau], ed. 1968. *Sekitanseisaku no Gaikan* [Overview of coal policies]. Tokyo: Zaimushuppan.
Yada, Toshifumi. 1975. *Sengo Nihon no Sekitansangyō* [The coal industry in Postwar Japan]. Tokyo: Shinhyōron.
Yada, Toshifumi. 1977. *Sekitangyōkai* [The coal industry]. Tokyo: Kyōikusha.
Yamamoto, Junko. 1959. Tankō Chitai ni okeru Shitsugyō Mondai [The unemployment problem in coal- mining regions]. In *Shakai Seisaku Gakkai Nenpō*, vol. 7. Tokyo: Yūhikaku.

Chapter 4
The Relationship Between Labor Management Reform and Inter-Company Relations at the Industry Level: A Case Study of the Japanese Steel Industry

Hiroshi Sugiyama

Abstract This work analyzes the relationship between labor management reform and inter-company relations within the Japanese steel industry of the 1950s and 1960s, through a case study of the 1962 introduction of the job-based wage system at Yawata Steel, Fuji Steel and Nippon Steel Tube. Previous research has examined institutional changes of this kind mainly in terms of the internal characteristics of individual companies with little regard for macroeconomic conditions. This study demonstrates that any important institutional change within a given company necessarily requires cooperation and coordination with similar companies in the same industry: companies that were similar in size, covered similar areas of the market and had similar labor problems. It also emphasizes that one company within an industry had to exercise leadership for institutional reform to be implemented successfully. On the basis of these findings, this study presents a framework to schematize patterns of labor management reform, with intercompany relationships taken into consideration.

Keywords Industrial relations • Management rationalization • Job-based wage system • Japanese steel industry

1 Introduction

This study aims to analyze the relationship between labor management reform and intercompany relationships within the Japanese steel industry during the 1950s and 1960s, through a case study of Yawata Steel Co., Ltd. (Yawata Seitetsu), Fuji Steel

H. Sugiyama (✉)
Osaka University of Economics and Law, Osaka, Japan
e-mail: h-sugiyama@keiho-u.ac.jp

H. Takeda (ed.), *Micro-Performance During Postwar Japan's High-Growth Era*, Monograph Series of the Socio-Economic History Society, Japan,
DOI 10.1007/978-981-10-0709-5_4

Co., Ltd. (Fuji Seitetsu) and Nippon Steel Tube Co., Ltd. (Nippon Kōkan). These three companies introduced job-based wage systems in 1962.

During the 1950s and 1960s, every large Japanese company, irrespective of industry, attempted to implement labor management reforms. The job-based wage system examined in this study was designed to replace the conventional seniority-based wage system. At the time, its introduction brought about a heated debate, the so-called 'job-based wage controversy,' that involved many scholars and business practitioners.[1]

Ample research has been conducted on the process of labor reform and the introduction of the job-based wage system, providing important historical insights. However, most of these studies have examined only individual companies, emphasizing factors internal to each company and explaining the causes and effects of institutional changes.[2] In order to overcome the limitations of the traditional approach, this study stresses intercompany relationships within a given industry.[3] This point will be discussed further in relation to the wage reform.

First, it is important to recognize that although changes in wage systems depend on the particular managerial conditions of individual companies, it is in fact difficult in practice for a company to carry out reforms based solely on its own internal needs. Grievances and discontent are highly likely to spread if the newly revised wage systems differ too greatly from conventional seniority-based systems. Companies therefore either wait for other companies to implement similar reforms and then ride the tide, or they seek to build cooperation with other companies in order to reinforce their own reforms.

Whether a company adopts the 'opportunistic strategy' or seeks 'cooperation' with other companies, a crucial element is which company takes the lead in the industry's reform process. In the former case, a company within the industry will take the lead and bear the greatest burden of the reforms. In the latter case, too, a leader company has to emerge to take the initiative. Otherwise, the process inevitably slows to a standstill, with all the companies merely watching one another for signs of movement. In order to understand labor reform, we must show how leader companies emerge and the nature of the cooperative relationship among companies.

---

[1] In this study, 'the seniority-based wage system' means a payment system in which wages are raised regularly according to length of service, although performance evaluations are applied to various extents. On the other hand, 'the job-based wage system' means a payment system in which wages are set through a job assessment method.

[2] Regarding changes in wage systems during the high economic growth period, see Hyōdō (1997). For case studies on labor management, see Saguchi and Hashimoto (2003). Regarding general problems about personnel management including wage systems, see Nitta and Hisamoto (2008). Regarding changes in the wage systems at Yawata Steel (Nippon Steel Corporation) through the early 1970s, see Sugiyama (2005). Regarding the influence of Yawata Steel's 1962 introduction of the job-based wage system on the personnel management, see Sugiyama (2008b). On the relation between workers' notion of wage and trade unions' demand for wages, see Sugiyama (2008a).

[3] Among studies on the relation between wages and intercompany relationships are Koike (1962), Takanashi (1967) and Sano et al. (1969). However, these studies mostly concentrate on the analysis of general wage levels and wage increases due to the annual spring wage bargaining.

However, the new labor management system is not likely to take strong root even where a leader company of this kind does exist, unless the other companies have long-term expectations for the new system. If they don't, they will adopt a passive position easily give up on the new system as soon as the leader changes its own policy. Hence, we must examine how a leader company generates reform in order to analyze the interaction between institutional reform and intercompany relationships.[4]

This analysis is accordingly conducted at two different levels, industry and company. Yawata Steel is the focus of the company-level investigation because it had considerable influence industry-wide, as reflected in its crucial role in introducing the job-based wage system into the steel industry. The first section outlines the steel industry's preliminary efforts to introduce the job-based wage system, which paved the way for the 1962 wage reform. Next, it analyzes the characteristics of the job-based wage system that was introduced in the three major steel companies (Yawata Steel, Fuji Steel and Nippon Steel Tube). This is followed by an examination of Yawata Steel's managerial efforts at institutional reform, and finally, the Conclusion presents a framework, applicable to various industries and companies of that era, for conducting further research on the relationship between labor management reform and intercompany relationships within the steel industry.

2 The Process of Introducing a Job-Based Wage System in Major Steel Companies

2.1 Preliminary Stages

Major steel companies utilized wage systems that were similar in terms of gross wages and composition ratios (Sōhyō Chōsabu 1962, p. 11). Yawata Steel in the early 1960s, for example, had the following three wage categories. (1) Basic wages (kihonkyū): Initial salaries were determined according to academic background and age, and a "scheduled yearly raise" (teishō) was added annually. These basic wages constituted 45 % of fixed wages (kijun-nai chingin). (2) Performance allowances (gyōseki teate): These were efficiency wages designated for particular groups of workers. In practice, however, this allowance was allotted to individual workers based mainly on seniority. Performance allowances constituted 45 % of fixed wages. (3) Various types of work allowances, including danger pay (gyōmu teate). These allowances constituted 10 % of fixed wages (Komatsu 1963).

Sumitomo Metal Industries Co., Ltd. (Sumitomo Kinzoku Kōgyō) was the first of the major steel companies to attempt the introduction of a job-based wage

[4] This viewpoint is also instructive when dealing with the labor management reform of the present time. How it is affected by intercompany relations and how it is different from the reforms of the 1950s and 1960s are important questions to be asked.

system.[5] In September 1947, the company set up a committee to study labor management and to review the existing job classifications. Implementation of its proposals was called off, however, because of high estimated costs and the large discrepancy between the existing system and the reform plan.

Nippon Steel Tube and Fuji Steel took other approaches. Nippon Steel Tube began conducting job analyses and making preliminary job evaluations in 1948, which eventually led to a comprehensive job evaluations in 1952. Fuji Steel made its first job evaluations in 1954. The aim in both cases was to calculate the precise number of employees the companies required. It was also these two companies that first used the results of job evaluations as a basis for setting wages. In 1956, Nippon Steel Tube tried introducing a job-rating system based on 'job-point scores' (shokunōten), calculated through job assessments, as a means of determining 'performance allowances' (nōritsukyū). The system took effect in July 1958, after 2 years of negotiation with the unions. In December 1956, Fuji Steel also completed the job-grading it had been working on in preparation for wage reforms, whereby 'job-point scores' (shokumuten) were used to determine 'performance allowances' (nōritsukyū). This 'job-point score' system was implemented in July 1957. It should be noted, however, that at both companies the job evaluation results affected only 20 % of the performance allowance. Part of the reason that job evaluations were incorporated into the wage determination system was the companies' need to ease the growing discontent of union members with traditional wage-setting practices (Shin Nihon Seitetsu (Fuji) Rōdō Kumiai Rengōkai 1974, pp. 355–362; Orii 1973, pp. 52–56). In this sense, the wage-system revisions made in this period had a slightly different historical significance than those carried out later.

Sumitomo Metal Industries introduced its 'job-ranking system' (shokubun seido) in 1960, which incorporated the idea of 'job-based wage.' Employees were classified into four ranks, and each rank was further divided into several grades. Wage rates were set for the various grades (ordinary blue-collar workers were at grade number nine.) Each grade corresponded to a certain range of 'job-point scores' (shokubunten) given to employees. Their 'job-point scores' were added each year through work assessments conducted by management, and when the accumulated 'job-point scores' reached a stipulated level, the worker concerned was promoted to a higher grade (Sōhyō Chōsabu 1962, pp. 13–14).

As has been shown, the shift away from the traditional seniority-based wage system began in the latter 1950s. The new wage systems, however, "were applied only to a tiny part of the wages . . . and such attempts were made only sporadically by individual companies" (Sōhyō Chōsabu 1962, p. 16). In fact, Yawata Steel, the most influential company within the industry at the time, did not make any significant moves to change the traditional wage system. It can be assumed that steel companies had decided not to take any radical action in order to avoid unnecessary industrial turmoil. As stated by a top official of the Japan Federation

[5] As to the process leading up to the 1962 wage reform, see Nihon Keieisha Dantai Renmei (1962), pp. 55–63.

of Steel Workers' Unions (hereafter, JFSWU) in preparation for the upcoming 1962 spring labor offensive:

> [Yawata Steel] has taken enough time preparing for the introduction of a job-based wage system that we must assume it is aiming for fundamental reform. It is sure to act decisively and to take the initiative within the industry. Once Yawata Steel decides to press forward with a radical reform plan, Fuji Steel and Nippon Steel Tube will follow suit and seek to establish a job-based wage system across the board, though they have made only piecemeal attempts so far (Sōhyō Chōsabu 1962, p. 17).

There are several reasons that only these three among a number of large steel companies introduced the job-based wage system in unison. First, they shared many characteristics, including similar product lines and work forces, because all three developed from integrated steelworks of the prewar period. By contrast, other steel companies such as Sumitomo Metal Industries, Kōbe Steel Co., Ltd. (Kōbe Seikōsho) and Kawasaki Steel Co., Ltd. (Kawasaki Seitetsu) constructed their blast furnaces only after World War II. Yawata, Fuji, and Nippon Steel Tube also faced comparable industrial relations problems, including wage issues (Iida et al. 1969, pp. 536–539). Coping with labor unions, therefore, called for cooperation among these three companies (Chiba 1998, pp. 407–416).

Yawata Steel in particular introduced job-based wages for the following reasons. (1) They needed an appropriate way to handle frustrated younger workers who, with the modernization of facilities, were becoming the core of the workforce but whose wages were kept low. (2) The modernization of the steel facility rendered traditional performance-standard allowances obsolete. (3) The company needed to develop new labor management practices to accord with its new management methods, including the line and staff system and the new foreman system. (4) The unions' demand for an across-the-board wage increase was intensifying. Yawata Steel had introduced the new foreman system (sagyōchō seido) into its steelworks at Tobata in 1958. Therefore, when the job-based wage system was introduced 4 years later, the chain of command was no longer uniform but could be based either on the new foreman (sagyōchō)/new group leader (kōchō) or on the traditional foreman (kumichō)/traditional group leader (gochō) depending on the workplace (Komatsu 1963).

2.2 *The 1962 Spring Labor Offensive and the Introduction of the Job-Based Wage System*

The Situation at the Industry Level

JFSWU demanded an across-the-board wage increase of 5000 yen in 1962; in response, the five major steel companies – Yawata Steel, Fuji Steel, Nippon Steel Tube, Sumitomo Metal Industries and Kōbe Steel – proposed an 1800 yen raise on 7 April. At the same time, Yawata Steel, Fuji Steel and Nippon Steel Tube proposed the introduction of job-based wage systems. The plan was to pay each employee an

Table 4.1 The wage systems of Yawata Steel and Fuji Steel: before and after the wage reform

	Before the reform		After the reform		
	Wage item	Amount (yen)	Amount (yen)	Wage item	Amounts of wages tansferred between wage items
The Yawata Steel	Basic wage (kihonkū)	14,253	15,230	Basic wage (kihonkū)	Increase: 488 yen
					From performance allowance: 488 yen
	Performance allowance (gyōseki teate)	15,351	11,684	Performance allowance (gyōseki teate)	To basic wage: 488 yen
					To job-based wages: 3179 yen
	Work allowance (gyōmu teate)	117	4567	Job-based wage (shokumukyū)	Increase: 1271 yen
					From performance allowance: 3179 yen
					Work allowance: 117 yen
The Fuji Steel	Basic wage (kihonkū)	15000	16000	Basic wage (kihonkū)	Increase: 500 yen
					From performance allowance: 500 yen
	Performance allowance (gyōseki teate)	14700	11200	Performance allowance (gyōseki teate)	To basic wage: 500 yen
					To Job-based Wages: 3000 yen
	Work allowance (gyōmu teate)	200	4500	Job-based wage (shokumukyū)	Increase: 1300 yen
					From performance allowance: 3000 yen
					Work allowance: 200 yen

Note: The figures indicate wages per employee. Figures for Fuji Steel are rounded
Source: Sōhyō Chōsabu (1962), p. 19

average of 4500 yen as a 'job-based wage' (shokumukyū), transferring 1300 yen out of the proposed raise of 1800 yen to this wage category.[6] Table 4.1 shows the composition of wages at both Yawata Steel and Fuji Steel before and after the introduction of job-based wages.[7]

[6] On the 1962 spring labor offensive, see Nihon Tekkō Sangyō Rōdōkumiai Rengōkai (1971), pp. 519–533. Incidentally, the job-based wage was called not 'shokumukyū' but 'gyōmukyū' at Nippon Steel Tube.

[7] The discrepancies between the initial proposal by the companies and the amount of job-based wages shown in Table 4.1 were due to the negotiations between the companies and workers who sought compensation for the disadvantages the employers' proposal would bring about. See Yawata Seitetśusho Rōdōbu, *Sokuhō* [Prompt Report], no.46 (1962a). *Sokuhō* was a document Yawata Steel's Labor Department made and delivered to its employees for the purpose of notifying them of the results of the ongoing negotiations.

Conversion of financial resources similar to Table 4.1 can also be found in the case of Nippon Steel Tube. See Konda (1963).

At its twenty-second special conference, held shortly before the 1962 spring labor offensive in anticipation of the reforms, JFSWU decided that it would fight against the new wage system. It would demand a repeal or, if that proved difficult, demand revision of the employers' plan. However, the union anticipated difficulty in preventing the reform's implementation, and found itself in a defensive position in the ongoing industrial power struggle. A JFSWU official recounts the situation as follows:

> "Given the actual balance of power, there was no realistic hope for us to change the proposed wage plan to our advantage. The best we could do was to demand an across-the-board wage increase, trying to minimize disparities among workers. Even this aim was going to be hard to achieve unless we concentrated fully on it. It was a hard, painstaking task. It was not easy to organize a strike. That was the reality in which JFSWU found itself" (Sōhyō Chōsabu 1962, p. 75).

The spring labor offensive did not in fact proceed as JFSWU had hoped. In order to prevent, or alter to its advantage, the intended wage reform, JFSWU had to establish a strong united front among its member unions for taking strike action, if necessary. At the time, JFSWU's call for strike action depended on whether the labor unions of the five major steel companies – namely, Yawata Steel, Fuji Steel, Nippon Steel Tube, Sumitomo Metal Industries and Kōbe Steel – were ready to walk out in unison.[8] But a strike that was planned to take place just prior to the companies' response was postponed due to a difference of opinion among the unions. In addition, union members at Nippon Steel Tube, Sumitomo Metal Industries and Kōbe Steel voted against the strike plan proposed by JFSWU. In an attempt to oppose the proprosed wage reforms, JFSWU established a 'Joint Struggle Committee Against Job-Based Wages.' However, it proved difficult to organize a joint struggle because the details of the three companies' reform plans differed. The settlement was therefore left to negotiations at the company level, and eventually, agreements were reached at all three companies: on 1 June, 1962 (in effect from 31 May, 1963) at Nippon Steel Tube; on 30 June, 1962 (in effect from 1 July, 1962) at Yawata Steel; and on 5 July, 1962 (in effect from 1 April, 1962, applied retroactively) at Fuji Steel.

Negotiating the Introduction of the Job-based Wage System at Yawata Steel

This section presents the process of negotiating the introduction of the job-based wage system at Yawata Steel. Presented with the wage reform plan, the Yawata Steel Union (Yawata Seitetsu Rōdōkumiai) decided, in line with JFSWU's policy,

[8] As to JFSWU's attempt to build a united front of its member unions, see Takanashi (1967), pp. 155–166. The trade unions of the five major steel companies were defeated badly in their industrial struggles over wages in both 1957 and 1959. After these defeats, they became rather reluctant to take strike action, realizing that such action would be fruitless unless the unions of the five companies could build a solid united front.

that it would enter into negotiations with the management to amend the reform plan.[9] As a strategic matter, the union decided not to question the basic framework of the proposed wage system because "the proposed system was very clear and concise, compared with the wage systems at Fuji Steel and Nippon Steel Tube, so it seemed difficult to change the framework itself."[10] The negotiations therefore focused on the validity of management's proposed job evaluation method and on the practical means of operating the system. In any case, the union gained little from the negotiations, which bred discontent among union members. Still, union officials stuck to their original policy, arguing that, "there was no use fighting for the amendment of the classificatory framework without sufficient preparation, which would only lead to internal conflict among union members over the allocation of wages."[11] Eventually, an agreement was reached in line with the policy of union officials.

It should be noted that management was fully prepared for the negotiations. In four meetings – from the 18th meeting on 11 April to the 21st meeting on 18 April – managers explained how the new wage system would work. At the same time, they delivered documents explaining to workers the basic plan and the need for the new system, in an effort to reduce misunderstanding and resistance. Therefore, it was only at the 31st meeting held on 19 May that management first disclosed all the job categories and grades.[12] Managers took this approach deliberately in order to avoid a situation in which indignant rank-and-file workers might move beyond the control of union officials. Management was also waiting for the right moment to launch fruitful negotiations on concrete issues: in other words, it was waiting for the enthusiasm over JFSWU's joint anti-reform campaign to recede.[13] Moreover, the initial reform proposal had had enough margin that management was able to make concessions. Managers were ready from the outset, for example, to make 3 month compensation payments to those whose wages would be reduced because of the new system. They did not specify this in the initial proposal, however. On hearing the union's demand for 10 month compensation payments, managers made a concession in the form of 6 month compensation payments in the final agreement (Yawata Seitetsusho Rōdōbu 1962b, p. 298).

---

[9] For details of negotiations over the introduction of job-based wages into Yawata Steel, see Shin Nihon Seitetsu Yawata Rōdōkumiai (1975), pp. 332–364.

[10] Yawata Seitetsu Rōdōkumiai (1962a).

[11] Yawata Seitetsu Rōdōkumiai (1962b).

[12] On the process and schedule of the negotiations over the introduction of job-based wages, see *Sokuhō*, nos. 26, 27, 29, 36 and 60 (1962). The agreement was reached in the forty-sixth negotiation meeting held on 30 Jun.

[13] Yawata Seitetsusho Rōdōbu (1962e), p. 4. *Shin Kyūyoseido*, edited in three volumes by Yawata Steel's Labor Department in August 1962, describes in details the process leading up to the introduction of the job-based wage system. Vol. 1 is titled "The Outline of the Introduction of the Job-based Wages," Vol. 2, "The Outline of Job Assessment, nos.1 and 2" and Vol. 3, "Reference Materials."

It also should be noted that the content of the reform plan was meticulously structured such that the union would not be able to refute it. Therefore, the union was forced to accept the basic framework of the wage reform, and furthermore, in discussions on the validity of the job assessment process, all the union's claims were refuted by management either as a matter of theory or on the basis of research on actual jobs.[14] Yawata Steel Union had no prior experience with the job-based wage system, so it was in a defensive position from the start (Sōhyō Chōsabu 1962, pp. 67–68), but in any event, it was management's thorough preparation that decided the outcome of the negotiations.

2.3 *Summary*

On the occasion of the 1962 spring labor offensive, the three major steel companies addressed wage reform in unison, creating momentum for the full-scale introduction of the job-based wage system into the steel industry. As JFSWU pointed out, Yawata Steel played a crucial role in this move. These points will be examined further in the following section.

3 The Job-based Wage System and Its Introduction in the Major Steel Companies

3.1 *The Job-Based Wage System at Yawata Steel*

This section will begin with an introduction of Yawata Steel's wage system and then go on to the details. The company created a new wage category, the 'job-based wage' (shokumukyū), to be applied to blue-collar workers. When it was first introduced, it averaged 4567 yen per employee, or about 15% of total fixed wages.[15]

There were about 9000 types of jobs (kata) at Yawata Steel, the wage rate of each of which was determined by a 'point rating method' based on job analysis. Three hundred and ten jobs (kata) from 58 workplaces were singled out as 'standard jobs' (kijun shokumu). These standard jobs were evaluated according to the eight factors indicated in Table 4.2, and their 'job-point scores' (shokumuten) were calculated by adding up the scores of each factor. As shown in Table 4.3, a certain range of 'job-point scores' corresponded to a 'job-grade' (shokkyū). As shown in Table 4.4, a wage rate was prescribed for each job-grade. The job-point scores of

[14] On the discussion over the results of the job assessment, see see *Sokuhō*, nos.38–42 and 48 (1962).

[15] As to the job-based wage system of Yawata Steel, see Komatsu (1963).

Table 4.2 Job-points by job evaluation factor

Rank	Basic knowledge	Experience	Responsibility	Judgment	Mental stress	Physical effort	Environment	Danger
A	10 points	10 points	10 points	10 points	10 points	10 points	10 points	10 points
B	18 points	18 points	18 points	15 points	15 points	15 points	13 points	13 points
C	32 points	32 points	32 points	22 points	22 points	22 points	16 points	16 points
D	56 points	56 points	56 points	33 points	33 points	33 points	20 points	20 points
E	100 points	100 points	100 points	50 points	50 points	50 points	25 points	25 points
Weight	20	20	20	10	10	10	5	5
Geometric ratio	1.78	1.78	1.78	1.5	1.5	1.5	1.26	1.26

Note: Figures for geometric ratios are rounded. For example, the job-points for 'Rank D' of the factor 'Basic Knoledge' is 56. 56 multiplied by 1.78 is 100, the job-points for 'Rank E' of the same evaluation factor

Source: Komatsu (1963)

Table 4.3 Job-grades at the Yawata Steelworks

Job-grade	Job-point score	Job-grade	Job-point score	Job-grade	Job-point score	Job-grade	Job-point score
1	80–87	6	129–141	11	208–228	16	336–368
2	88–96	7	142–156	12	229–251	17	369–406
3	97–106	8	157–171	13	252–276	18	Foremen
4	107–117	9	172–188	14	277–304	19	Foremen
5	118–128	10	189–207	15	305–335	20	Foremen

Note: Foremen's job-grades were determined according to the job-grades of group leders under their supervision. The geometric ratio between successive ranks is around 1.1
Source: Komatsu (1963)

jobs outside this category were determined through comparison with the standard jobs. In creating the job evaluation system shown in Table 4.2, management took into consideration both its own needs and union criticisms of the job-based wage system. Managers thoroughly studied the experience of Fuji Steel, which had conducted a wage reform in 1957.[16] This point will be discussed later.

To take the example of a blast-furnace keeper (group leader) engaged in slag discharge (shussen shukkai kata gochō), his wage rate was determined in the following way. He was graded 'D' in 'Basic Knowledge' and, according to Table 4.2, this corresponded to a score of 56 points. 'Experience' and 'Responsibility' were both classified as 'E, 100 points'; 'Judgment,' 'D, 33 points'; 'Mental Stress,' 'B, 15 points'; 'Physical Effort,' 'B, 22 points'; 'Environment,' 'C, 16 points'; 'Danger,' 'B, 13 points.' This worker's 'job-point score' totaled 355 points, which, according to Table 4.3, corresponds to 'Grade 16.' Table 4.4 shows that his 'job-based wage' therefore came to 7810 yen. Incidentally, three 'sub-grades' ('Elementary,' 'Standard' and 'Advanced') were set within the same 'job-grade,' and 7810 yen was the rate for 'Standard.' Promotion within the same 'job-grade' was based on the length of service and job performance. The 'Standard' wage rate of Grade 17, the top grade for 'group leaders' (gochō, kōchō), is about three times as high as that of Grade 1. Thus, the wage gap ratio, previously about four times, was narrowed significantly by the reform.

Had this wage system simply been mechanically applied, the new industrial order would have differed too radically from the traditional order already established within and among workplaces. An upper limit was therefore set for the 'job-grades' for which employees who had worked for the company for 7 years

[16] 'Performance allowances' (nōritsukyū) that Fuji Steel introduced in 1957 caused many problems. Job assessment was based on as many as nine evaluation factors: 'Knowledge,' 'Experience,' 'Adaptability,' 'Mental Stress,' 'Physical Burden,' 'Danger,' 'Environment,' 'Duty' and 'Supervisory Responsibilities.' In addition, there were 14 evaluation grades for each evaluation factor. Moreover, the difference in the point scores between the highest evaluation grade and the lowest was too wide. In the case of the evaluation factor 'Knowledge,' for instance, the point score for the highest grade was 378.6 and that for the lowest was 10.0. It was difficult for the employers to accept this system. See Tozawa (1962a).

Table 4.4 Job-based wages (shokumukyū) at the Yawata Steel (Unit: Yen)

Job-grade	Elementary	Standard	Advanced	Gap	Job-grade	Elementary	Standard	Advanced	Gap
1	2650	2750	2950	–	11	5830	5950	6170	340
2	2950	3050	3250	300	12	6170	6290	6530	340
3	3250	3350	3550	300	13	6530	6670	6910	380
4	3550	3650	3850	300	14	6910	7050	7290	380
5	3850	3950	4150	300	15	7290	7430	7670	380
6	4150	4250	4470	300	16	7670	7810	8050	380
7	4470	4590	4810	340	17	8050	8190	8430	380
8	4810	4930	5150	340	18	8430	8570	8810	380
9	5150	5270	5490	340	19	8810	8950	9190	380
10	5490	5610	5830	340	20	9190	9330	9570	380

Note: 'Gap' means the difference between successive job-grades
Source: Komatsu (1963)

or less were eligible. This 'upper limit regulation'[17] was necessary because of the enormous differences in lengths of service between Yawata and Hikari steelworks workers. In addition, 'performance allowances' (gyōseki teate) were maintained for certain types of jobs even after the wage reform, in order to compensate for the disadvantages incurred by the mechanical application of a job assessment system comprised of only eight evaluation factors.[18]

3.2 Comparing the Job-Based Wage Systems Adopted by Major Steel Companies

Only Yawata Steel and Fuji Steel presented concrete plans for job-based wages at the 1962 spring labor offensive. The investigation that follows therefore focuses chiefly on these two companies.

The similarities between the wage systems of the three companies are as follows. First, they had a common framework, on which their wage and labor-management systems were based[19]: the 'job-based wage' (shokumukyū) as an independent wage category, along with the 'basic wage' (kihonkū) and 'performance allowance' (gyōseki teate) categories.

Table 4.1 shows the similarities between the job-based wage averages, the amounts of money transferred between wage categories for adjustment, and the amount and compositional ratio of each wage portion. It is important to note that the wage gap ratio (the highest wage rate/the lowest wage rate) was around 3.5 times at both Yawata Steel and Fuji Steel. Further, though Yawata Steel originally planned to transfer a much larger amount of money from the 'performance allowance' to the 'basic wage' category for adjustment, it reduced that amount to 500 yen as a result of consultations with Fuji Steel and Nippon Steel Tube (Yawata Seitetsusho Rōdōbu 1962b, Preface and p. 375).

The companies also had similar processes for determining wages. At both Yawata and Fuji, all blue-collar workers were subject to job evaluation based on

[17] On account of this regulation, those employees who had worked for the company for 7 years or less were classified into no higher than the ninth job-grade, whatever high-grade jobs they were actually assigned to. The upper limitation was the sixth job-grade for those whose work experience with the company was 4 years or less, and the third job-grade for those whose experience was 2 years or less. For those employees who had worked for the company for less than a year, probationer's rates were applied.

[18] At Yawata Steelworks the average length of service was 12 years and the average job-grade was the seventh, whereas at the Hikari Steelworks 2 years and the eighth, respectively. See Yawata Seitetsusho Rōdōbu (1962b), p. 232 and (1962e), p. 178. As to the treatment of 'performance allowances,' see (1962b), pp. 457–462.

[19] The discussion about the job-based wages of the three companies is based on the following sources. Komatsu (1963). Shin Nihon Seitetsu (Fuji) Rōdō Kumiai Rengōkai (1974), pp. 545–555. Tozawa (1962a, b). Sōhyō Chōsabu (1962).

the 'point rating method.' As a result, each job was classified into one of twenty 'job-grades' at Yawata Steel, or nineteen at Fuji.[20] The evaluation points set for each grade rose in geometric progression with each higher grade.[21]

The wage systems of the three companies also differed from each other. Job evaluation methods comprised eight factors at Yawata, but only five at Fuji Steel (namely, 'Knowledge,' 'Experience,' 'Mental Stress,' 'Physical Effort' and 'Environment'), which did not include 'Responsibility.' Its 'Knowledge' and 'Experience' factors conformed to seven grades, however, though a five-grade evaluation was applied to all the other factors. As mentioned above, the number of points set for a given evaluation factor increased geometrically with each higher grade. Although this feature was common to both companies, the geometric ratios were different. For example, in the case of 'Basic Knowledge' ('Knowledge,' for Fuji Steel) Yawata's geometric ratio was 1.78 times (Table 4.2), and Fuji Steel's 1.4. Fuji Steel's system reflected company union requests,[22] as will be explained later.

Another difference was the distribution of workers among job-grades. In comparison with Yawata Steel, Fuji classified a relatively small number of workers into lower job-grades. This difference reflected the difference in the companies' policies on job assessment. At Fuji Steel, "most workers were classified in Grades 7 to 10, even if they were not high-skilled workers," whereas "Yawata Steel's grading was severe and restrictive of wages" (Sōhyō Chōsabu 1962, p. 62). Fuji Steel's leniency was a response to the discontent of union members who had been classified into low-grade jobs in the 1957 wage reform.

The relationship between job evaluation and wage rates also differed. Under Fuji Steel's wage system, job evaluation results were more closely reflected in wage rates. At both companies, the 'job-grades' into which workers were classified were determined by 'job-points' calculated in the job evaluation. At Fuji Steel, 'job-grade points' were also set for each 'job-grade,' and wage rates were calculated according to the following formula:

[20] Fuji Steel also initially planned to set twenty job-grades. As a result of the actual job assessment, however, it decided to eliminate the lowest job-grade on the ground that there was no job that fell into that category (Tozawa 1962b). Incidentally, when Nippon Steel Tube introduced the job-based wage system in 1963, ten job-grades were set.

[21] The evaluation points of the same evaluation factor were set in geometric progression on the basis of the psychophysiological idea called the Weber–Fechner law. According to the law, when a man feels that his physical burden has doubled, the actual burden has been increased by four times. If so, the gap ratio of evaluation points should be four times. See Motobayashi (1957), p. 58.

[22] JFSWU's criticism of the job-based wage system can be summarized as follows. (1) Jobs were evaluated mostly in terms of the 'contribution to the company' rather than factors like 'physical burden' which mattered more to workers. (2) The evaluation method was also more favorable to management. (3) High grades were only given to a small number of supervisory jobs, whereas most of the workers were classified into low grade jobs. As a result, competition and division among workers were precipitated, while labor management was intensified. See Nihon Tekkō Sangyō Rōdōkumiai Rengōkai (1971), pp. 531–532. Fuji Steel Union requested to put away the 'Responsibility' factor in line with JFSWU's criticism, especially with regard to points (1) and (2).

$$[\text{Wage Rate}] = [\text{Job} - \text{Grade Points}] \times [\text{Unit Rate(yen) per job} - \text{grade point determined by the steelworks}] \times [\text{Adjustment Coefficient}] + 300\,\text{yen}.$$

Adjustment coefficients varied according to a worker's length of service. For workers who had worked for the company less than a year, the adjustment coefficient was 0.85; 1–3 years, 0.95; 3–10 years, 1.0; over 10 years, 1.05. This measure was adopted out of consideration for seniority. In Yawata Steel's system, by contrast, 'job-points' were not so strongly reflected in the 'job-grade'-based wage rates. The ranges of job-points corresponding to the same job-grade were relatively broad, and the wage gaps between two successive job-grades relatively small, whereas, at Fuji Steel, the wage gaps between two successive job-grades widened progressively as the job-grade itself rose.[23] Fuji Steel probably adopted this wage structure in order because to maintain some structural consistency with its 1957 wage system. As mentioned earlier, Yawata Steel's system divided any given job grade into Elementary, Standard, and Advanced 'sub-grades,' a rough counterpart to Fuji Steel's 'adjustment coefficients,' though promotion within the same job-grade was at management's discretion.

The following observations can be made. First, Yawata Steel's system was more 'severe,' or, in other words, more convenient to management needs than Fuji Steel's.[24] Since Yawata was the industry's leading company, its restrictiveness must have affected the process by which the job-based wage system was introduced into the steel industry as a whole.

Next, the wage systems of the three companies shared many characteristics. In particular, the degree of similarity in average job-based wages, the amounts of money transferred between wage categories for adjustment, and the ratios of highest to lowest job-based wages would be inexplicable without assuming there was close consultation among the three companies. At the same time, however, the companies' wage systems differed enough to suggest significant limitations in the cooperation between the three companies. The next section will investigate the company's different stances towards wage reform in order to elucidate this point.

---

[23] As indicated in Table 4.4, Yawata Steel's wage system had only three levels of wage differences between successive job-grades: that is, 300 yen, 340 yen and 380 yen.

[24] Yawata Steel's wage system can be regarded as 'more severe' for the following reasons. (1) Promotion within the same job-grade was at the discretion of management. (2) Compared with Fuji Steel, a relatively large number of jobs were classified into low job-grades at Yawata Steel. Although many jobs were classified into relatively high job-grades (the seventh to tenth job-grades) at Fuji Steel, that had the effect of weakening the motivation to further climb up the career ladder, even if the wage gaps between successive job-grades increased in geometric progression.

3.3 The Companies' Stances Towards the 1962 Wage Reform

The companies' stances towards wage reform differed as of the 1962 spring labor offensive. For Yawata Steel management, the 1962 reform represented the first attempt to change the traditional seniority-based wage system. Managers drew up the reform plan without consultation with labor unions and pressed on with it. Their authoritarian attitude originated in part from the company's history, including its origins as a state-owned steelworks in the prewar period (Chiba 1998, p. 411). Furthermore, Yawata Steel Union was poorly prepared and lacked its own wage plan (Sugiyama 2008a), perhaps leading managers to conclude that consultation would be futile and would only bring turmoil.

For Fuji Steel and Nippon Steel Tube, by contrast, the 1962 wage reform was the second stage of a reform that had already started in the late 1950s. However, there were differences between these two companies as well. Fuji Steel managers sought for a higher portion of 'performance allowances' to be determined by 'job-points' and eventually did increase it from 20 to 25 % in 1960. Fuji Steel Union opposition intensified, however, such that the company became unable to increase that proportion further. In addition, management itself started to recognize various problems with this system. It was at this time that Yawata Steel made a move towards wage reform. Management must have regarded it as a good opportunity to modify the system, but for Fuji Steel, consultation with labor unions was unavoidable. The company proposed a revision of the job-point system to Fuji Steel Union in August 1961, conveyed its basic policy on job evaluation to the union in September, and even after that, continued to consult with the union. Fuji Steel Union took the matter into consideration and presented management with *Requests Concerning the Wage Revision* in April 1962. Eventually, these requests were reflected in the new job-based wage system agreed to by both parties in July 1962 (Shin Nihon Seitetsu (Fuji) Rōdō Kumiai Rengōkai 1974, p. 539–555; Tozawa 1962a, b).

Nippon Steel Tube's management, by contrast, was not so keen on the introduction of the job-based wage system. Although the company also addressed the introduction of a job-based wage system at the time of the 1962 spring labor offensive, management announced that it would discuss the details of the system employees so as to make it workable and acceptable to both parties. The company established its new wage system in 1967, but the system emphasized seniority, with many 'sub-grades' within the same job-grade (Orii 1973, pp. 56–67; Konda 1963). It can be assumed therefore that when Nippon Steel Tube, like Yawata and Fuji, took up reform in 1962, its real intention was to introduce a system different from the other two companies, even if it supported the general idea of a 'job-based wage.' It kept pace with the two companies, probably because it sought to maintain cooperative relations with them.

Judging from these findings, it is obvious that Yawata Steel played a leading role in the 1962 wage reform. Fuji Steel and Nippon Steel Tube were the followers in this process because they had no strong incentives to implement the reform at that point. In fact, Fuji Steel itself recognized that its wage reform plan had "many deficiencies due to insufficient preparation" (Tozawa 1962a).

It is instructive, in this respect, to examine how Yawata Steel's preliminary wage reform plan was affected by those of the other two companies. According to the report *Shin Kyūyoseido* [The New Wage System], edited by Yawata Steel's Labor Department, which describes the process of introducing the job-based wage system, the only provision of the plan that was revised as a result of consultation with Fuji Steel and Nippon Steel Tube was how much money would be transferred from 'performance allowances' to the 'basic wage.' This report purports to have been written on the understanding that "a detailed record of the reform process was indispensable for the proper operation of this job-based wage system" (Yawata Seitetsusho Rōdōbu 1962b, Preface). Had there been other cases of Yawata Steel's revising its original reform plan due to consultation with other companies, the report would have included them, because any such 'unwilling' revisions had to be remembered and 'corrected' in the future. It is reasonable to conclude that the report cites only one such case because that was in fact the only case. It can be assumed in addition that the coordination between the three companies was confined to 'conspicuous' issues that were likely to attract union criticism; these included the average amount of the job-base wage, its proportion of total fixed wages, the amount of money transferred between wage categories for adjustment and the gap ratio between the highest and lowest wage rates. Incidentally, it was in December 1961 that Yawata Steel decided to introduce a job-based wage system, and in March 1962 that Yawata's president made the final decision on the raise and the amount of money transferred to the 'job-based wages' (Yawata Seitetsusho Rōdōbu 1962b, pp. 224 and 474). It was presumably around this period that the three companies consulted on the conditions of the wage reform.

One reason that coordination between the three companies had only limited scope was that Yawata Steel and Fuji Steel had similar wage structures since they had originally been formed by the 1950 breakup of Japan Steel Co., Ltd. (Nihon Seitetsu). There were other reasons as well. Yawata Steel had thoroughly investigated Fuji Steel's job-based wage system and used the results of the investigation when designing its own system.[25] As mentioned earlier, Nippon Steel Tube made no concrete proposals to its union about wage reform details at the time of the 1962 spring labor offensive, which would also have reduced the need for coordination among the companies.

It is worth mentioning here an observation made by an official of JFSWU regarding the wage structures of Yawata Steel and Fuji Steel. As noted earlier, in Fuji Steel's wage system, the wage rate set for each 'job-grade' increased

[25] "[Yawata Steel and Fuji Steel were] originally the same company. Even after the separation, information was exchanged frequently. Therefore, there was no large institutional difference between the two companies" (Yawata Seitetsu Shoshi Hensan Jikkō Iinkai 1980, p. 422). Moreover, in order to study the job evaluation method, Yawata Steel "dispatched its staff to various companies around the country including the Fuji Steel Hirohata Steelworks which had already conducted job analysis and job assessment" (Yawata Seitetsusho Rōdōbu 1962b, p. 65).

progressively as the 'job-grade' went higher, whereas wage rates increased almost proportionally to 'job-grades' in Yawata Steel's wage system. "Despite the difference in the wage structures, however, the average wage per employee was, strangely enough, around 4,500 yen at both companies" (Sōhyō Chōsabu 1962, pp. 61–62). This was only possible because the distribution of workers among 'job-grades' was adjusted.[26] Since Yawata Steel did not allow other companies to influence its plan, it is likely that Fuji Steel adjusted the distribution of workers among 'job-grades' so as to match the average wage and the gap ratio between the highest and the lowest wage rate Yawata Steel's standard as closely as posible.[27]

3.4 Summary

Cooperation and coordination among the three companies were indispensable for the introduction of job-based wage systems in 1962. At the same time, however, both had their limits. The three companies had different stances towards wage reform, so introducing identical systems would have been impractical. Their cooperative activities were limited to the minimum necessary for the purpose of establishing a job-based wage system.

Two important aspects to their relationship should be noted. First, Yawata Steel took the initiative and exercised leadership, encouraging the other two companies to introduce the new wage system. The second aspect was 'cooperation and coordination.' Fuji Steel and Nippon Steel Tube followed, although to a limited extent, the policy line set by Yawata Steel. Such cooperative relationships should not be taken for granted, considering the situations in other industries in the same period. That such cooperation was possible in the steel industry was due largely to Yawata Steel's thorough preparation and the integrity of its reform plan. Yawata Steel "sought to establish the principle of the 'job-based wage,' which was tantamount to 'equal pay for equal work,' and reconciling the principle with reality was the most difficult part" of the reform process (Yawata Seitetsusho Rōdōbu 1962b, Preface).

It is wrong to assume that the job-based wage system was introduced successfully and then took root in the steel industry merely because of Yawata Steel's leadership. Had the new system failed to dampen union opposition to the efforts at labor management, it could not have lasted even at Yawata Steel. The next section therefore examines how Yawata Steel management designed the new system.

[26] As mentioned earlier, Fuji Steel reduced the number of job-grades from twenty to nineteen. There is a possibility that this curtailment was also a measure to adjust the wage gap between high job-grades and low job-grades. To obliterate the lowest job-grade was a much easier way of adjustment than to change the job evaluation method.

[27] The fact that Yawata Steel had great initiative not only in the spring labor offensive but also in the establishment of the new wage system within the industry is an important discovery.

4 Designing the Job-Based Wage System at Yawata Steel

4.1 *Basic Policy*

Yawata Steel's management drew up the reform plan itself, although it was aware of the possibility that lack of consultation with unions could trigger discontent and resistance among its employees. Its preparations took the possibility into consideration.

Full-fledged preparation for the introduction of the job-based wage system started in February 1960.[28] Key to the system were the rules and methods of job evaluation. In designing this part, the company emphasized two points: (1) The new industrial order based on job-based wages should not conflict with the traditional order based on the shop floor authority of 'foremen' (kumichō) and 'group leaders' (gochō, kōchō), and (2) the principle and results of job evaluations had to be acceptable to workers in general. Regarding procedures for preparation, the following was made clear. "First, a purely theoretical exploration of the most appropriate job-evaluation method should be undertaken. Then, the practical validity of the results should be examined. Finally, a balance between the two should be made" (Yawata Seitetsusho Rōdōbu 1962b, p. 102). In short, managers at Yawata Steel set themselves the difficult tasks of connecting a new industrial order to the conventional industrial one, meeting managerial needs, and making the new wage system acceptable to workers and unions.

4.2 *Establishing the Rules and Methods of Job Evaluation*

The Selection of Job-Evaluation Factors

If the point rating method were to be adopted, the choice of evaluation factors and the stationing of points would determine the framework of the wage rates and industrial order. Since these would be the issues of greatest concern to labor unions, management needed to be thoroughly prepared. The following is an analysis of how Yawata Steel dealt with one of the job-evaluation factors: 'Responsibility.'[29]

At the time, the point-rating method of job evaluation included two ideas of 'responsibility.' One was 'responsibility for property,' which concerned damage to the company's property. The other was 'responsibility for people' which included both supervisory responsibility for subordinates and responsibility for the safety of others. However, some people were of the opinion that 'responsibility' should not be one of the factors since some element of responsibility was inevitably included

[28] As to how Yawata Steel came to decide the introduction of the job-based wage system, see Sugiyama (2008b).

[29] As to the discussion over the evaluation factor, 'Responsibility,' see Yawata Seitetsusho Rōdōbu 1962b, pp. 109–113 and 120–121.

in other factors. Labor unions in general strongly supported this opinion. From management's point of view, however, 'responsibility' needed to constitute an independent factor for evaluation; otherwise, it would be impossible to properly assess responsibility in terms of 'basic knowledge,' 'experience' and 'judgment.' Moreover, U.S. Steel had adopted 'responsibility' as one of its job-evaluation factors. Hence, managers generally supported the idea that 'responsibility' should be included among the job evaluation factors.

While drawing up its reform plan, Yawata Steel, like the other companies, discussed whether to adopt 'responsibility' as an independent evaluation factor. Management had to take the 'job's importance' into account, and particularly for Yawata Steel, which was trying to launch a job-based wage system for the first time, the factor of 'responsibility' had the merit of connecting the conventional job hierarchy to the new one through an evaluation of 'responsibility.' Assuming that all workers had a natural sense of a 'job's importance,' management expected unions to accept the inclusion of 'responsibility' into job-evaluation factors, as long as it was appropriately weighed against other evaluation factors.

The management of Yawata Steel divided 'Responsibility' between 'responsibility for property' and 'responsibility for people.' 'Responsibility for property' covered both 'responsibility for losses,' meaning damage to the company caused by workers' operational errors, and 'the importance of the job' to the company. It ultimately proved difficult to evaluate individual workers' 'responsibility for losses,' because Yawata Steel was not able to implement cost management beyond the 'group- leader' level even at its most advanced steelworks in Tobata. At its steelworks in Yawata, it was even harder to account for each worker's actual tasks, because there was no clear demarcation between line and staff personnel. It was therefore decided that evaluation should be on the basis of the 'job's importance' and that 'responsibility for losses' would be treated as a supplementary factor.

The company at first considered dividing 'Responsibility for people' into 'responsibility for the safety of others' and 'supervisory responsibility.' 'Responsibility for the safety of others' had been adopted as a job-evaluation factor by U.S. Steel, and Yawata Steel was fully aware of the importance of safety measures. Eventually, however, it concluded that 'responsibility for the safety of others' should belong to the category of 'Mental Stress,' in order to make it possible to specify the source of the mental stress in question.[30] The discussion of 'supervisory responsibility' centered on whether it should be evaluated according to the number and quality of subordinates or to the importance of a supervisor's discretion as leader. Ultimately, Yawata chose the latter, because management feared that, determining 'supervisory responsibility' by number and quality of subordinates would undermine the 'group-leader' rank and the workplace authority of the 'group leaders' and 'foremen' on which the traditional industrial order was based.

[30] The problem of double evaluation also occurred concerning other evaluation factors. Managers dealt with this problem by clarifying evaluation criteria. In the case of 'Experience' and 'Judgment,' for example, it was specified that the former should be used for the evaluation of practical knowledge and skills whereas the latter should be used for the evaluation of the job's difficulty and urgency. See Yawata Seitetsusho Rōdōbu 1962b, p. 103 and pp. 113–114.

Technological development meant that highly skilled individuals were handling more and more of the jobs, as management was aware. It was in order to protect these particular workers against the leaders of simpler group work that management decided not to give too high a valuation to 'supervisory responsibility.'

Ultimately, the decision was made to evaluate all 'group leaders' equally regardless of their workplaces so far as 'responsibility for property' and 'responsibility for people' were concerned, and that the relative importance of these evaluation factors should be limited. This led to the realization that there was little sense in having two separate evaluation factors for responsibility. 'Responsibility for property' and 'responsibility for people' were therefore combined into 'Responsibility,' and in this category, workers were classified into the following five ranks according to the content and importance of their work: 'group leader,' 'responsible,' 'skilled,' 'general' and 'hammering.' As will be shown later, the policy of uniform evaluation of all group leaders would ultimately be altered due to the need for further adjustment.

Determining the Allocation of Job-Evaluation Points

Allocation of evaluation points rested on the following basic principles: It should be acceptable to employees; the industrial order based on the new point rating method should accord with the industrial order based on the 'classification method' (bunruihō)[31]; and the gaps in wage rates should be relatively small compared with the gaps in job-point scores.

Yawata Steel began by studying the 'Motobayashi method,' adopted by Fuji Steel and Nippon Steel Tube when they introduced the job-based wage system in the late 1950s. In this method, an evaluation point 'Y' allotted to the evaluation grade 'x' of a certain job-evaluation factor was determined by the formula, $Y = 10(1 + K)^{4(x-1)}$, 'K' being a constant set for each evaluation factor based on the level of perceptibility of that factor. For example, 'K' was assigned relatively smaller values when applied to evaluation factors such as 'physical burden,' and relatively larger values when applied to 'responsibility' and 'experience.'[32] In August 1960, Yawata Steel launched a simulation of the method,[33] but it proved too problematic to apply both theoretically and in practice.

---

[31] As to the allocation of job-points, see Yawata Seitetsusho Rōdōbu 1962b, pp. 118–142.

[32] According to Fujirō Motobayashi, who developed the Motobayashi method, the appropriate value of 'K' for 'physical burden' was 0.1–0.125 and that for 'responsibility' was 0.15–0.2 (Motobayashi 1957). Yawata Steel adopted 0.2 as the value of 'K' for 'Responsibility.' As a result, the job evaluation points for the factor 'Responsibility' were set as follows: Rank A 100; Rank B 207; Rank C 427; Rank D 891; and Rank E 1,848. (The formula used was $Y = 100(1 + K)^{4(x-1)}$.)

[33] Yawata Steel tried three methods of job evaluation including the Motobayashi method, checking the distribution of the job evaluation points concerning 64 types of workers. In the case of foremen, two jobs were examined in this way; for group leaders, four jobs; and for average workers, nine jobs. At this stage of preparation, foremen's jobs were evaluated in the same way as those of group leaders and average workers.

First, the company was unable to give a solid theoretical basis for the values of 'K.' Management feared that if this method was presented to workers, they might suspect that the company had manipulated those values for its own convenience. Moreover, the results of the simulation suggested that this approach would produce large differences in job-point scores among highly-graded workers, including foremen. It became obvious that manipulations of 'K' would not be enough to create job-point systems that were acceptable for both management and workers.

The company next attempted a 'percentage method,' but also in vain, because this method was incompatible with the existing industrial hierarchy. Eventually, management came to the conclusion that practicality should take precedence over theoretical rigidity, and adopted a 'freehand method' that gave managers room for discretion.[34] The results can be seen in Table 4.2. The characteristics of this method were as follows. First, as was mentioned above, the relative importance of the 'Responsibility' factor was reduced. Next, the weights placed on various evaluation factors were carefully adjusted lest the results of the job evaluation threaten the existing industrial order either within or between workplaces. Finally, the five-grade assessment was applied to all eight evaluation factors, despite early efforts to adopt different numbers of grades for different factors. These plans had been discarded because it was obvious that they would draw worker criticism. The uniform five-grade system also had other practical merits for management. For instance, if managers wanted to treat a certain job at an advanced steelworks as equal to another job at a conventional steelworks, all it needed to do was to grade the former 'D' in 'Basic Knowledge' and 'C' in 'Experience,' while grading the latter 'C' in 'Basic Knowledge' and 'D' in 'Experience.'

The Process of Formulating Job-Grades and Prescribing Wage Rates

The question of how to connect 'job-point scores' to actual wage rates was a critical issue that attracted union attention. The central concern in setting job grades was whether the range of job-point scores corresponding to a job-grade should be the same for all job-grades or be widened in geometric progression moving up the grade scale. In the former case, differences in the 'job-point scores' of such high-ranked workers as 'group leaders' were strongly reflected in their wage rates, widening wage gaps among them. In order to prevent the breakdown of high-ranked workers, therefore, it was decided that the job-point scores corresponding to a job-grade should increase geometrically.[35]

[34] Fuji Steel also did not adopt the Motobayashi method at the time of the 1962 wage reform. It allocated job points in a similar way to Yawata Steel. See Tozawa (1962b).

[35] As to the setting of job grades, see Yawata Seitetsusho Rōdōbu 1962b, pp. 141–143.

Next comes the question of how wage rates were prescribed to job-grades.[36] Yawata Steel introduced its first job-based wage plan in August 1960, basing it on the 'performance allowances' (gyōseki teate) of June 1960 (paid in July). Twenty job-grades were created, with the highest and lowest wage rates set at 13900 and 2500 yen, respectively. The gap ratio between the highest and lowest rates was slightly lower than in the June allowances. Meanwhile the number of sub-grades in each job-grade increased with each rise in job-grade. The complication caused by these subgrades resulted in too many cases of the same wage being assigned to jobs in different job-grades. Since management wanted to minimize wage rates' overlapping and to retain discretion in the promotion of workers within the same job-grade, it began to reconsider the plan in February 1961. Eventually, it was decided that each of the twenty job-grades should consist of three sub-grades.

In March 1962, the president of Yawata Steel decided to increase fixed wages by 1800 yen, of which 1300 yen would be transferred to the 'job-based wage' (shokumukyū). At the same time, the following conditions were set regarding wages: (1) About 10% of workers would have wages reduced by the reform (in other words, to whom compensation allowances would be paid); and (2) The wage gap ratio between 'Job-Grade 1' and 'Job-Grade 17' (the job-grade of 'group leaders') would be around 3 times. It should be noted that these conditions represented a loosening of previous plans. In the December 1961 plan, for instance, the proportion of the 'job-based wage' were around 25 % of total fixed wages, and the wage gap ratio between 'Job-Grade 1' and 'Job-Grade 17' was four times. As the economic recession deepened, the company had less and less money to spend on establishing the new system. It therefore lowered the proportion of the 'job-based wage' to fixed wages in February 1962. It was becoming more concerned about the smooth introduction and secure operation of the new wage system than about its merits for labor management. At this point, the proportion of workers whose wages would be reduced by the new system was a little over 20% and the wage gap ratio between 'Job-Grade 1' and 'Job-Grade 17' was 3.84 times. As shown above, these proportions were brought down further in the March decision (final results in Table 4.4). This indicates how careful the company was about the introduction of the new system.

As noted above, Yawata Steel did not make a strong connection between 'job-point scores' and wage rates. Although *The New Wage System* does not reveal anything on this matter, it can be assumed that the company never had any intention of linking them closely, because its primary concern was worker opposition to the new system. That was why management was so keen on making wage gaps relatively small compared to the gaps between job-point scores. It should be pointed out in this regard that JFSWU, usually more critical of Yawata Steel than Fuji Steel, praised the former only on this point (Sōhyō Chōsabu 1962, p. 60).

[36] As to the prescription of wage rates for job-grades, see Yawata Seitetsusho Rōdōbu 1962b, pp. 201–225.

4.3 Fine-tuning the Job-Evaluation Results

A desirable industrial order cannot be established simply by mechanically applying a point-rating method. The job-evaluation results have to be examined and carefully fine-tuned before they are actually put to use. At Yawata Steel, this process proceeded as follows.[37] First, on the basis of the job assessment conducted by a nine-member job-study unit, Labor Management Department selected 'standard jobs,' drew up implementation guidelines, and presented the original job-evaluation plan.[38] The Job Investigation Committee examined and endorsed the the basic framework of the new system, including the rules, method and selection of 'standard jobs.' The secretariat (placed within Labor Management Department) of the Job Investigation Committee and a sub-committee of the same Committee did the preparatory work for fine-tuning the evaluation results, before the Job Investigation Committee gave its endorsement. Then the Labor Management Department made final adjustments to address problems both within and across sections of the steelworks. At coordinating meetings with the 'Section Chiefs' (kachō) and 'Senior Staff' (kakarichō) who supervised workplaces, the Labor Management Department "asked them to give any opinion on the job-evaluations (kata)" (Yawata Seitetsusho Rōdōbu 1962b, p. 186) in order to solve whatever problems had arisen during the process of preparing for reform. The Labor Management Department also examined the results of the evaluations of all jobs before making its final adjustments. It is evident that enormous effort was put into modifying the evaluation results. The Yawata Steel job evaluation process took place as follows: (1) April 1960 – January 1961: making the original job evaluation plan; (2) February 1961 – April 1961: discussions on 'standard jobs' in the Job Investigation Committee; (3) April 1961 – December 1961: adjustments of job evaluations; (4) October 1961 – February 1962: adjustments of job evaluations across sections; and (5) February 1962–April 1962: final adjustments (Yawata Seitetsusho Rōdōbu 1962b, p. 147 and 152).

A number of problems were raised during this process, ranging from how to define a 'job' (kata) to how to evaluate it in terms of specific evaluation factors. Discussion focused in particular on the question of how to achieve a balance between production workers and production support staff. As mentioned earlier, all 'group leaders' had equal valuation in the category of 'Responsibility.' This treatment, however, contradicted conventional wage-setting practice, according to which production and production support 'group leaders' were treated differently. Conventionally, performance allowances for workers in the production section were higher than those for production support workers. As opposition to equal treatment intensified during the discussion, some kind of accommodation became

[37] On the process of job evaluations, see Yawata Seitetsusho Rōdōbu 1962b, pp. 147–187.

[38] The implementation guideline and the original job evaluation plan were made simultaneously. The former was completed in January 1961. The making of the original job evaluation plan confirmed the validity of the implementation guideline. See Yawata Seitetsusho Rōdōbu 1962b, p. 144 and pp. 151–152.

inevitable. One way to solve this problem was to add the element of 'responsibility for production (properties)' to the 'Responsibility' factor. As discussed above, however, it was hard to determine a given group leader's responsibility for production. But if, however, the validity of the evaluation method itself was called into question, the entire wage reform project might be placed in jeopardy. This problem was eventually settled by revising the results of job assessments only insofar as 'group leaders' in the production support section were concerned.

The problem concerning the balance of job evaluations between different sections arose again, when a survey on individual workers' jobs was conducted in August 1961. The investigation revealed that the job-evaluation results contradicted the conventional industrial order, with regard not only to 'group leaders' but also to average workers in the production and production support sections. In the production section, a large number of workers were engaged in simple, physical jobs whose 'job-point scores' were relatively low, whereas many jobs in the production support section had 'job-point scores' for 'Basic Knowledge' that were relatively high. If these job evaluation results were directly to reflect wage rates, management anticipated, production section workers would not accept them. The company therefore revised the job evaluations of workers engaged in 'transportation,' 'power' and 'maintenance.' Once again, these revisions were made without changing the basic framework of the planned job evaluation system. These revisions were to conform to the following principles: (1) that they should bring about a desirable balance between the 'job-point scores' of jobs in question; and (2) that they should have accountability toward all parties concerned. Under this rubric, suitable, or convenient, evaluation factors were chosen for revision as needed. Hence, evaluation factors chosen for revision differed by case.[39] For each revision made, concrete reasons had to be presented. It is recorded, for instance, that: "[the] evaluation of the factor, 'Responsibility,' of the job (kata), 'assistant locomotive engineer' (kikanshi daimu) is downgraded from 'C' to 'B,' because, unlike 'locomotive engineer' (untenkata), he does not assume responsibility for a locomotive all by himself."[40] Yawata Steel took these troublesome adjustment measures first, in order to show the validity of the evaluations to both unions and 'Section Chiefs' and 'Senior Staff' who were supervising workplaces, and second, because in rationalizing labor

[39] These two conditions for the revision of job evaluation are mentioned frequently in Yawata Seitetsusho Rōdōbu 1962c, d.

[40] Yawata Seitetsusho Rōdōbu (1962c), p. 23. This is an example of a revision of job evaluation concerning the transportation section. There were many ways to adjust working conditions within and between workplaces: (1) Introducing the upper limit regulation. (2) Making continuous use of various allowances. (3) Changing (abolishing) job categories. (4) Changing job categories from the blue-collar to the white-collar category. There were also cases in which the management did not make these adjustments on the grounds that necessary adjustments were already included in the basic wage and in performance allowances.

management, the company could not afford to jeopardize the job-evaluation method itself, which was the very basis of the intended job-based wage system.[41]

4.4 Statistical Investigations of the Job-Based Wage System

Yawata Steel conducted statistical surveys on individual workers' jobs (*kata*) three times: in August and October of 1961 and January of 1962. The first was only for the Yawata steelworks; the second, for the Yawata and Hikari steelworks; and the third, for all works including the Sakai steelworks and the Nagoya factory. The company thought that the introduction of new wage categories such as the 'job-based wage' (shokumukyū) needed more deliberate preparation than usual. Following the results of these surveys, further investigations were made into the distribution of workers by both job-grade and the length of service; the relationship between 'job-grades' and the company's traditional 'job qualification system' (shokubun seido); the amount that individual workers' wages would increase or decrease as a result of the planned reform; and the amounts of compensation payments the company would have to pay workers for wage reduction. The results of these investigations were used to compare the new working conditions with the conventional ones and to demonstrate the validity of the reform. In addition, the surveys on individual workers' jobs had the advantage of making supervisory staff think about the proper deployment of workers (Yawata Seitetsusho Rōdōbu 1962e, pp. 177–226). These investigations also helped management to deal with the unions' criticism of the reform.

The investigations were fruitful. The 'upper limit regulation' mentioned in Sect. 3.1 was introduced as a result of the survey of the distribution of workers by job-grade and length of service. In addition, the investigation into the relationship between job-grades and the traditional job qualification system led to the conclusion that "the introduction of job-based wages [was] consistent with the traditional job qualification system, and could serve, in an indirect way, as a support for the traditional system" (Yawata Seitetsusho Rōdōbu 1962e, p. 182). The results of these investigations gave management confidence in the new wage system and put it in an advantageous position in negotiations with unions.

4.5 Summary

Yawata Steel proceeded with preparations for the new job-based wage system, trying to make two opposing requirements compatible: advantages for labor

[41] Regarding the meaning of the 1962 introduction of the job-based wage system to Yawata Steel, see Sugiyama (2008b).

management and acceptability for employees. The company put a great deal of time and energy into the task, conducting a series of investigations and taking considerable trouble to fine-tune the system. It ultimately was successful. Yawata Steel was of course making the effort in order to achieve labor management rationalization. However, Yawata Steel's effort laid the foundation for the cooperative relationship between the three major steel companies. At the industry level as well, Yawata Steel's deliberate preparation gave strength to the job-based wage system. This wage system therefore went on to operate within the major steel companies for a long period.

5 Concluding Remarks

As has been shown, intercompany relationships were indispensable to the introduction of the job-based wage system into the three major steel companies in 1962. In addition, the existence of a company to lead the reform process was crucial to its success. There was elaborate coordination between the companies. It should be stressed that an in-depth analysis of industrial relations and labor management is only possible by taking into account macro factors such as intercompany relationships within the industry as well as micro factors concerning individual companies. What implications, then, can be drawn if this approach is applied to the broader context of labor management reform carried out by Japanese companies in the 1950s and 1960s?

During the period in question, industries differed greatly regarding the necessity of institutional reform, the nature of intercompany relationships and the existence of a leading company in the industry. Table 4.5 presents patterns of company activities within these complicated circumstances. To take the example of the steel industry wage reform examined in this study, Situation II in the table corresponds to the period in which Yawata Steel had not yet moved towards wage reform. It was in this situation, around the late 1950s and the early 1960s, that the 'job-ranking system' of Sumitomo Metal Industries and the 'performance allowances' of Fuji Steel and Nippon Steel Tube were introduced. When Yawata Steel decided to introduce 'job-based wages' in 1962, Situation I emerged and fundamental institutional reforms were put into place. There then was a return to Situation II, in which Yawata Steel retained the job-based wage system. Under these circumstances, it was hard for other companies to abolish, or radically change, the system, even when problems with it became apparent.[42]

[42] The Kōbe Seikōsho Steelworks Co., Ltd. introduced job-based wages based on the point rating method in October 1965. See 80-nenshi Hensan Iinkai (1986), p. 601. Kawasaki Seitetsu Steelworks Co., Ltd. introduced 'performance allowances' (nōritsukyū) based on job evaluations in October 1968, and then revised them to 'job-based wages' (gyōmukyū) based on the job-grade system in July 1973. See Kawasaki Seitestu Kabushiki-kaisha Shashi Henshū Iinkai (1976), pp. 526–528.

Table 4.5 Company-specific labor reform and intercompany relations

		Stance of leading company		
		Motivation for institutional reform: Strong	Motivation for institutional reform: Weak	Absence of leading company
Need for institutional reform within an industry	Strong	I: Full-scale institututional change at the industy level	II: Partial reform influenced by actions of the leading company	III: Reform on a limited scale within individual companies
	Weak	IV: Initiative by a leading company; Limited followership by other companies	V: Stable maintenance of the existing system within the industry	

This analytical framework, however, has to be used with caution. The general applicability of the patterns in Table 4.5 needs to be tested through an examination of various industries and companies with a variety of labor management systems. Moreover, the patterns in Table 4.5 cannot be applied to all periods. The framework requires some revision when applied to a period in which companies acted either more distinctly from one another or in closer cooperation or more distinctly from each other. The former case corresponds to the late 1940s, when Sumitomo Metal Industries sought to introduce the 'job-ranking system,' whereas the latter corresponds to the period after the 1970s in which industrial relations were adjusted across major steel companies.[43] These points need further investigation.[44]

Acknowledgements The author is thankful for the help offered by Nippon Steel Co. Ltd., the Federation of Nippon Steel Workers' Unions and the Japan Federation of Basic Industry Workers' Unions. As for the content of this study, however, the author assumes full responsibility.

References

80-nenshi Hensan Iinkai. (ed.). 1986. *Kōbe Seikō 80-nen* [The eighty-year history of Kōbe Steel]. Kōbe: Kabushiki-kaisha Kōbe Seikōsho.

Chiba Toshio. 1998. *Sengo Chingin Undō: Kiseki to Tenbō* [Postwar labor struggles for wages: History and outlook]. Tokyo: Nihon Rōdō Kenkyū Kikō (JIL).

Hyōdō Tsutomu. 1997. *Rōdō no Sengo-shi Jo* [The history of industrial relations in Japan, 1945–1989, vol. 1]. Tokyo: University of Tokyo Press.

[43] In the early 1970s, workers in major steel companies shifted the focus of their demand for wage increases from the average amount of wages per person to the amount of wage increase of a 'standard worker' (hyōjun rōdōsha). Under these circumstances, a new industrial situation emerged. Incidentally, 'standard worker' designates a worker who was employed by a company immediately after graduation and then worked there continuously. See Chiba (1998), pp. 424–426.

[44] With regard to today's labor management of Japanese companies, the role of intercompany relationships within an industry seems to be losing its importance due to mergers and acquisitions and the widening financial disparity between companies. It can be said that leading companies among all Japanese companies are becoming more and more influential.

Iida Ken'ichi, Ōhashi Shūji and Kuroiwa Toshirō. (eds.). 1969. *Gendai Nihon Sangyō Hattatsu-shi IV: Tekkō* [The history of modern Japanese industries, vol. 4: Iron and steel]. Tokyo: Kōjunsha, 1969.

Kawasaki Seitestu Kabushiki-kaisha Shashi Henshū Iinkai. (ed.). 1976. *Kawasaki Seitetsu 25-nenshi* [Twenty-five year history of Kawasaki Steel]. Kōbe: Kawasaki Seitetsu Kabushiki-kaisha.

Koike Kazuo. 1962. *Nihon no Chingin Kōshō* [Wage negotiations in Japan]. Tokyo: University of Tokyo Press.

Komatsu Hiroshi. 1963. Yawata Seitetsu ni okeru Shokumukyūka to Shomondai [Problems in the introduction of the job-based wage system at Yawata Steel]. In Nihon Keieisha Dantai Renmei Kantō Keieisha Kyōkai, *Rōmu Shiryō* [Labor management material], no.75, pp. 1–30.

Konda Masaharu. 1963. Nihon Kōkan no Shokumukyū ni tsuite [Job-based wages introduced at Nippon Steel Tube]. In Nihon Tekkō Renmei, *Tekkō Rōmu Tsūshin* [The bulletin of steel labor management], no. 846 (11 Jul), pp. 2–11.

Motobayashi Fujirō. 1957. *Jitsumu no tame no Shokumuhyūka* [Job evaluation for business practice]. Tokyo: Rōdō Kagaku Kenkyūsho Shuppanbu.

Nihon Keieisha Dantai Renmei. (ed.). 1962. *Shokumukyūka e no Michi* [The road to the introduction of a job-based wage system]. Tokyo: Nihon Keieisha Dantai Renmei.

Nihon Tekkō Sangyō Rōdōkumiai Rengōkai. (ed.) 1971. *Tekkō Rōdō Undō-shi: 20 Nen no Ayumi* [A twenty-year history of the Steelworkers' Labor Movement]. Tokyo: Nihon Tekkō Sangyō Rōdōkumiai Rengōkai .

Nitta Michio and Hisamoto Norio. (eds.). 2008. *Nihonteki Koyō Shisutemu* [Japanese employment systems]. Tokyo: Nakanishiya Shuppan.

Orii Hyūga. 1973. *Rōmukanri 20-nen* [A twenty-year history of labor management]. Tokyo: Tōyō Keizai Shinpōsha.

Saguchi Kazurō and Hashimoto Shūichi. (eds.). 2003. *Jinji Rōmukanri no Rekishi Bunseki* [Historical analysis of Japanese personnel management]. Tokyo: Minerva Shobō.

Sano Yōko, Koike Kazuo and Ishida Hideo. (eds.). 1969. *Chingin Kōshō no Kōdōkagaku* [Behavioral science of wage negotiations]. Tokyo: Tōyō Keizai Shinpōsha.

Shin Nihon Seitetsu (Fuji) Rōdō Kumiai Rengōkai. 1974. *Fuji Seitetsu Rōdō Undō-shi* [Fuji Steel Labor History]. Shinnihon Seitetsu (Fuji) Rōdō Kumiai Rengōkai.

Shin Nihon Seitetsu Yawata Rōdōkumiai. 1975. *Yawata Seitetsu Rōdōundō-shi: Zokuhen Chūkan* [The history of the Yawata Steel Union: Supplementary Volume, 2] (Shin Nihon Seitetsu Yawata Rōdōkumiai).

Sōhyō Chōsabu. (ed.). 1962. *Tekkō Shokumukyū no Naiyō to Mondaiten* [Job-based wages in the steel industry: Outline and problems]. Tokyo: Rōdō Shuppansha.

Sugiyama Hiroshi. 2005. Tekkōgyō ni okeru Shokumukyū Dōnyū to sono Henyō [The introduction of the job-based wage system in the steel Industry and subsequent changes]. *Shakai Keizai Shigaku* [Socio-Economic History], vol. 71, no. 4 (Nov), pp. 71–91.

Sugiyama Hiroshi. 2008a. Shogū no Arikata wo meguru Rōdōsha Ishiki: 1960-nendai no Yawata Seitetsu wo Jirei to shite [Blue-collar workers' consciousness regarding the personnel system: A case study of Yawata Steel in 1960s]. *Ōhara Shakaimondai Kenkyūshozasshi* [The Journal of Ōhara Institute For Social Research], no. 590 (Jan), pp. 1–22.

Sugiyama Hiroshi. 2008b. Tekkōgyō ni okeru Shokumukyū Seido Dōnyū to Jinji Rōmukanri no Gōrika: Yawata Seitetsu wo Jirei to shite [Labor management rationalization and the introduction of job-based wages: A case study of Yawata Steel Co.]. *Shakai Keizai Shigaku* [Japan Business History Review], Vol. 42, no. 4 (Mar), pp. 33–57.

Takanashi Akira. 1967. *Nihon Tekkogyō no Rōshikankei* [Industrial relations in the Japanese steel industry]. Tokyo: University of Tokyo Press.

Tozawa, Takumi. 1962a. Fuji Seitetsu no Shokumukyū ni tsuite Jo [The job-based wage system at Fuji Steel, vol. 1]. In Nihon Tekkō Renmei, *Tekkō Rōmu Tsūshin* [The steel industry labor management newsletter], no. 803 (16 Aug), pp. 2–8.

Tozawa Takumi. 1962b. Fuji Seitetsu no Shokumukyū ni tsuite Ge [The job-based wage system at Fuji Steel, vol. 2]. In Nihon Tekkō Renmei, *Tekkō Rōmu Tsūshin* [The steel industry labor management Newsletter], no. 804 (23 Aug), pp. 2–9.
Yawata Seitetsusho Rōdōbu. 1962a. *Sokuhō* [Prompt report], nos. 26–60
Yawata Seitetsusho Rōdōbu. 1962b. *Shin Kyūyoseido Dai 1-hen* [The new wage system, vol. 1].
Yawata Seitetsusho Rōdōbu. 1962c. *Shin Kyūyoseido Dai 2-hen* so no 1 [The new wage system, vol. 2, no. 1].
Yawata Seitetsusho Rōdōbu. 1962d. *Shin Kyūyoseido Dai 2-hen* so no 2 [The new wage system, vol. 2, no. 2].
Yawata Seitetsusho Rōdōbu. 1962e. *Shin Kyūyoseido Dai 3-hen* [The new wage system, vol. 3].
Yawata Seitetsu Rōdōkumiai. 1962a. *Chūi News* [The Yawata Steel Union central committee news], no. 325 (27 Apr).
Yawata Seitetsu Rōdōkumiai. 1962b. *Neppū* [The hot blast: Newspaper of the Yawata Steel Union], no. 522 (14 Jun).
Yawata Seitetsu Shoshi Hensan Jikkō Iinkai. (ed.). 1980. *Yawata Seitetsu Hachijū-nenshi Sōgōshi* [An eighty-year history of the Yawata Steelworks: General history]. Yawata: Shin Nihon Seitetsu Kabushiki-kaisha Yawata Seitetsusho.

Part II
Book Reviews

Chapter 5
Review of Tsuyoshi Numagami, *Ekisyō Display no Gijyutsu Kakushin-shi* (The History of Technological Innovation in Liquid Crystal Displays)

Hakuto-Shobo, Tokyo, 1999

Juroh Hashimoto

This work's reputation is already well established in the academic world. It has been the recipient of Economist Award and numerous others, and it is in fact a monumental achievement. Its methodological approach is clear and incisive; its research on the LCD sector and analysis of the patents acquired is comprehensive; and its research methods include careful attention to the accounts of many people who have worked in this sector. As the discussion that follows can only begin to show, this research, rather than give way to passing trends, seeks to explain the very essence of technological innovation.

It is, however, very difficult to offer an ample review of this work. I would use up my page allotment just trying to summarize the first few chapters. So I will approach this in a slightly unorthodox way, and present several aspect of this work that might be called concerns.

Since this is a review, let me begin by parsing the phrase, "history of technological innovation." The very title, "The History of Technological Innovation in Liquid Crystal Displays," is perhaps a little misleading. The work certainly qualifies as a history, given that it covers the more than 100 years that passed between the discovery of the liquid crystal phenomenon in Europe, America, and Japan, and its actual application. The story is one of "Technology as an Action System [a system of linked actions]" according to the subtitle. The author explores liquid crystal displays as an example of that system, so in that sense, the LCD case is used to depict "technological innovation," and "history" is not quite an appropriate term.

Juroh Hashimoto
Author was deceased at the time of publication

H. Takeda (ed.), *Micro-Performance During Postwar Japan's High-Growth Era*, Monograph Series of the Socio-Economic History Society, Japan,
DOI 10.1007/978-981-10-0709-5_5

At the same time, the author's commitment to addressing the full century and treating it systematically is rooted in a deep skepticism about the popular argument that the Japanese enterprise system is suitable for technological development in the form of improvements, but not for the breakthrough developments that are generally regarded as the province of American enterprises. This commitment signifies his insistence that we consider the weight of the entire 100 years in our efforts to understand present conditions. In other words, it is an interpretation of history from the "vertical" vantage point of development over time. At the same time, it shows that the effort to explain the liquid crystal phenomenon and to develop liquid crystal materials was at first purely academic in Europe. In this sense, it considers history from a "horizontal" point of view, examining particular periods in time, and also from the point of view of the comparative history of Europe and America.

All of which is to say that Numagami's work comprises the three points of view that I believe are essential to historical analysis.[1] It may therefore indeed represent a challenge to what we ordinarily think of as historical analysis.

To turn to the contents of the work: According to Numagami, technology does not determine people's actions, as is conventionally assumed, but rather people's actions determine technology. Because this requires that actions be explained as part of a social system, Numagami's object of study is not limited to the enterprise, but is expanded to include universities and research facilities. The objective he has established for himself is to "capture technology as a system of linked actions."

The term, "action system," or "chain of actions," refers to the long-term historical process by which technologies are born, developed, and transformed, involving actors across many generations in many countries. In the case of the liquid crystal display, we must begin all the way back in 1888 with the discovery of the liquid crystal phenomenon.

With this aim, Numagami examines technological innovation in LCDs over the course of more than 600 pages of print. Given that he was addressing the essence of technological innovation through research into a particular case, even these 600 pages were not enough to cover all the methodological considerations he regarded as necessary. He therefore proceeded to publish "Toward an Action System Theory of Management" (Hakuto Shobo, 2000). He pursued this theme, in other words, for more than 13 years. It is not a simple matter to determine either how to define the concept of essential technology, or whether the findings in this case study offer much of universality (what Numakami calls 'validity' or 'generality'). In fact, the undertaking itself would not be possible for one whose intellect was not at once vigorous and acute.

The book's contents are as follows. The two chapters in Part 1, "The Development of Technological Innovation Over Time and Across Space," consider previous research on the problems raised above, while also giving an overview of the current state of the LCD industry. Part 2, "The Discovery and Early Commercialization of

[1] On economic-historical analysis as a vantage point, see my introduction in "Modern Japanese Economic History," Iwanami Shoten, 2000.

the Liquid Crystal Phenomenon in Europe and America," in four chapters, begins with Austrian botanist Reinitzer's discovery of the beautiful color phenomenon that occurs in the liquid state between two melting points. The scientific exploration of this liquid crystal phenomenon initially unfolded in Europe, principally in Germany. Chemists and biologists carried it forward, but until the 1960s, they had little consistent interaction with each other, and in this sense "linked actions" were at best intermittent. At that point, RCA's Sarnoff Research Lab in the US began developing LCDs and launched the first enterprises associated with the technology. This began a period of interaction between scientists and technologists, but efforts were not yet consistent enough to turn the interaction into businesses. Nevertheless, the research advances being made in the US stimulated European interest, and the fruits of research on liquid crystal materials gradually accumulated. This was the beginning of a chain-like development, or technological innovation as a system of "linked actions."

The two chapters of Part 3, "The Early Commercialization of Liquid Crystal Displays in Japan," show how Japanese scientists and technologists, who had not initially produced much from RCA's research, began all at once in the late 1960s to become very active. Japan's early commercialization of liquid crystals for batteries and watches was characterized by long-term transactional relationships built on abundant exchanges and interactions, which in turn established trust in these first-generation liquid crystal displays.

Numagami covers the 1970s and 1980s over the course of three chapters in Part 4, "Japan's Technological Innovation," including (a) the development of reliable automated LCD production processes, (b) the establishment of mass production systems, (c) the product innovations made for high information capacity in LCDs based on high performance LCD drivers, (d) the formation of networks between Japan's LCD makers and Japanese and Europe's liquid crystal materials makers, and (e) the integration of chemistry and biology.

It is in the two chapters of Part 5, "The Development of the Liquid Crystal Display Industry," that he shows how LCDs underwent active development on the foundation of these networks, in such new areas as active matrix LCDs. Through this point in the book, Numagami's analysis focuses on the process of technological innovation in LCDs.

Part 6, "A Reconsideration of Japan's System of Technological Innovation, " is comprised of Chap. 14, "A Reconsideration of Fundamental Concepts about Japan's Enterprise Systems"; Chap. 15, "Invention Generation Systems – A Science-and-Technology 'Bilingualism'"; Chap. 16, "Enterprise Systems and Technological Choice – the Flexibility Trap"; Chap. 17, "Internal Technological Progress – The Economics of Advance"; and Chap. 18, "Technological Innovation as a Process of Forging Agreements." As the chapter subtitles suggest, the author, having summarized his analysis through Chap. 13, next undertook to reconsider the relationship between science and technology, the influence of transactional relationships, etc.

Before wrapping up, I'd like to add one thought on the question of whether Numagami shares the conventional view that Japan does not lend itself to radical innovation. Allow me to present it in some detail. Back at the stage when the prospects of LCD research were at best uncertain, Japanese enterprises put their efforts into the research and development of LCDs, the improvement of production processes, and the building of networks among diverse elements of production, and they thereafter created new markets and built even more diverse interconnections: this is itself radical technological innovation. Which should answer the question posed at the beginning of this paragraph.

Having summarized chapter-by-chapter in this way, I'm afraid readers will come away with the impression that the book is dry and flavorless. So I will conclude by describing my experience as a reader of this volume. All the way through my reading, I was overwhelmed by its depth and precision and by the tenacity of the thinking it represents. I was literally shaken by the experience of reading a work with such fresh and novel content. It has fired shots of such range and weight that the force of its impact can hardly be measured. There is no question that it poses a serious challenge to the existing social sciences and history studies.

Chapter 6
Review of Woo Jong-Won, *"Mibun no Torihiki" to Nihon no Koyō Kankō* ("Transactions Over Status" and Japan's Employment Practices)

Nihon Keizai Hyouronsha, Tokyo, 2003

Hiroshi Ichihara

One of the features of Japanese labor history research in recent years is that it has largely turned away from its previous emphasis on the history of labor relations. Woo's work, by contrast, which focuses on Japan National Railways, seeks to analyze the formation of postwar Japanese hiring practices from the vantage point of labor relations. Strongly evidence-based, and introducing a methodology, too, that raises important and stimulating questions, this work may well prove epochal when we look back at the history of this kind of research. I feel considerable awe for the author, who produced such impressive work from his period of study abroad.

The author takes up postwar Japanese labor practices. By this he refers to the seniority wage structure and "permanent employment" (employment guarantees) that extended even to blue-collar workers. This meant the payment of wages to blue-collar workers as "compensation for indeterminate types and indeterminate amounts of work" in exchange for according the same treatment to blue-collar and white-collar work, or in other words, imposing on blue-collar workers the same flexible work expectations and employment adjustment methods that governed white-collar work.

This is not a new approach to this subject. What is new about the author's argument, however, is the argument that these practices were born of the clash between the viewpoints of management and labor.

He presents the process as a transaction between labor and management over "status," which included wages and benefits and focused on the extension of "membership" and position to blue-collar workers. This "regularization" concept stressed that contributions of blue-collar workers, through the cultivation of their

H. Ichihara (✉)
Department of Economics, Dokkyo University, Saitama, Japan
e-mail: hitihara@dokkyo.ac.jp

H. Takeda (ed.), *Micro-Performance During Postwar Japan's High-Growth Era*,
Monograph Series of the Socio-Economic History Society, Japan,
DOI 10.1007/978-981-10-0709-5_6

skills, were comparable to those of white-collar workers, and it was the formulation of the laborers themselves. Management, in exchange for accepting this premise, demanded that blue-collar workers accept flexible assignments in the way white-collar workers did, and labor in its turn accepted these requirements: it was this mutual engagement and transaction, the author stresses, that gave birth to postwar employment practices. The author thus places laborers and their viewpoints in the driver's seat, arguing that they took the lead in producing postwar Japanese employment practices.

This review is a weighty undertaking. The book analyzes JNR's employment system and the history of labor relations in detail, but the explanations are not easy to grasp, and to be very frank, there were a number of passages that I did not have sufficient prior knowledge to understand. What follows is a chapter-by-chapter summary of the principal arguments, and the questions that they suggest.

Chapter 1, *Changes in the Prewar Status System*, covers in detail the changes already underway in JNR's status system in the prewar period due to labor demands for higher status, and stresses this background as necessary to understanding postwar employment practices. The rise in the position of laborers, who sought clerical-assistant status, spread extensively between the two world wars, while during WWII, everyone including manual workers became clerical assistants and the status system was abolished. In the process, a job ladder was created to include principal transport and engineering jobs in the clerical-assistant class; internal training and promotion were forwarded in the years around WWI, and even among construction, track maintenance, and engineering workers who were not incorporated as clerical assistants, a system of foremen with junior-official status was developed for railroad hands. The author shows that promotion to all these positions progressed in the years between the wars.

Moreover, it was laborers' own stance on skill development that led to that rise in status. That is, they stressed the skill development that came with long tenure in the same type of work, and took the stance that the acquisition of skills made laborers comparable to salaried bureaucrats. According to the author, these skills served as a weapon for labor groups in the prewar period, and established a prototype for the concept of laborers becoming salaried bureaucrats, which ultimately supported the seniority conventions that became the norm in the postwar. As the author points out, there was a limit to how far this concept reached: it did not extend to manual workers, and employment guarantees and clerical-assistant status did not extend either to manual workers. The part of this work that is hardest to understand is the presentation of evidence for the argument that it was laborers themselves who formulated the proposition that they could develop their skills by staying in the same job over the long term. The citations are fragmentary, so I was not able to assess the persuasiveness of this part of the argument.

From Chap. 2 on, using materials from the Japan National Railway Worker's Union, the author analyzes JNR's negotiations on the employment system, and traces the process by which the aforementioned employment practices were formed. Chapter 2, "The Introduction of a Job Classification Wage System" is a detailed consideration of postwar thinking about labor relations in terms of wage systems. Labor regarded the introduction of the job-classification wage system as a way to shrink the status-based wage gap with white-collar work. In order to break down the JNR administration's insistence on containing seniority-based blue-collar wage hikes, labor extended its position that "technical skill is proportional to number of years in a given job" to cover even skilled workers. In other words, it linked tenure with the value of the job. As a result, the job-classification wage system gave way to a wage system that enabled wage hikes for workers who remained in the same position. In other words, the system changed from job-based pay to grade-based or "merit"-based pay.

Chapter 3, *The Formation of Labor Practices in Postwar Japan*, discusses how employment guarantees, which before the war had been limited to salaried bureaucrats, were extended to blue-collar workers after the war, and the process by which laborers acquired "membership" status at the management level. The labor negotiations concerning post-surrender personnel adjustments are discussed in detail: the author argues that following the administrative reorganization of 1949, laborers built on their entrenched strength within JNR to advance the idea that their work constituted a contribution to JNR. By reaching agreements with JNR officials over employment guarantees, they extended flexible personnel changes and scope of occupations covered include even the shopfloor employees, and in exchange for labors' acquiescence to employment adjustments in the form of voluntary retirements, they won the status guarantees according to which regular employees = union members. The author argues strongly that the employment practices that have bearing even today were formed on the basis of this kind of thinking by labor.

Chapter 4, *Occupational Hierarchies and Promotion Practices*, discusses the promotion system, which was the focal point for position or status within the firm. The promotion ladder was established to address both labor and management aims, and one of the special features of this volume is that it explains this system. While labor aimed to expand access to high-status positions by extending the reach of the promotion ladder higher and higher, the JNR administrations' concern was the flexible operation of the labor force. Both sides turned their backs on the task-oriented promotion ladder, which had been based on an attempt to analyze and rate tasks or jobs, and ultimately in the 1950s, shopfloor entry jobs and clerical employees were combined into a single category; the names given assorted tasks were standardized by both sides, and in that sense, the "simplification of status lines," which had been the aim of the promotion ladder, was achieved, while those in the upper ranks gained in power as well. Meanwhile, laborers without university education, including shopfloor employees, could also compete with their university-educated counterparts and climb the ladder based on tests and other evidence of skill.

In Chap. 5, *The Postwar Transformation of the Quota Problem*, the author analyzes the aims and negotiating positions of labor and management regarding JNR's quotas on regular employees. He starts with the premises that the fundamental aim of labor relations is to create rules governing worker compensation and benefits and that the main concern of both labor and management was controlling the quotas on regular employees. He seeks to elucidate how the accumulated experience of labor and management behavior viz. union regulations in the workplace gave JNR's labor relations their special character. Labor's aim was to increase the number of regular workers in upper-level work so as to achieve the status and occupation systems of the upper ranks. After the administrative adjustments of 1949, an attempt was made to create a single set of standards for regular workers nationwide, categorized by institution and by task, but the effort was abandoned when it collided with labor's demand for a reversion to a more flexible system. The employees created a "comprehensive task diagram, per the individual worker" that allowed for the flexible adoption of work tasks fitted to the occupational realities, and carried out assessments of regular workers and management in every workplace. In the process, the unions carried out talks regarding regular workers, region by region and in workplaces, which turned the shopfloor into the venue of the transaction. This part of the argument, too, is connected to the book's overall point that the jobs were not configured based on labor and management aims but were the result of transaction-based promotions and flexible work assignments.

The author has read and analyzed an enormous amount of material on labor negotiations from the National Railway Workers' Union, and therefore brings an empirical basis to his argument that postwar labor practices incorporated the aims of labor. By explaining JNR's labor relations and employment system, and how the behavior and thinking of those involved gave shape to that system, and additionally by taking the approach of analyzing the formation of the employment system from the labor relations point of view, this volume raises many stimulating issues. It takes a positive stance regarding Japanese labor's stress on "skills," something that is usually regarded as injurious to labor's claims, and I also sympathize with his presentation of this process not as the result of competition among laborers but as a path for demands for equality relative to the status system of those with university education.

I would, however, like to raise a number of questions about this book.

My greatest doubt was whether laborers' opinions can in fact be grasped quite so tidily as this. The myriad conflicts within the Japan Railway Workers' Union over the question of employment practices are already well known; and the fact that the National Railway Motive Power Union split off from the Japan Railway Workers' Union and went independent is evidence of just how serious these conflicts were. There were also serious standoffs on the question of leadership within the Railway Workers' Union itself. The author points this out here and there, but the differences of opinion within labor is mostly left out of the discussion, and, while stressing the central importance of labor's stance, the book does not show how these conflicting opinions combined to become that united stance. Additionally, the viewpoints of laborers themselves are completely overshadowed by the viewpoint of the union in the negotiations, so the reader is not able to access the opinions and feelings of actual laborers. This is no doubt due to the fact that the author depended principally on Railway Union materials, but the demands and statements of the union in labor negotiations also derive from complex tactics that we cannot understand simply by taking the union's declarations at face value. I am therefore not able to agree with the author's conclusions without further consideration.

It is hard in this work to get a sense of the flesh-and-blood laborer and his world. The labor market and labor's strength are analyzed, but the differences in occupation types and career development due to educational background are hard to make out. Overall, I was unable to develop an image of the reality of the JNR laborer. That is likely due to my own ignorance. However, the book does not analyze the content of the various jobs or skills involved, and likewise, does not refer to a central problem, which is how the situation changed due to rationalization. Given the argument that labor promoted the concept of skill development based on tenure, we need to understand the actual foundation of those skills. If the concept did not rest on that foundation, the laborers would have been unable to take action in their own interest, or rather, if they did take action, the tensions among them would have been seriously damaging. The argument would be more persuasive if the author had addressed these questions.

How shall we assess the path by which the laborer on the shopfloor rose; the impact of exams and training on that rise; and other special features of the JNR organization? According to the author, these features were ideas developed by the laborers themselves, but we need more research to show whether they were likewise central to the formation of postwar Japanese employment practices more generally. This work demonstrates the author's strong drive for research, and I have great expectations for the contributions he will make going forward.

Chapter 7
Review of Junko Watanabe, *Sangyō Hatten, Suitai no Keizai-shi—"10-dai bō" no Keisei to Sangyō Chousei* (The Economic History of Industrial Development and Decline: The Formation and Industrial Readjustment of the Cotton Industry's "Big 10")

Yuhikaku, Tokyo, 2010

Kyohei Hirano

This volume is unusual in that it considers industrial stagnation and decline from the point of view of industrial structural adjustment. It is well known that cotton manufacturing was, along with silk, a leading industry in pre-World War II Japan, but as the author records, the industry saw its peak in the 1930s, and aside from a brief uptick during the postwar recovery era, underwent long-term stagnation and decline. Managers, workers, and policy-makers in the Japanese cotton industry were, however, well aware of the experience of Lancashire's cotton industry, whose decline preceded that of Japan's, and sought to avoid following in its footsteps. It was in that spirit that the cotton industry undertook its first large-scale industrial readjustment, the historical process of which is described in this volume.

By industrial structural adjustment or readjustment, the author is referring first, on a micro level, to companies' entry into new businesses through diversification or change of business, and second, on a macro level, to changes in the industrial structure through shifts in resource allocation from declining industries to growth industries. Readjustment approaches included both the market-based, such as the abandonment of declining industries and entry into growth sectors; and the intra-organizational reallocation of investment from existing businesses to new growth-sector ventures. These approaches to industrial structural adjustment were furthered by government policy interventions. The author points out that, "While organizational adjustment was to some extent spurred by market mechanisms and competitive industrial organizations, it was the adjustments carried out by large enterprises

K. Hirano (✉)
Graduate School of Business Administration, Kobe University, Kobe, Japan
e-mail: k-hirano@b.kobe-u.ac.jp

H. Takeda (ed.), *Micro-Performance During Postwar Japan's High-Growth Era*, Monograph Series of the Socio-Economic History Society, Japan,
DOI 10.1007/978-981-10-0709-5_7

that carried a greater weight… and these rested on a delicate balance between market and non-market approaches" (p. 13). This book focuses chiefly on the organizational adjustments carried out by large enterprises. The following is a brief introduction of its contents.

Themes and Methods pulls together previous research touching on the question of industrial structural adjustment, and outlines the analytical themes of the volume as a whole. The author concentrates chiefly on the period from the 1930s to the 1960s, which was the transition period preceding the 1970s, by which time industrial adjustment was in full swing. The "prototype" of large-firm organizational adjustment is found in the spinning industry of the prewar period, when the Big 10 were formed and undertook their initial diversification. The introductory chapter, *The Dynamics of Industrial Development*, recounts the century-long history of the textile industry while showing that industrial structural adjustment in cotton proceeded gradually over a long period between the 1960s and the 1990s. The Japanese textile industry of the time was characterized by a dual structure of large and small enterprises, and industrial adjustment was characterized by a similar "dual" structure: large firms with abundant management resources could advance into overseas markets, for example, and diversify by reallocating enterprise resources, while small firms with meager management resources were divided between those that entered the market and those that pulled out.

Chapters 1–3, *The Formation of the "Big 10," Prewar Diversification of the "Big 10,"* and *The "Big 10" as an Established System*, consider, as their titles suggest, the Big 10, which are taken to be the prototypes for large-firm organizational readjustment. Japan's cotton firms were amalgamated into ten companies under wartime controls, and the author shows that the diversification that had already been underway in the prewar textile industry advanced both through reequipping enterprises and through shifts into non-textile businesses in response to military procurement. The companies themselves acted to diversify during the war, spurred by military demand, and approaches to diversification into alternative sectors was developed on the foundation of management resources that the companies had built up internally. The author argues that these developments differ from industrial structural adjustment, and that they are not therefore directly related to the companies' postwar actions, but the means that were developed of reallocating resources within a given company formed the prototype for large-firm organizational readjustment. The author's consideration of the post-surrender period shows that the Big 10's reconstruction policies, in concert with the economic democratization policies of those years, fell into two categories: plans for comprehensive textile enterprises based on the textile diversification of the war years, and plans for non-textile businesses.

The author makes a positive assessment of the non-textile ventures, but others' evaluations may differ when the accompanying flows of technology and personnel are also taken into consideration. Chapter 6, *Intra-firm Adjustments by the Big 10*, launches the discussion of postwar organizational adjustment in the form of diversification and penetration of overseas markets. The author notes the following particulars in intra-firm adjustment: (a) diversification based on a foundation of resources internal to the firms, including capital formation, technology, and human resources; (b) entry into new sectors by absorbing external resources through M&A, mergers and *keiretsu* formation; (c) advances into growth sectors, synthetic fibers, auto-related enterprises, pharmaceutical goods, and foods. The author also shows that this kind of diversification being undertaken by large firms was virtually unseen in small- and medium-size enterprises.

To return to the chapter outline, chapter 4, *A New Competitive Environment: The Emergence of "New Cotton" and "New, New Cotton,"* addresses the problem of new small- and medium-sized firms' entering the cotton sector and their impact on chronic over-competition and excess capacity, which were principal factors in the textile sector depression. New entrants exacerbated low returns and low wages with price competition, and the Big 10 adjusted for the rise in labor costs by increasing productivity through equipment modernization. From the latter 1950s, as the Big 10 started to enter synthetic fibers and non-textile businesses, they began their partial withdrawal from the cotton industry. In Chapter 5, *Structural Adjustment Through Government Intervention*, the author approaches the problems raised in the previous chapter from the government side. Discussing industrial policy of the 1950s as it concerned the textile industry, she finds that it often ran counter to the trends of the times, with supports for cotton exports, policies for developing the synthetic fibers industry, and plans to address the depression in textiles. These were discrete ad hoc policies formed in response to short-term conditions, but in the long-term, they added up to a consistent policy of industrial adjustment focused on making the shift from natural to synthetic fibers. The author shows that the government's moderate guidance helped ameliorate the impact of the pressures for readjustment in these years, and that the Big 10 were accordingly able to start making the shift while they still had some remaining strength.

Chapter 7, *The Formation of International Rules Governing Readjustment*, takes a new vantage point that considers Japan's industrial adjustment vis-a-vis trade policies and relations with the international economy. Especially interesting are the establishment of new international trade rules under the leadership of the US, at a time of US-Japan trade friction over textiles, and the declaration of industrial adjustment assistance policies by advanced nations in connection with these rules. The author demonstrates that these approaches emerged and became firmly established in the form of the OECD's "positive adjustment policies."

In *Conclusions and Outlooks*, the author summarizes her previous chapters and reasserts her findings on the organizational adjustment of large firms and the role of policy interventions. While acknowledging that these show a certain wasteful excess, she accords them high points for effecting a gradual and peaceable adjustment. As subjects for future analysis, she suggests the 1970s, when industrial readjustment was fully established.

This volume covers the 1930s–1960s transition years and addresses the concept of industrial adjustment from the point of view of markets and organizations, industrial policy, trade, and international conditions, and in so doing, makes a meaningful contribution. It will take its place in the ongoing research and debate in business studies and business history over diversification by postwar cotton firms, in particular because of the author's elucidation of her positive assessment of the significance of large firms' organizational adjustment through diversification.

I would like to complete my duty as reviewer by raising three questions, while noting that these do not detract from the value of this work.

The first regards industrial readjustment in non-cotton textile industries. The spinning industry, for example, peaked in the prewar just as cotton textiles did, and reached the world's highest standards technologically in the postwar, but struggled to compete with the low prices of the later developing nations. What was its industrial readjustment process? The pressure for readjustment must have been even stronger in this area than in the cotton industry, given the loss of the principal market, the US, due to the emergence of nylon, which was a particularly strong competitor. Similarly, although synthetics were a postwar growth industry, they, too, faced the need to readjust, though later than the cotton industry. How did they fare? Given the technological issues, their need for readjustment was probably even greater than that of the cotton industry. The author's positive evaluation of the effectiveness of organizational adjustment by large firms would be strengthened by a consideration of textile industries other than cotton.

My second question regards the using large-firms organizational adjustment as a "prototype." I understand the author's emphasis on the importance of the wartime years, but as the author herself mentions in the introduction, the interwar period has a comparable significance. Production peaked in the 1930s, but the shadow of falling revenues was already apparent, and with the retained earnings from World War I, the major cotton companies were already focused on textile diversification from the 1920s on, and were making strides in the reallocation of resources to sectors outside cotton textiles. In that sense, the fact that cotton-firm managers felt a sense of crisis even prior to the industry's peak in the 1930s meant that they had already begun planting the seeds of organizational adjustment. In that case, would it not be correct to seek the "prototype" of industrial readjustment in the interwar period? Should the diversification of the war years not be understood simply as a situation-specific response to military demand for non-textiles?

Third regards the friction within companies that was part and parcel of organizational adjustment. The author says that "the firm's internal resource allocation (diversification) was comparatively lower in friction and adjustment costs than resource allocation through the market," (pp. 326–327), but what about the friction that took place at the company level? The Big 10's non-textile businesses did not necessarily start out in a strong position within the larger companies; many earned their success through their own efforts, while along the way, the variance between them and the managers and outlook of the parent cotton businesses caused considerable struggle. It is also important to consider the kinds of conflicts that arose on account of the same organizations' having within them both growing and declining sectors. It is important to consider the problem of intra-company friction and the responses to that friction in order to understand organizational readjustment from the point of view of business history.

This reviewer has felt in recent years that we are beginning to see an environment more conducive to accessing materials on Japan's textile industries and companies. It is my hope that with this volume will serve to stimulate interest and questions about Japan's postwar textile industries and firms and that many researches will henceforth undertake dynamic research into the industrial and business history of the textile sector.

Chapter 8
Review of Juroh Hashimoto, *Sengo Nihon Keizai no Seichou Kouzou: Kigyō System to Sangyō Seisaku no Bunseki* (The Structure of Postwar Japan's Economic Growth: an Analysis of Enterprise Systems and Industrial Policy)

Yuhikaku, Tokyo, 2001

Seiichiro Yonekura

1 Introduction

If Professor Juroh Hashimoto were still living, I would certainly not have taken on the task of writing this review. Whether positive or critical, it was not likely to elicit a good response. Still, it was only when I began writing that I realized how empty it would feel to write a review when the author cannot respond.

Juroh Hashimoto was something of a giant in my eyes when I was student. The first time we met was when I was writing my master's thesis, in the dim light of the company's archives at Onoda Cement Ltd. Juroh was an Assistant Professor at the University of Electro-Communications at the time, and was editing a 100 year history of the company along with Haruhito Takeda, also still an Assistant Professor at University of Tokyo then. As it happened, I was researching Onoda Cement for my master's, and therefore was also spending time at the archives. Those of you who know Professors Hashimoto and Takeda will be able to imagine just how daunting it would be to meet these two as a first-year master's student. I'd go so far as to say that they were the last people whom graduate students writing their theses would want to meet. They were sharp-tongued and incisive, and even the way they looked was altogether imposing. Juroh gave me a sharp glance and asked what I was doing. I don't recall my answer but remember that he just grinned.

S. Yonekura (✉)
Institute of Innovation Research, Hitotsubashi University, Tokyo, Japan
e-mail: yonekura@iir.hit-u.ac.jp

H. Takeda (ed.), *Micro-Performance During Postwar Japan's High-Growth Era*, Monograph Series of the Socio-Economic History Society, Japan,
DOI 10.1007/978-981-10-0709-5_8

As I subsequently went to the United States to study under the late Professor Alfred Chandler, I did not have any further opportunity to meet Professor Hashimoto, but it was in the U.S. that I read with great admiration his *Japanese Capitalism in the Great Depression*. "This is an amazing book!" I kept thinking there in the university library stacks. In fact, he won the Nikkei Prize with this book.

Many of those who admired Hashimoto's writings at that time have apparently been less satisfied with his recent work. Haruhito Takeda, another giant, for example, speaking at the November, 2002 meeting of the Business History Association committee reviewing *The Structure of Postwar Japan's Economic Growth*, pointed out "the ambiguity of the relationship between his research on the capitalist economy and his research on postwar history, ever since [the volume] *Japanese Capitalism in the Great Depression*." Although his previous and more recent works differ greatly in style, however, I do not share this impression.

I think Hashimoto's recent work is an extension of the work he presented in *Great Depression*. That is, it is part and parcel of his evolving viewpoint on history. It is clear that as he refined his macroeconomic analysis of industrial structure and economic policy, he reached the conclusion that the dynamism of the Japanese economy could not ultimately be explained by macroeconomic developments alone. This emerges clearly in a passage from one of his posthumous publications, "Market Ignorance, Entrepreneurship, and Creative Adaptation," in *Hitotsubashi Business Review*, (Vol. 49, No. 3, December, 2001), where he says, "The engine of economic development is entrepreneurial activity, and entrepreneurial activity in its organized [form] is the enterprise." (p. 33) In other words, his focus shifted to what are the primary actors in economic development according to microeconomic analyses: (a) "entrepreneurial activities," (b) the government as creative respondent, and (c) industrial policy. This shift came about as a result of many years of developing macroeconomic analyses.

2 The Organization of Hashimoto's *The Structure of Postwar Japan's Economic Growth*

With this background in mind, we can readily identify the issues Juroh Hashimoto seeks to explore in this volume: "First, how did Japanese companies react creatively and innovatively to the extremely limiting conditions of the early postwar period and create an enterprise system adapted to that environment?" and "Second, given the extreme constraints [of the period], how did the government seek to alleviate them and to lend its support to company efforts to respond creatively?" In this work, in other words, he places companies and the government, and their adaptive and creative responses to the harsh conditions of the time, at the very center of "postwar Japanese economic development."

This volume is therefore composed of two parts. The first part, *Postwar Enterprise Systems and Business Innovations*, explores companies. Part 2, *The Particular*

Features of Postwar Industrial Policy, examines the government role, which is also a microeconomics. Both are more commonly the focus of studies in microeconomics.

Part 1, chapter 1, *The Birth, Refinement, and Systematization of Enterprise Systems*, presents an overview of enterprise systems in their Japanese form; chapter 2, *The Formation of Japanese-style Specialization Systems*, addresses specialization within and among companies. Here he analyzes the very core of the Japanese enterprise system from the viewpoint of specialization, covering "labor relations, career formation, product development and technologies, and *keiretsu* transactions, etc." In so doing, he is able to isolate the features that were particular to Japanese enterprise systems as distinct from the broad frameworks that "had hitherto been vague assumptions in economic [analyses]." Hashimoto concludes that the competitiveness of Japanese firms lay in the system's flexibility, the key word here being "soft specialization," the flexible system that transcended the boundaries between specific duties or functions within a company or between companies.

Chapter 3, *The History and Logic of Long-term Transactions*, analyzes *keiretsu* transactions in Japan through the cases of four companies: Toyota, Matsushita Electric, Fuji Xerox, and Mitsubishi Heavy/Yawata Steel (New Japan Steel), and explains the logic behind their strength. Chapter 4, *Leaps in Mass Production Industries through Innovation in Production Systems*, presents the case of Kawasaki Steel and Chiba Steel as prime examples of creative response and adaptation by postwar businesses. It happens that this chapter takes a critical look at my "Kawasaki Paradigm" argument and sets about refining it – I expect that's why this review came round to me. My "Kawasaki Paradigm" did indeed leave many loose ends, as Juroh Hashimoto points out, but its argument did not differ fundamentally from his. His contributions here have made its argument that much clearer, and I therefore have a particular appreciation for this chapter.

Chapter 5, *The Development of Enterprise Management by Entrepreneurs*, discusses the development of Matsushita Company under Matsushita Konosuke's leadership. This is the least satisfying chapter, both vis-à-vis Hashimoto's usual perfectionism and in terms of the structure of this volume. Nevertheless, in reading it now, I sense that Hashimoto was taking up a new field. He uses the case of Matsushita Konosuke and Matsushita Electric Industries to explore in detail the entrepreneurial activities that supported postwar economic development. Those who know Juroh Hashimoto as an economic historian may be put off by this subject, but this chapter should be read as his first foray into the field of entrepreneurial history.

In Part 2, *The Special Features of Postwar Industrial Policy*, Hashimoto places the actions of private firms at the center of postwar economic development, which necessarily results in a repositioning of the role of "industrial policy," which had for too long been ascribed undue credit for Japan's postwar growth. He provides evidence demonstrating that the role of government was to alleviate the constraints of the postwar, to enable companies to be resilient, and to guide private firms in their creative responses and adaptations. The author's intent is well expressed in chapter 6, *A Viewpoint on Analyzing Industrial Policy*, whose subtitle reads, *The*

Undue Weight Given to Government Policy and the Discovery of Policy Challenges in Industrial Policy. The evidence for this vantage point is presented in the discussion of the shipbuilding industry in chapter 7 (*The Government Role as Coordinator of Strategy: Shipbuilding Plans in Postwar Recovery and the Role and Activity of the Transport Ministry*), the machine industry in chapter 8 (*Relationships Among Government, Industry Associations, and Enterprises*), and the Japan Development Bank in chapter 9 (*The Effectiveness of the Temporary Recovery Measures for the Machine Industry Recovery*). Each case study presents evidence of private firms' creative responses and adaptations, and by elucidating the inside workings of policy development and decision-making and the reactions of individual firms, clearly elucidates the realities of postwar industrial policy. The quantitative analysis applied to the company histories is especially interesting as a new analytical approach to business history. Less satisfactory is his open avowal of the idea that, "the personnel of Japan's bureaucratic institutions, including MITI, had a strong sense of autonomy" and that "we can assume strong professional ethics." Certainly, the bureaucrats who implemented particular policies for specific industrial sectors had broad discretionary powers and were upstanding in comparison to those in Southeast Asia or South America. However, the corruption that has come to light in the Japanese bureaucracy since the 1990s suggests the need to address the fact that Japan's bureaucratic system could not withstand corruption indefinitely.

Hashimoto's evidence-based analysis of the industrial-policy implementation process by the government and private sector reveals that "industrial policy was formed and implemented according to the particular conditions of specific industries," that we need to produce more evidence-based research so as to avoid facile generalization, and that he, for one did not begrudge the time and labor involved.

I want to conclude by offering my honest thoughts about the work. My first impression on reading it through was that that this was after all a medley of topics he'd already addressed elsewhere. I could not help but think that Juroh Hashimoto at his most careful would have produced a more solid book if he had taken more time. It is only in hindsight, of course, that we realize that he didn't have that time. It is worth giving the work a careful rereading with that in mind: the lines of thought that are true to Juroh Hashimoto begin to emerge with greater clarity. The title notwithstanding, *The Structure of Postwar Japan's Economic Growth* is not really aimed at economists or economic historians, but rather, is a rich gift to business historians who endeavor to analyze how enterprises, through their activities and innovation, drive economic development. My dear Professor Hashimoto – thank you. Please rest in peace, and watch over our work.

Index

H. Takeda (ed.), *Micro-Performance During Postwar Japan's High-Growth Era*, Monograph Series of the Socio-Economic History Society, Japan,
DOI 10.1007/978-981-10-0709-5

The manufacturer's authorised representative in the EU is Springer Nature Customer Service Centre GmbH, Europaplatz 3, 69115 Heidelberg, Germany. If you have any concerns regarding our products, please contact ProductSafety@springernature.com

Printed and bound by CPI Group (UK) Ltd, Croydon, CR0 4YY
25/09/2026
02222850-0007